CONSTRUCTIONS OF DEVIANCE IN SOCIOLOGICAL THEORY

The Problem of Commensurability

Charles Wright
Oklahoma City University

UNIVERSITY
PRESS OF
AMERICA

LANHAM • NEW YORK • LONDON

Copyright © 1984 by

University Press of America,™ Inc.

4720 Boston Way
Lanham, MD 20706

3 Henrietta Street
London WC2E 8LU England

Printed in the United States of America

Library of Congress Cataloging in Publication Data

Wright, Charles, 1943-
  Constructions of deviance in sociological theory.

  Bibliography: p.
  Includes index.
  1. Deviant behavior—Labeling theory. 2. Functional
analysis (Social sciences) I. Title.
HM291.W74   1984   302.5'42   84-7501
ISBN 0-8191-3993-9 (alk. paper)
ISBN 0-8191-3994-7 (pbk. : alk. paper)

TO NANINA AND TERRY

PREFACE AND ACKNOWLEDGMENTS

This study involves an analysis of two theories of deviance. Each, for a time, dominated the understanding of deviance within sociology, and each continues to have adherents. The two theories which are the subject of this work are most widely known as "Functionalism" and "Labeling Theory." The method of analysis which the study employs leads to a focus upon the meaning associated with the core conceptual features employed by each theory group. The use of these concepts *within* each group is treated here as nonproblematic. However, upon those relatively rare occasions of inter-group communicative exchange, there appears to occur what Kuhn (1970--first published in 1961) refers to as a "communication breakdown." It is with an interest in the quality of communication of this type--inter-scientific, theory-group communication-- that this study is written. The character of inter-group communication between sociological theory groups, and these two groups in particular, appears to rest upon deeply erroneous assumptions made by members of both groups concerning fundamental aspects of the approach of the other. To put the matter most radically, the communication is affected problematically by a "shared belief" that the members of the two groups speak with reference to the same "world." To put the matter less radically, much of the "failure in communication" and the controversy which occurs between the practitioners within each group is a result of their somewhat ironic assumption that there is more in common between them than is actually the case, i.e., the practitioners within each group believe that they share the same conceptual universe with members of the other group to a greater extent than is actually the case. This work stands the system associated with each group against the other, feature by feature, so as to see the two perspectives in the sharpest possible relief.

The analysis of these two ways of thinking occurs within the framework of what Kuhn refers to as a "disciplinary matrix"--a term which replaced one of the many usages and meanings which came to be associated with the more prominent term, "paradigm." The major elements of a "matrix" are "basic concepts in use" (e.g., in the thought examined here, "deviance"), the structure and method of "understanding" (e.g., "explanation"), philosophical and methodological underpinnings, and value commitments. Each of these are central in the composition of "the world of the theorist"--the sociological practitioner.

The conclusion at which we arrive suggests that the disparity and controversy between these two approaches may not easily lend itself to resolution, as many sociologists (e.g., Jack Gibbs and Edwin Shur) had hoped. Rather, the two groups of thinkers share little with respect to the most fundamental aspects of their world-view or the problems to which they direct their attention.

In light of this lack of resonance between the two perspectives and the lack of reciprocal understanding of the meanings associated with the basic concepts employed, the question is raised as to whether or not the two "theories of deviance" are, in any sense, commensurate with one another, i.e., do they "speak" to one another. This issue is much more important than that usually implied by the phrase, "failure of communication," in that it raises questions concerning the cumulative nature of science (in this case, sociological knowledge), and, more generally, leads to reflection upon the nature of "culture" and its transmission. Of course, issues such as these are not easily resolved and perhaps are not the types of issues which are subject to resolution at all. Certainly, this study does not pretend to arrive at a firm conclusion regarding the commensurability of the two perspectives under consideration. Any conclusion, even at this level, would require a further and even more painstaking investigation into the relationship between Functionalism (and Parsons' Theory of Action) and Symbolic Interactionism, the general systems of thought with which the Functionalist Theory of Deviance and Labeling Theory are respectively associated. This study concludes that it is incorrect to argue that the Functional Theory of Deviance and Labeling Theory are commensurate or that the two yield a historical accumulation with respect to the understanding of some phenomenon (called "crime" or "deviance") which stands independent of each system of thought. Possessed of radically disparate world-views as to the nature of social life, the two groups of thinkers arrive at incommensurate ideas regarding the nature of "deviance" and "conformity."

With respect to the use of the masculine pronoun, "he," and, from time to time, the generic, "Man" (rather than "person," "human being," or other gender-nonspecific word choice), which occasionally occurs within the text, I can only offer the following explanation. My editor, a thoroughly modern woman in most all respects, is quite traditional with respect to the long-standing customs of the mother tongue.

Many people have been instrumental in the formulation of the perspective which guided this study and in the selection of its subject matter. Accordingly, I wish to express my gratitude to Fred Silberstein, David Whitney, Ed Manier, David Dodge, Andy Wiegart, Lincoln Johnson, and Susan Randall. I also wish to acknowledge a special indebtedness to R.E. Hilbert for his untiring effort to lead me to understand "Functionalism" and Parsons' Theory of Action with the precision which it demands and deserves. None of the above is due any blame for the foibles contained herein, for I have deviated, perhaps too frequently, from what each suggested.

I also wish to extend my appreciation to my friend and colleague Larry Wieder for encouraging me to proceed with the publication of this manuscript and for instructing me as to the broader implications of aspects of the methods herein employed. Finally, this work could not have been completed without the support and assistance of my friends Pat and Jan Chesley, the careful, competent, and laborious processing of the final manuscript by Carolyn Clark, and the production of "his last index" by my brother, Michael. To Karen Wieder, I owe more than I shall ever be able to repay for having graciously, and too often, put aside her other responsibilities, in order to complete this project by editing, with the greatest of care, the entire manuscript, compiling the bibliography, and aiding me in the checking of each and every quotation.

C.W.
December, 1983

TABLE OF CONTENTS

FIGURES AND TABLES

CHAPTER I

THE PROBLEM AND THE APPROACH

A. Introduction

This study is an analysis of divergent ways of thinking about deviance within sociology. There are two major traditions of thought upon which the study will concentrate. The first is sociological Functionalism as it has been applied to the attempt to understand the sources of deviant behavior. The second tradition involves primarily, although not exclusively, the application of Symbolic Interactionist Theory to the phenomenon of deviance. This latter tradition is most often referred to as "Labeling Theory." In the study which follows, a good deal of attention will be devoted to the relationship between these theories of deviance and the more general systems of thought from which they derive.

The objective here is to locate and analyze basic conceptual components of the two approaches to deviance. However, the task is not to review all of the intellectual production associated with each perspective. Rather, it is to focus on those components which can be said to characterize a theoretical program.[1] This method is not unlike that of the field ethnographer, who "pretends" that the "community" speaks with a single voice. He listens for the more or less consistent themes which can be discovered from selected informants. The idiosyncrasies, the individual departures and divergencies from the central themes, although important for other purposes, are not of primary interest here. Through the employment of this method, the characteristic components of the approaches, as well as their major applications, can be discovered.

---

[1] The term "theoretical program" is used here rather than simply "theory," because of the rather specific and limited meaning often associated with the latter term. This study will focus on more than the system of explanation, which is what the term "theory" usually connotes. It will also focus upon fundamental assumptions, method, values, etc. which are found to be associated with a theory and which are sponsored by the practitioners within a "theory group."

The "Etiological-Functional"[2] approach may be broken down into two related variants: the "Anomic" and the "Systemic" wings of Functional Theory. The two possess somewhat distinct emphases, and, therefore, it is useful to analyze them separately. However, the sense in which they remain within the same general framework will be established.

The Anomic variant was initiated by Emile Durkheim and further elaborated by Robert Merton and, later, Richard Cloward and Lloyd Ohlin. The most prominent works associated with the theory are Durkheim's *Suicide* (1951; originally published in 1895), Merton's "Social Structure and Anomie" (1967), and Cloward and Ohlin's *Delinquency and Opportunity* (1960).

The "Systemic" variant of the Functional approach is most closely associated with the works of Talcott Parsons and Albert Cohen. Parsons' influence on this approach is mainly through his view of science, his general theory, and his approach to deviance as put forward in *The Social System* (1951). Cohen's most prominent work is *Delinquent Boys* (1955).

The Symbolic Interactionist approach to deviance, Labeling Theory, is represented here by a number of scholars and works: Edwin Lemert, *Social Pathology* (1951) and *Human Deviance, Social Problems, and Social Control* (1972); Howard Becker, *Outsiders* (1963); Thomas Scheff, *Being Mentally Ill* (1966); Edwin Schur, *Labeling Deviant Behavior* (1971); David Matza, *Delinquency and Drift* (1964) and *Becoming Deviant* (1969); Richard Quinney, *The Social Reality of Crime* (1970); and John Lofland, *Deviance and Identity* (1969). This approach has its internal divergencies and separate patterns of influence, which will be discussed along with the way in which the approach diverges from the Anomic and Systemic traditions. However, the major task of this study is to characterize and examine a general approach which is shared by a group of scholars, not to examine internal divergencies. As a result, the main task of this section will be to separate the Labeling approach from the other theories of deviance under consideration.

The selection of the personnel within these theory groups and the designation of them as "groups" was made with some consideration of the criteria which Nicholas Mullins suggests in his recent work, *Theories and Theory Groups in Contemporary American Sociology* (1973).

---

[2] The use of the term "Etiological-Functionalist" is necessary to properly narrow the focus of this investigation. Neither variant of analysis considered here has really developed a functional analysis of the patterns of conduct which it has isolated for consideration. The approach does not carry out Functional analyses in the same manner as do the works of Kingsley Davis (in his analysis of prostitution, 1961) or Daniel Bell (in "Crime as an American Way of Life," 1953). Rather, the mode of analysis examined here is etiological in that it seeks the source of deviance. However, the approach is rooted in the Functional tradition in sociology, hence the notation "Etiological-Functionalism."

Mullins states:

> Briefly, two or more pieces of theory work are considered to be similar if their authors (1) cite similar sources; (2) are known to be colleagues or students, of one another, or all of yet another person; and (3) are considered to be similar by themselves and others. (Mullins, 1973:12)

Mullins' objective, to establish the structure of scientific theory groups, requires him to do extensive research on the membership of such groups. Two of the groups of interest to him are of concern to this study--the Functionalists and the Symbolic Interactionists. Examining his description of the membership of these groups uncovers some discrepancies, but no real contradiction exists between his designation of a scholar as associated with a theory group and those designated in this group. Each scientist designated here as a Functionalist is also placed in that group by Mullins (see Mullins, 1973:56). However, only two (Becker and Scheff) of the five scholars who are described here as having been influenced by the Symbolic Interactionist tradition are within Mullins' designation of that group's membership (see Mullins, 1973:84-85). The others, Lemert, Matza, and Quinney, all prominent sociologists, do not appear in Mullins' work; i.e., they are not included in any of eight theory groups which he isolates. However, the inclusion of Matza and Lemert within this group would probably spark little argument from Mullins. Their publications have been specialized, largely within the area of deviance, and this probably accounts for their absence from Mullins' work. The placement of Quinney within this approach is perhaps more controversial. Quinney does not exhibit the influences of the Symbolic Interactionist tradition as clearly as the others. In fact, as will be shown, his later work is more affected by Marxian sociology. However, the major test of the validity of the designations (especially the selection of Lemert, Matza, and Quinney), is not, as in Mullins' work, the structural ties among a body of practitioners, but the similar employment of certain concepts associated with a single approach. The analysis will show that Quinney, as well as Lemert and Matza, shares root concepts with others (e.g., Becker and Scheff) who are more clearly bound structurally to the Symbolic Interactionist theory group.

A brief diagram (see Figure 1) will tentatively convey the relationships within the theory groups which are the subject of this analysis. Scholars placed on the top line are not necessarily associated with the modern subdisciplinary theory group, but are either classical influences on the modern group (as are, e.g., Durkheim and Mead) or provide a general theoretical underpinning for the more specialized scientific work (as do, e.g., Mead, Schutz, and Blumer). Within the Functionalist group, Parsons has been important in developing general philosophical and theoretical grounding for the specialized area and has, as well, written specifically in the area of deviance itself. Merton has also been important in this regard, although to a lesser extent than Parsons. In the course of this study, these relationships will become more clear. However, it should be emphasized that although allusion will be made to the patterns of influence which have shaped statements on deviance, this is not the major objective of the work. The goal of this

3

project is to examine the relations among theoretical programs.

Summary Chart of Theory Groups and Directions of Influence

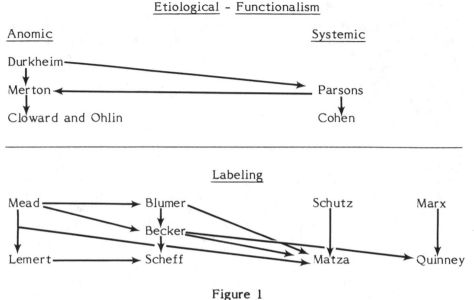

Figure 1

This task will require: (1) attention to the question of the existence of distinct conceptual apparatus and (2) examination of the components of such apparatus. Employed here will be a concept developed by Thomas Kuhn in a postscript to the Second Edition of *The Structure of Scientific Revolutions* (1970). To refer to a set of shared conceptual elements among members of a scientific community, Kuhn suggests the term "disciplinary matrix." He states:

> Scientists themselves would say they share a theory or a set of theories. . . As currently used in philosophy of science, however, 'theory' connotes a structure far more limited in nature and scope than the one required here. Until the term can be freed from its current implications, it will avoid confusion to adopt another. For present purposes I suggest 'disciplinary matrix;' 'disciplinary' because it refers to the common possession of the practitioners of a particular discipline; 'matrix' because it is composed of ordered elements of various sorts, each requiring further specification. (Kuhn, 1970:182)

Kuhn does not provide an exhaustive list of the components of a disciplinary matrix, but he does suggest four fundamental points of consideration: (1) symbolic generalizations, (2) metaphysical parts of

4

paradigms, (3) value commitments, and (4) exemplary problems. By symbolic generalizations, Kuhn means "those expressions, deployed without question or dissent by group members, which can be readily cast in logical form. . ." (1970:182). Symbolic generalizations are the anchoring point of scientific activity within the scientific community. They are viewed as both "law-like and definitional." An example from sociology is the suggestion by Herbert Blumer (1969) that "social action is an outcome of symbolic interpretation."

The next component, the metaphysical parts of paradigms, involves a commitment to particular models. This commitment may refer to either "heuristic" or "ontological" models. In the former case, Kuhn provides the example of "the electric circuit" which may "be regarded as a steady state hydrodynamic system. . ." (Kuhn, 1970:184). In sociology, viewing society as a "social system" tending toward equilibrium, or as an "imperatively coordinated system of authority" represents heuristic, and at times, ontological commitments.

The third element of the matrix, value commitments, may be broken down into two major classes: (1) "intra-scientific" values, i.e., values internal to the practice of science (e.g., consistency, predictive success, description, interpretation, explanation, etc.) and (2) "extra-scientific" values, i.e., values external to science (e.g., conservatism, radicalism, etc. in socio-economic matters).

The last component which Kuhn offers, and which is of primary importance, is "exemplary problems." "By it [exemplar] I mean, initially, the concrete problem solutions that the students encounter from the start of their scientific education. . ." (1970:187). The importance of "exemplary problems" is that they, more than any other element of the paradigm, "signal the gestalt" in which the world is seen. The student is confronted with problems which he is taught to solve via the employment of certain anchoring points (symbolic generalizations). These generalizations may be conceived as basic elements of "exemplary solutions." The student is then introduced to other problems (upon which the anchoring points should also shed light) which he comes to see in terms of the gestalt in which he is being trained. That is, he is taught to see the similarity of this problem to the exemplary problems which characterize a certain approach.[3] Ultimately, the student comes to view all sorts of problems from the point of view of the appropriate gestalt. A sociological example might be drawn with reference to the study of "race." How is the student to understand "race" and the theoretical problems associated with the concept? That is, what gestalt is used? Perhaps the phenomenon is viewed in terms of economic and power relations (e.g., a Marxist gestalt). Minorities, in this case, are viewed as an exploited class. Alternately, race may be viewed in terms of the institution

---

[3]Kuhn avoids the use of the term "paradigm" in this context, because he has used it in two ways in his text. First, in the way he now employs the concept of "disciplinary matrix," and, second, as what is now viewed as a component of such a matrix--a set of exemplars. In order to avoid confusion, he has dropped the term "paradigm" in favor of the two separate meanings: (1) disciplinary matrix and (2) exemplary problems.

of racism and its relation to the societal system as a whole, as well as the institution's consequence on the pattern of life of racial minorities (a system gestalt). Or "low" racial status can be viewed as a form of "stigma" and, hence, understood in the theoretical terms associated with that concept ("managing" problems of social identity in face-to-face interaction). How any phenomenon is defined and viewed--just what "race" is--depends upon the gestalt, the set of exemplars with which one becomes acquainted and in terms of which one is trained to "see." In this regard, Kuhn states what is a fundamental proposal of his perspective:

> What a man sees depends both upon what he looks at and also upon what his previous visual-conceptual experience has taught him to see. In the absence of such training there can only be, in William James' phrase, "a bloomin' buzzin' confusion." (Kuhn, 1970:113)

The scope of Kuhn's concerns with disciplinary matrices includes the whole of science. The purpose of this current work--the treatment of sociological world-views and particular issues in the sociology of deviance--requires a narrowing of focus. Therefore, certain elements of the Kuhnian scheme must be modified.

In relation to Kuhn's first component, "symbolic generalizations" constitute fundamental anchoring points of "doing science" within the world-view which guides the scientist. To illustrate such generalizations--which are part law-like and part definitional--Kuhn refers to the statement, "action equals reaction." Such a statement functions in part as law, but also in part as a definition for certain symbols which scientists employ (Kuhn, 1970:183). Although such statements may be located within sociological matrices, they may not be intended as they are in the natural sciences (i.e., readily cast in logical form, part law-like, etc.). At the very least, any suggestion that sociological statements could be made with such force would probably generate unnecessary controversy.

To capture the essence of Kuhn's "symbolic-generalizations" category, while avoiding some of its problems, it is appropriate for the purposes here to substitute the term "fundamental anchoring points." Such anchoring points designate basic theoretical concepts that go unchallenged and unreflected upon by practicing scientists within the respective approaches. With regard to the theoretical programs which center upon the study of deviant behavior, the primary anchoring points are the conceptions of deviance which are built into the respective programs. An example, drawn from the disciplinary matrix of the Labeling school, is Becker's (1963) part definitional, part law-like conception that *deviance is that which is referred to as such in society's reaction to conduct*. This conception both defines the phenomenon and indicates its explanation. It signals the gestalt in terms of which deviance is to be understood, and it points to the kinds of problems to be solved. In short, it exemplifies the "fundamental anchoring point" of the perspective.

In similar fashion, Kuhn's category, "metaphysical parts of paradigms," has been translated into terms more comfortably applied to issues of sociological theory. The concept employed here is that of "Domain Assumptions," taken from Alvin Gouldner (1970), which he conceives as follows:

6

Background assumptions of a more limited application, for example, about man and society, are what I shall call "domain assumptions." Domain assumptions are the background assumptions applied only to members of a single domain: they are, in effect, the metaphysics of a domain. (Gouldner, 1970:31)

The appropriation of the concept of domain assumptions narrows the "metaphysical parts of paradigms" in such a way as to increase their manageability. In relation to the examination of "sociological matrices," it raises such questions as: (1) What is the basic nature of humanity? (2) What is the status of human consciousness in human affairs? (3) Is human behavior predictable? and (4) Is human conduct the result of determinant causes, or is it in some sense contingent upon the "creativity" of the actor? In conjunction with these questions, a second aspect of domain assumptions will be considered, and that is the philosophy of science or method associated with the matrix. Here the most general questions are (1) What is the nature of "science"? and (2) How can a "science of persons" be accomplished?

In regard to the component of values, a distinction will be drawn between: (1) *expressed* extra-scientific values and (2) value implications embedded in the matrix regardless of whether or not they are expressed. This latter focus departs somewhat from the thrust of the rest of the study, in that it involves an assessment of the value implications of the various approaches. However, there has been much discussion of this matter by practitioners of the theories concerned, and this analysis will draw heavily upon that discussion.

The table below exhibits, in summary form, the modifications of Kuhn and the applications which will be developed in the course of this study.

Summary Table of Matrix Components

	Fundamental Anchoring Point (Exemplary Problem)	Exemplary Solution (or Mode of Explanation)	Domain Assumptions and Methods	Values Intra-Science	Extra-Science
Etiological-Functionalism					
Labeling Theory					

Table 1

7

B. The Phases of Scientific Activity

In *The Structure of Scientific Revolutions* (1970), Kuhn is concerned with the processes taking place within scientific communities. He informs his readers of two basic phases of scientific activity. The first, "normal science," characterizes the recent history of the "mature sciences." The description of scientific practice as being in the "normal science" phase locates the scientist in a community which shares with him certain basic scientifically relevant assumptions. There is, then, a high level of consensus within this community. The direction of activity is, in a sense, plotted, and what remains is to follow it through. Moreover, within the community, the character of solutions to fundamental problems is agreed upon. The scientists share, in Kuhn's terms, a set of exemplars—which is the first situation that captures the sense of the concept of paradigm as Kuhn has employed that term. In this phase of scientific activity—amidst generalized agreement over fundamentals—practitioners are directed toward typified tasks and problems to which model solutions can be applied.

The second phase, described as "revolutionary" by Kuhn, is quite the opposite of the "normal science" phase. In this phase, there is a lack of consensus among scientists concerning the basic "program" and appropriate "method" of doing science. A disciplinary matrix is not established. In the terms of some sociologies, there is not a well institutionalized, shared "world-view" within the "community."

This revolutionary stage (which involves a "struggle" between paradigms for the allegiance of members of the scientific community) is descriptive of science in its "immature," i.e., "pre-paradigmatic," state. Maturity, in this sense, is indicated by the establishment of a relatively high level of consensus among a group of scientists and, as a result, the appearance of the science as "hard." A scientific discipline is immature insofar as it is "pre-consensual" in terms of the successful institutionalization of an overarching paradigm; hence, it appears as "soft." In these terms, as well as others, the social sciences must be "soft," i.e., they lack consensus concerning fundamentals. Sociology is done in an environment of "softness"—an environment characterized by widespread theoretical confrontation among practitioners.

There is not, nor has there ever been, a period in which a set of exemplars has ascended to such a high level of control over the field that the practice of sociology, as a whole, could be described as being in a period of "normal science." This is not to say that there are not shared exemplars among sociologists or that there is no "normal sociology," i.e., a sociological practice which involves the working out of the problems a theory poses through extending model solutions. Many sociologists do work out of particular theoretical programs. However, no program has ascended to such a level of influence that it successfully controls the discipline. There is perennial confrontation among supporters of various sociological approaches. Most sociologists realize that there are contemporary sociologists of some prominence who do not accept their basic assumptions. Although confrontation does generally characterize the environment in which sociology is done, there are periods when the disputes are more intense, direct, and heated than at other times. The

8

situation in this instance is similar to Kuhn's description of the case of the pre-paradigmatic study of physical optics.

> Being able to take no common body of belief for granted, each writer on physical optics felt forced to build his field anew from its foundation. . . Under these circumstances, the dialogue of the resulting books was often directed as much to members of other schools as it was to nature. (Kuhn, 1970:13)

The situation in sociology is not quite so "loose," but, nevertheless, paradigms are constantly being built by someone who seeks to "shake sociology to its very foundations." In this situation, similar to both the pre-paradigmatic and revolutionary phases of science, there are several characteristic aspects of sociological work. First, discourse within the discipline reflects a concern for fundamentals--basic questions of theory and method are in the forefront. Second, there is a relatively greater focus on the philosophical underpinnings of the activity. Third, communication is often heated and direct--books (which typically deal with fundamentals), rather than journal articles (which typically deal with the solution to problems), proliferate. And, in the revolutionary situation, the dominant but "shaky" paradigm is contested either by the invention of new paradigms or by attention to alternate, but formerly subordinate, paradigms. Sociology is always, relative to the natural sciences, in such a state.

There are times when this situation of conflict among the practitioners of sociology is heightened. The early nineteen-seventies, following the "breakdown" of Parsons' systemic paradigm (see Friederichs, 1970), was clearly such a time. One need only to note the proliferation of new journals and the publication of edited volumes (often containing articles unacceptable to the established journals), the interest in the sociology of knowledge (with sociological knowledge as the subject), and the sudden prominence of such works as *The Coming Crisis of Western Sociology* (1971), in order to become aware that sociology was, not so long ago, in a peculiar state of conflict and self-reflectiveness, even for such a usually volatile and self-conscious discipline.

The situation of the subdisciplinary area, the sociology of deviant behavior, was not then and is not now exempted from this heightened state of confrontation. If anything, the conflict was and is more intense in this area than in others. In the face of the formerly dominant Functional approach of Merton and Parsons, there emerged the important, and now perhaps dominant, new orientation of Labeling Theory.

Although much recent communication among sociologists has been inter-paradigmatic and heated and direct within deviance literature, it is more so now than ever before. A brief excursion into some of the recent statements in the area should make this obvious. Such an excursion should offer some limited documentation for the suggestion that there is a clear dispute over fundamentals in the area.

John Lofland, a representative of the Labeling approach, made it clear in his work, *Deviance and Identity* (1969), that he was, in part, reacting to other approaches. In two rather striking statements in his opening chapter, his attitude toward previous works is established. The first remark is located within a discussion of the "history" of the

9

emergence of the concept of deviance. Noting that the concept's modern development emanated primarily from Harvard and Columbia in the works of Parsons, Cohen, and Merton, he states: "These strangely brief statements of the field were ubiquitously recounted, cited as major statements and read seriously by active sociologists of the time" (Lofland, 1969:6). Within the context of his work, the suggestion of this statement is clear: (1) brief statements cannot be very significant, (2) insignificant statements have been "ubiquitously recounted" and cited as if they were important, (3) the statements were "read seriously" when they should not have been taken seriously, and (4) all this took place in a time now far removed. Lofland's contempt for the older model is hardly contained in the above and shows up even more clearly in the following remark: "social scientific theories of these matters [deviance] tend to reproduce, in more abstruse language and in more complicated manner, the folk theories of mass culture" (1969:10). He then follows with this statement in a footnote to the above quotation:

> . . . instructive have been the writings of students in courses on juvenile delinquency who, upon being asked on the first day of the course to write what they believed to be the causes of delinquency, would handily produce reasonably accurate versions of Cohen, 1955, Cloward and Ohlin, 1960, and various psychologistic perspectives. (Lofland, 1969:10)

The works to which Lofland refers are, of course, highly respected from other perspectives within the area and are hardly regarded as warmed-over folk knowledge. Nor is it the case that the students of those who teach out of the matrix from which such theories flow are viewed as capable of "handily" reproducing these theories even after a few semesters of work, let alone on the first day of class. [4]

At the same time, similar statements have been made by spokesmen of the traditional programs and directed toward those engaged in the development of more recent alternative systems of thought. Robert Merton (the primary figure in the development of the "theory of anomie"), upon reviewing a "staple" passage of basic theoretical content (definitional) by the noted Labeling Theorist, Howard Becker, remarks:

> This passage puts forward a variety of theoretical claims. The first which it shares with every other theory of deviance, is blatantly true and trivial: namely the statement that behavior cannot be considered "deviant" unless there are social norms from which that behavior departs. It seems banal and safe to stipulate: no rule, no rule-violating behavior. (Merton and Nisbet, 1971:827)

---

[4] In discussing Lofland's statement with some of my colleagues, who happen to work from the theoretical system at issue, I found that the position unanimously expressed by them was that Lofland could not have fully understood the theories which he mentioned. Their suggestion was that Lofland most likely did understand the theory at about the same level as his students. That says little of his students, or of the theories at hand, but much about Lofland.

Clearly, there are some basic disputes among sociologists who are concerned with the explanation of deviance. Such exchanges as those which have been recounted here are taken for granted by sociologists. However, such exchanges are not characteristic of most scientific communication among natural scientists or *within* sociological paradigms. The fact that such disputes are (more or less) part of the everyday life of the sociologist indicates something about the structure of the social scientific community and the character of the scholarly work done therein. It is the major task of this work to examine the nature of the differences that encompass such disputes, specifically those which distinguish sociological approaches to deviance, one from another.

C. The Nature of the Examination of the Disciplinary Matrices

Most works that consider separate approaches in sociology, and there are many, seek to do one of two things. One type, which might be called "paradigm histories," seeks a review of past achievements associated with a discipline in order to show how these events have led to the present state of knowledge in the particular field. Usually it is argued that past "discoveries" or "insights" have led inexorably to the point of view from which the work is written. These works take a form similar to "post-revolutionary" histories (e.g., Part I of David Matza's *Becoming Deviant*, 1969). From the perspective of these works, scientific knowledge and insight appear to be a result of a process of cumulative progress, however such progress may be defined. A second type of work focuses upon contemporary paradigms which appear to be in confict with one another, with an eye to the potential synthesis of at least some of their elements (e.g., Walter Wallace's *Sociological Theory*, 1969).

The approach which guides this effort is somewhat removed from either of the types of tasks mentioned above. Under the influence of Kuhn, it is not possible to be sanguine about the potential for historical inter-paradigmatic accumulation of scientific knowledge or the synthesis of inter-matrix conceptualization. Thus, the perspective employed here looks to the various approaches under consideration not with potential synthesis or cumulative development necessarily in mind, but, rather, to *locate* and *elucidate* what may be insurmountable differences between "incommensurable universes of discourse." Kuhn's thesis reflects affinity with some variants of German Historical Idealism and contemporary phenomenology, in that it induces the historian or sociologist of science to locate scientific production within specific paradigms. The concept of "paradigm" (and historically later, "matrix") functions within the framework of Kuhn's theory in a manner akin to the German Idealists' conception of *Geist*. It indicates a (sub)cultural epoch in terms of which action or thought is cast and has meaning.

Consistent with Kuhn's thought, the focus of this study, and its limit, is the "world as it is understood" by the subjects being investigated. The focus of investigation here is not the "everyday life-world" of the subjects, but the theoretical enclaves into which they withdraw while doing their sociology. Specifically, what this study attempts is to decipher, describe, and report the "world as it is constituted" by

11

sociologists in their scientific-theoretical activity. Thus, this work is primarily a study in the sociology of sociology. Its data is, by and large, the documents produced by sociologists for publication in the context of their professional lives.

At the same time, it is a work in comparative sociological theory. In this connection, a question which influences the work throughout is, "Do these theories speak to each other in a meaningful way?" This course of action is recommended by Kuhn in the following statement:

> Taking the differences between their own intra- and inter-group discourse as itself a subject for study, they [scientists] can first attempt to discover the term and locutions that, used unproblematically within each community, are nevertheless foci for trouble for inter-group discussions. . . Having isolated such areas of difficulty in scientific communication, they can next resort to their shared everyday vocabularies in an effort to further elucidate their troubles. . . Each will have learned to translate the other's theory and its consequences into his own language and simultaneously to describe in his own language the world to which that theory applies. . . As translation proceeds, furthermore, some members of each community may also begin to understand how a statement previously opaque could seem an explanation to members of the opposing group. (Kuhn, 1970:202-203)

Following this suggestion, this study analyzes "troublesome terms" in the discourse between the theoretical groups which are its subjects. Further, insofar as it is possible, the work aims to translate these terms into a more widely shared vocabulary--one closer to that of everyday life than the vocabulary of either theoretical group, and one which the practitioners of both groups are presumed to understand. Although this work involves a process of translation, the extent of the translation is limited. The work does not seek to translate the terms of one theory into the terms of another, although to do so would be a very significant accomplishment. However, the view of science which guides this work is pessimistic concerning such a possibility. For those who are hopeful regarding such a possibility, this study can be regarded as a step in that process. Be this as it may, this project emphasizes the distinctiveness of the matrices under consideration. The assumption in this work is that the matrices represent distinct gestalts and that such gestalts cannot be combined, i.e., it is unlikely that one can "see" in both ways at the same time. Although one cannot "view" from several gestalts simultaneously, it is possible to "know" them simultaneously. It is then possible to employ each gestalt as one chooses. However, the most direct result of such "simultaneous knowing," and the primary goal of this work, is a more general understanding of the theoretical world of the sociologist. The value which might be found in such understanding will be considered as this project is brought to a close.

CHAPTER II

THE SETTING OF THE STRUCTURAL-FUNCTIONAL APPROACH TO DEVIANCE

A. Introduction

Before establishing the basic components of the study of deviance within the Anomic and Systemic approaches, it will be useful to consider some basic elements of the more general perspective of "Structural-Functionalism." It is not the intent of the present study to isolate the major elements of this system of sociology in its entirety. However, the study will pinpoint the elements of the general approach which have influenced the development of the theory of deviance. This requires that the focus be primarily upon the nature of the concept of "social structure," rather than the other major concern of the perspective, that of the functional significance of structural patterns. The study will be *less* concerned with the issues which surround the emergence and functional consequences of institutions than with the impact of social structure on conduct.[1]

Four major concepts associated with this aspect of the Structural-Functionalist perspective will be considered. These are concepts which allow the establishment of the setting from which the problem of deviance emerges. These four central concepts are: (1) institutions, (2) internalization, (3) norms and values, and (4) society. Discussion of these will allow consideration of the sense in which, from this perspective, a person may be viewed as a "member" of society. This is of primary importance in establishing the perspective on deviance employed by the Functionalists.

Although these four terms are widely employed in sociology, they

---

[1]Such an interest may include concern with the "functional consequences of behavior." However, the study is not concerned with the issues usually associated with that phrase (i.e., issues which refer to the fulfillment of functional prerequisites or the establishment of functional relations within systems). Rather, the study is concerned with behavioral outcomes regardless of their functional consequences.

are used in a particular way by the Functionalists. However, their meaning and employment is not necessarily the same amongst all sociologists.

B. Institutions

Perhaps the central concept of the Structural-Functional approach is that of "institution." For Durkheim, the social institution was the social fact *par excellance*:

> But in order that there may be a social fact, several individuals, at the very least, must have contributed their action; and in this joint activity is the origin of a new fact. Since this joint activity takes place outside each one of us (for a plurality of consciousnesses enters into it), its necessary effect is to fix, to institute outside us, certain ways of acting and certain judgments which do not depend on each particular will taken separately. It has been pointed out that the word "institution" well expresses this special mode of reality. . . One can, indeed, without distorting the meaning of this expression, designate as "institutions" all the beliefs and all the modes of conduct instituted by the collectivity. Sociology can then be defined as the science of institutions, of their genesis and of their functioning. (Durkheim, 1938:lvi)

The concept of institutions is equally central in the modern Functionalist approach. Marion Levy suggests in his work, *The Structure of Society*:

> The most general form of these concepts oriented to normative patterns and the problem of conformity is the concept, *institution*. This concept is a focal point of interest for the entire volume. (Levy, 1952:102)

Talcott Parsons, perhaps the major figure of influence among the modern Functionalists, also views institutions and institutionalization as the central organizing concept of his work. He states, "The focus of this view has been on the importance of institutions and institutionalization as the primary concern of sociology as a science" (Parsons, 1951:547).

A primary element of the definition of the concept has already been established in the quotation from Durkheim--that institutions are a joint (shared) product. Levy adds, in his definition, the element of "sanctions" which is associated with institutions.[2] He suggests that an institution is a particular type of normative pattern,

> . . . (1) conformity with which is generally to be expected, and (2) failure to conform with which is generally met with moral indignation of those individuals who are involved in the same general social system. . . (Levy, 1952:102)

---

[2] See, also, Johnson, *Sociology: A Systematic Introduction* (1960: Chapters 1 and 2).

Hence, when an institution is violated, punishment (or at least disapproval) ensues, and when it is adhered to, rewards (or at least approval) are forthcoming. In sum, a pattern of social life is regarded as institutionalized when it is not only repetitive[3] but shared. The pattern is an outcome and representation of a joint commitment among a collectivity of actors, that is, adherence to it must be diffused among the members of the group. Furthermore, an institutionalized pattern is supported by a system of sanctions. When such a pattern exists, and that which is shared is a specific expectation concerning activity, it can be called an "institutionalized norm." To suggest that a norm is institutionalized does not imply that all actors within the collectivity are committed to it, but, rather, that most certainly are and that the pattern is operative. That is, if the pattern is institutionalized, it is at least something with which all actors within the setting must contend. However, institutionalization is a matter of degree,[4] i.e., a norm may be more or less institutionalized.

C. Internalization

The concept of internalization does not have the wide use among Functional Theorists that the concept of institutionalization has. The term was not at all fashionable in Durkheim's time. It is employed by Parsons and his closest students (e.g., Albert Cohen) who delve more systematically into the psychological level which includes internalization than do most Functionalists. Although the term was not current in Durkheim's time, Parsons argues that Durkheim was among the first to have had insight into the process.[5] Although the term is not widely used, modern Functionalists usually find themselves using terms which imply that internalization (or something similar to it) has taken place. For example, terms referring to the *actor's orientation, commitment,* etc. are often employed in lieu of a specific reference to internalization. These terms imply that the actor is committed to an institutional pattern.

Whereas institutionalization refers to the workings of a group, internalization refers to an individual's "taking on" the pattern of the group (literally, "taking into" such that the pattern is viewed as a constituent of personality).[6] A pattern is described as having been

---

[3]Idiosyncratic individual patterns may well be repetitive, but if they are not shared or supported by a system of sanctions, they are not viewed as institutionalized. The term "habit" usually refers to these repetitive, idiosyncratic behaviors of individuals.

[4]See Johnson (1960:20-21).

[5]See Parsons (1952), "The Superego and the Theory of Social Systems," *Psychiatry,* 15:15-25.

[6]From this point of view, personality is an abstraction which refers to aspects of the individual's orientation, without regard to whether or not the elements of orientation are shared by others. (See Parsons and Shils, *Toward a General Theory of Action,* 1951: Chapter 2.)

internalized when it is associated with the commitments or "needs" of a person. It is possible, then, to describe a pattern as having been institutionalized within a group, although there will be, at the same time, some individuals in that group who do not share in the collective commitment (i.e., some will not have internalized the norm). When referring to the way of life of a people (their institutions), it is always an "empirical question" as to whether or not a particular individual in the collectivity has internalized these institutionalized norms. The problem of "internalization of norms," then, always refers to an aspect of the individual's orientation.

D. Institutionalized Values and Norms

The Functionalists have generally discussed institutions in relation to two major forms: (1) institutionalized values and (2) institutionalized norms. Norms and values differ in their level of generality. Values provide the most general orientations. Smelser (1973:6) defines values as "cultural standards that indicate the general goals deemed desirable for organized social life." Norms are viewed as more specific guides to conduct. Smelser's definition of norms indicates that they "refer to expectations and standards that regulate the interaction among persons." The difference in the levels of generalization between norms and values can be exemplified by reference to a value such as "equality of opportunity," which is an institutionalized value in the United States of America. Whereas this value provides a general orientation for conduct, it does not indicate, in any specific way, how persons are to behave in a particular situation. However, specific guidelines may be derived from the general value. Such guidelines as "The personnel committee of academic departments should not discriminate against Blacks and Women in hiring practices"[7] represent such specific mandates to action, i.e., they are norms. The relationship between the two is generally such that a norm (a specific item of proposed or expected action) is legitimated by reference to a value (a broad belief which influences the designation of appropriate action).

E. Society

The concept of society within Functionalist literature may be derived directly from the concepts just reviewed. Society is not a group of individuals co-existing within certain geographical boundaries. Parsons makes clear the distinctiveness of his concept of society as he states:

---

[7]Norms are often embodied in law, as exemplified in the illustration above. Values are less likely to be specified narrowly enough to allow their codification into law. Only at the most general level might this occur (e.g., in the Constitution of the United States). Values are, of course, developed in the literature and documents of a people (e.g., in the Declaration of Independence).

16

This view [his own] contrasts sharply with our common sense notion of society as being composed of concrete human individuals. . . The core of society, as a system . . . is the patterned normative order through which the life of a population is collectively organized. As an order, it contains values and differentiated and particularized norms and rules, all of which require cultural references in order to be meaningful and legitimate. (Parsons, 1966:9-10)

The "primary" constituents of society, then, are not the individual people themselves, but, rather, their interaction patterns--institutions. "Institutions in the sense intended here are *found as parts of a society* [emphasis added] or as the result of intersocietal relationships" (Levy, 1952:111). Society, of course, is associated with a group of people (sometimes called a collectivity in the Functionalists' vocabulary); but society is *not* itself the concrete group.[8] Rather, it is a "social fact" which, along with other things, influences the conduct of persons. It is not the persons themselves.

F. Membership in Society

The last topic of this chapter involves the establishment of the sense, from the Functionalist frame of reference, in which persons are understood as *members* of society. Not all persons standing within certain geographical bounds to one another or even those who are in persistent interaction with each other need be viewed as members of the same society.

In the first place, members of a society share an institutional framework. That is, they are all oriented toward the same pattern of institutions. However, the extent to which they share this orientation is always a matter of degree. As Levy states:

The members of a society may and commonly do vary in the degree to which they orient their actions to the particular system of action concerned. They may, and certainly today commonly do, either directly or indirectly, orient their action to more than one such system of action. (Levy, 1952:122)

In order to determine whether or not a person is a member of a particular society, the observer/classifier must shift referents, according to the orientation of the actor. To put it another way, determining a person's membership in society (having specified the societal point of reference) necessitates answering the question: "Is the person oriented to, and involved in, the pattern of action?" The answer, for some Functionalists, revolves around the problem of whether or not the general pattern has

---

[8]Society, not being composed of concrete persons, is an abstraction. It is one of three major abstractions drawn from the concrete person and group which the Functionalists employ. The other abstractions are personality and culture.

been internalized by the actor. Other Functionalists, as previously indicated, are reluctant to employ the concept of internalization. But, one way or the other, most specify or imply that an actor who is a member of society is "psychologically involved with" a set of institutions, which is the societal pattern. Phrases such as, "the actor is oriented to" (Levy, 1952) or "shares the deposit of values" (Merton, 1967), are alternatives to directly saying that the actor has internalized the pattern.

Levy clarifies this conception of societal membership by pointing out that:

> An individual from a given society x may in fact reside among the members of a quite different society y. He may do so over long periods and may conform to a high degree indeed to the structures of society y. To the degree that such conformity remains an expedient from his point of view and an expedient entered into in order to orient his actions in terms of society x, the individual remains in the terminology of this study a member of society x, or, if one will, a *genuine member* of society x and *an expedient member* of society y. To the degree, whether realized or not, that this conformity ceases to be such an expedient, a shift takes place in his membership. (Levy, 1952:126)

Levy's distinction between a genuine and an expedient member of society clearly demands a reference to the individual level (i.e., it involves questions of the actor's orientation). The difference, it appears, has to do with whether or not the actor has "internalized" the pattern. If he has, he is a genuine member of society. If not, the person is simply involved in a set of institutional patterns with which he must contend but to which he is not committed.

The contention to be developed in the next chapter is that the Functionalists' "problem of deviance" focuses upon the departure from institutionalized patterns by "genuine" members of society.

CHAPTER III

ETIOLOGICAL-FUNCTIONALISM

A. Introduction

This chapter will consider Functionalism in relation to the development of a theory of the etiology of the deviant act. The focus of the chapter is upon what has been described as the "fundamental anchoring point" of a disciplinary matrix (See Chapter I). As indicated in the opening chapter, it is the conception of deviance associated with a perspective which is understood here to be its fundamental anchoring point, and as such establishes the nature of the "exemplary problem" found within the matrix. The first section of this chapter will be concerned with the conception of deviance associated with the Anomic variant of Functionalism, the latter portion will address the Systemic variant of Functionalism. This chapter will establish the differences in emphasis associated with the two variants and will also establish the sense in which the two wings of the approach are within the same general disciplinary matrix of Etiological-Functionalism.

As noted earlier, the contemporary approach of Anomie traces its origins to the work of Emile Durkheim. Of the classical sociologists, Durkheim exhibited the most explicit concern with what sociologists today call deviant behavior. It is not suggested that Durkheim's perspective on the subject of deviance is precisely the same as that of theorists within the Anomie tradition of our day. Rather, Durkheim established two fundamental aspects of the modern Anomie approach. First, he established a conception of crime and the criminal as existing within consensual societies. Second, he established a mode of explanation--structural explanation--which has been adopted by many modern theorists, not only those associated with the Anomie approach.

Important among those who have been influenced by Durkheim, and who have also elaborated his views, is Robert Merton. Merton may be described as the major architect of the "modern" theory of Anomie. Richard Cloward and Lloyd Ohlin have also contributed to the theoretical development of the approach. This chapter will focus upon the contributions of these scholars and Durkheim's influence on them.

B. Specification of the Fundamental Anchoring Points Within the Theory of Anomie

This section highlights the basic and most taken-for-granted aspects of the Anomie approach to deviant behavior. In the introductory chapter, it was suggested that the fundamental anchoring points are composed of basic positions that go unchallenged by those who "do science" within a particular disciplinary matrix. Among those adhering to the Anomie tradition, perhaps the most taken-for-granted assumption is that the idea of "social structure" may be employed in the explanation of human conduct, including deviant behavior. One part of this section will be devoted to a discussion of the role of social structure in the exemplary mode of the explanation of deviant behavior within the works of Anomie theorists.

The second aspect of the theory of Anomie which is fundamental and which signals the "exemplary problem" is the character of the concept of "deviance" which this group of theorists develops. The question here is, "What is it that is meant by deviance; what special qualities does an act have to possess, if any, to qualify as deviance and, hence, as an object requiring explanation within this approach?" In attempting to specify the meaning of deviance within the approach, reference must be made to the previous discussion of the two related concepts of institutionalization and internalization.

After a discussion of the concept of deviance employed within the framework, the Anomie theorists' use of social structure as a primary explanatory variable in the explanation of the phenomenon will be examined.

C. The Concept of Deviance Employed Within the Theory of Anomie

1. Introduction

The term "deviance," which is widely employed by contemporary sociologists, has its origins within the latter phases of the Anomie tradition. It has been appropriated by other perspectives within sociology, although it is doubtful that the concept, as originally conceived, fits neatly into their general framework. It is a term which emerged within the confines of a sociology which posits the existence of consensual orders, groups of persons characterized by a widespread sharing of belief concerning how man should live.

2. Durkheim's Concept of Crime

Although Durkheim did not employ the term "deviance" (but, rather, "crime"), it is clear that it is his conception of society and the character of departures from the dominant patterns of society, that has supplied the foundation for the concept of deviance which is embodied in the Theory of Anomie. The Durkheimian concept of "crime" is developed in two of his works: primarily in *The Division of Labor in Society* (1933) and, more briefly but perhaps more importantly, in *The Rules of Sociological Method* (1938).

As is well known, in *The Division of Labor*, Durkheim was concerned with describing the bases of solidarity in social life. In essence, the book proposes two distinct mechanisms by which different types of society are held together. First, there is "mechanical solidarity." In this instance, persons are held together by their basic homogeneity, i.e., their sharing of a similar world-view and set of commitments. The second Durkheim describes as "organic solidarity." Organic solidarity (characteristic of modern society) finds men held together not by essential similarity, but, rather, by their differences along the lines of a "functional division of labor." Men are held together by the functional reciprocity among their differentiated roles within a complex and highly segmented society.

These two types of society are characterized by the distinctiveness of the type of law which predominates in each. Mechanical solidarity is associated with the predominance of "repressive law." This type of law calls for a punitive reaction which aims at the suppression of the action which is "in violation." Such law is an outcome of the *mutual abhorrence* that members of society feel toward certains kinds of acts. Organic solidarity is characterized by "restitutive law." This form of law is associated with "contract." Contract law governs relations among persons who differ in some important respects, but who are reciprocally dependent, even though they may have separate interests. Restitutive law governs the relations between these parties to contract who exist together in an "under-institutionalized" relationship. The function of such law is to allow the establishment of relations among heterogeneous categories of persons, rather than to punish the party who does not meet his obligations under "contract." Restitutive law seeks to re-establish the situation which existed prior to the violation of the specific mandates of the contract and the consequent "injury" of the offended parties. It seeks, so to speak, to restore the status quo ante. Restitutive law corresponds to "civil law;" repressive law corresponds to "criminal law." Crime, then, is conceived by Durkheim in the terms of mechanical solidarity as consisting "of an act which offends very strong collective sentiments" (Durkheim, 1933:67). To Durkheim, deviance is a violation of institutionalized norms. An act is deviant (criminal) when it is institutionally proscribed.

Since Durkheim's concept of crime is found in relationship with his concept of mechanical solidarity, it may appear that it is only applicable to pre-modern societies. However, to arrive at such a conclusion would be an error. Durkheim did not argue that the emergence of modern society and "organic solidarity" signaled the disappearance of repressive law. The dichotomy between organic and mechanical solidarity which Durkheim discussed concerns which system of law (acting as the primary basis of solidarity) is dominant in the society and, thus, characterizes a type of social arrangement. In fact, mechanical solidarity,[1] a shared institutional framework, carries over into the organic setting, as is best

---

[1] It would be going too far afield to discuss the issues concerning the interpretation of Durkheim which suggests that he deserted the dichotomy of mechanical and organic solidarity altogether in his later work, concluding that mechanical solidarity was the basic cement of the moral order. There is no doubt, however, that this interpretation has been taken on by modern Functionalists (see Parsons, 1937: Chapter VIII).

exemplified by the *institution* of contract itself. What must be emphasized here is that Durkheim's conception of crime is drawn from the setting of mechanical solidarity. This conception of deviance, although it is appropriate to modern society (since mechanical elements remain in modern society), does not refer to the differentiation of persons and interests characteristic of organic solidarity, but rather to the continued existence of repressive law. The problem of deviance as conceived by Durkheim refers to "mechanical solidarity" and "homogeneity," even in the case of modern "pluralistic" society in which restitutive law is dominant. Hence, for Durkehim, deviance is defined in terms of the sentiments persons hold in common, rather than those which differentiate them. The realm of conflicting values and interests simply does not present the problem which, in this context, requires explanation. Deviance is, rather, conceived in terms of institutionally governed relations. Robert Nisbet summarizes succinctly the interpretation of Durkheim's work which is suggested here:

> Repressive law--which, as we have seen, is the mechanism of the maintenance of mechanical solidarity in tribes, clans, villages, and other manifestations of this type of solidarity--is the agency both of definition of deviance (and in degree at least of creation of it) and of punishment. (Nisbet, 1974:213)

This is true not only in the case of the application to "simple societal units" (those which Nisbet includes above), but to modern societies as well. If there is no consensus such as is characteristic of Durkheim's mechanical solidarity, then there is no "deviance," as he conceives the category.

Durkheim's view of deviance is further elaborated in *The Rules of Sociological Method* (1938). It has already been established that Durkheim views deviance as a violation of institutions--conceived as widely shared commitments. This position, established in *The Division of Labor*, goes unchanged in his later work. However, the question still remains as to how far this "sharing" extends. Specifically, in relation to deviance, where does the "deviant act" (as opposed to other failures to live up to expectations, e.g., failures to conform by strangers) stand in terms of the mutual commitments of the group? Does deviance involve only the violation of a sentiment which the deviant actor shares with the group? That is, must he be enmeshed in the institutional complex in order to "deviate" from it? This question might have been neatly answered in Durkheim's text if he had employed the concept of internalization. However, Durkheim was never systematically concerned with the psychological states of the actor and rarely delved into this realm. He was much more inclined to discuss collective commitments than individual ones. Further, the concept of internalization is associated with modern psychology and sociology. However, there are some clues in his work which indicate the intimate relation of the deviant actor to the sentiments which he violates. As Durkheim conceives crime, it is a phenomenon which is present even in the most highly consensual societies. In these cases, the consensus extends to include all of the individuals. That is, each member, including the actor engaged in deviance, shares the same sentiments. Under this condition (or better, because of it), deviance is

22

inevitable. The following statement indicates that individuals who commit "crime" may be committed to a social order which, in spite of the high degree of consensus associated with it, spawns deviance:

> Imagine a society of saints, a perfect cloister of exemplary individuals. Crimes, properly so called, will be there unknown; but faults which appear venial to the layman will create there the same scandal that ordinary offense does in ordinary consciousness. (Durkheim, 1938:68)

Crime, then, for Durkheim, is not just an outcome of pluralism, value conflict, or heterogeneity in general;[2] rather, it is an integral aspect of "society," of consensual order. Although it would be inappropriate to suggest that Durkheim views crime as so bound up with consensus that even if *all* the actors have *internalized* the same norms to the same extent, crime would nevertheless persist, he does come close to making such a statement, in the following quotation:

> In a society in which criminal acts are no longer committed, the sentiments they offend would have to be found without exception in all individual consciousnesses, and they must be found to exist with the same degree as sentiments contrary to them. *Assuming this condition could actually be realized, crime would not thereby disappear*; it would only change its form, for the very cause which would thus dry up the sources of criminality would immediately open up new ones [emphasis added]. (Durkheim, 1938:67)

How, then, do we account for the differences among persons which allow some behaviors to emerge which "violate" the sentiments which they share with others? If men all share the same sentiments in a particular society, how can deviance occur? Although all members of society--in order to be designated as members--are cognizant of the same sentiments, they do not necessarily reflect equal commitment to them. This fact is accounted for by the normal diversities among human beings and is an outcome of normal biological, psychological, and social processes. As Durkheim states:

> . . . the immediate physical milieu in which each one of us is placed, the hereditary antecedents, and the social influences vary from one individual to the next, and consequently diversify consciousnesses. (Durkheim, 1938:69)

Durkheim's view of deviance may be briefly summarized as follows. First, deviance occurs within the framework of a highly consensual setting. It is associated with mechanical solidarity, homogeneity, and repressive law, not with the heterogeneity of organic solidarity, pluralism, or conflicting interests. Crime is associated with and is a violation of

---

[2]This is not to say that such a situation might not generate crime, defined as the violation of "very strong collective sentiments," but this simply is not Durkheim's focus. Durkheim's focus is upon another problem: crime as a phenomenon of "society."

strong, mutually held sentiments. Second, this mutuality of sentiment (consensual commitment) extends to the potential deviant actor.

For Durkheim, deviance takes place within membership. The actor engaged in deviance is associated with the consensus which he violates. Durkheim admits that he, too, had made the mistake of seeing the criminal as an alien to society. He makes the following statement in the text of *The Rules*: "Contrary to current ideas, the criminal no longer seems a totally unsociable being, a sort of parasitic element, a strange and unassimilable body introduced in the midst of society" (Durkheim, 1938:72). He footnotes this statement by noting his "mistake" in *The Division of Labor*. "We have ourselves committed the error of speaking thus of the criminal, because of our failure to apply our rule. . ." (1938:72). Durkheim, then, does not go outside the consensus which is society to locate some aliens (in a biological, psychological, or sociological sense) in order to account for deviance. He finds it, rather, within the confines of society (defined as a consensual group), endemic to its structure and carried out by its members.

3. Merton's Concept of Deviance

The task undertaken in this section is to specify the qualities associated with the concept of deviance within the work of Robert K. Merton. Merton is concerned, as was Durkheim, with the explanation of deviance within societal groups. And "society," just as was ultimately the case for Durkheim, is also viewed by Merton as a consensual order. He states that, "Unless there is a deposit of values shared by interacting individuals, there exist social relations, if the disorderly interactions may be so-called, but no society" (Merton, 1967:141). Employing this concept of society, Merton seeks to explain the distribution and rates of deviance in "American Society." Merton's analysis assumes that, insofar as there is an "American Society," it contains a shared deposit of values among the membership.

While Merton operates with this assumption of widespread consensus, he is well aware that a significant portion of the population may *not* be committed to the dominant values. However, that portion of the population which does not share important elements of the "shared deposit of values" is, in the strict Mertonian sense, outside "society" (since they do not share the values), and, therefore, their behavior is irrelevant to the theory. Commenting on the distribution of the American success motif among the lower class, he states:

> . . . the hypothesis of the foregoing chapter [Social Structure and Anomie] requires that an appreciable minority, not all or most, of those in the lower strata will have assimilated the cultural mandate for monetary success, and that it *presupposes affectively significant assimilation of the value* rather than merely verbal acquiescence with it [emphasis added]. (Merton, 1967:172)

This quotation is important to Merton's analysis in two respects. First, and directly relevant to this present work, it aids in the specification of the category of deviant behavior within the theory of Anomie. This analysis presupposes *affectively significant assimilation* of the values of the actor. If he does not share commitment to the value at some point, then his behavior is not relevant to the theory. In other words, in the absence of "affective assimilation," the actor is "outside society," and, therefore, his behavior will not fall within the range of those behaviors which require explanation within the framework of the approach. Second, if the value is not ascribed to, there can be no "pressure" exerted on the actor by the fact that he does not have access to the means of its attainment. Hence, the actor's commitment to the values is a basic source of the *pressure* to *deviance* which Merton describes as impinging upon the actor.

There is further evidence in Merton's text that he begins his analysis of deviance with a view of the actor as having been committed to a set of standards from which he withdraws his support. Commenting upon the "emotional strains" associated with the commission of deviant acts, he states:

It appears unlikely that cultural norms, once interiorized, are wholly eliminated. Whatever residuum persists will induce personality tensions and conflict, with some measure of *ambivalence*. A manifest rejection of the once-incorporated *institutional* norms will be coupled with some latent retention of their emotional correlates. Guilt feelings, a sense of sin, pangs of conscience are diverse terms referring to this unrelieved tension. [emphasis added]. (Merton, 1967:136)

Merton, then, like Durkheim, is concerned with behavior as it is relevant to *membership* in society. However, more directly than Durkheim, Merton indicates that the actor engaged in deviance is himself caught up in the consensus which he violates. Merton's formulation (as can be seen from the above quotation) begins with an actor who is successfully socialized into the dominant pattern--an actor who is, in the fullest sense, a *member* of society. It is only under the "pressure" imposed by a "malintegrated" culture that the actor *withdraws* his support from the norms and, in a sense, becomes uncommitted. The relationship between this original commitment and the emergence of deviance is indeed dialectical. The actor is subject to the pressure to withdraw his commitment from the dominant pattern partially as a result of his commitment.

This formulation leaves us with a question. Can the behavior of an actor who does not share an element of the deposit of values, e.g., the goals, be considered "deviant"? Clearly, Merton's "ritualist," as well as other types of deviant adaptations, fits this case. The question as to whether or not this lack of commitment is "deviant" must be answered within the biographical experience of the actor. If the actor was "originally" committed to the value system but was "driven out" of this commitment, then the behavior is deviant. If, on the other hand, the actor was never committed to the pattern of goals and means (never oriented to the norms), his behavior--although it may not conform to the pattern-- does not meet the requirements of Merton's conceptualization of deviance. Nor, in this case, is the actor subject to the pressure which Merton describes.

Merton's conceptualization involves more than a consideration of a relationship between a pattern of behavior and the dominant institutions

25

of a geographical area (e.g., the United States) such that all behavior which departs from those institutions is deviant. The establishment of deviance requires a consideration of the actor's relationship to the institutional framework. The actor must be "hooked up" to the social structure (be a member of the group) before his behavior falls within the purview of the theory.

In sum, Merton's theory of deviance includes the violation of the institutionalized norms of the group by an actor who is viewed as once having been committed to these norms. The actor, under pressure, withdraws his commitment from the pattern--the disposition to follow the pattern is overcome. In such a case, deviant behavior, as a special case of human behavior, exists and requires explanation.

4. Cloward and Ohlin's Concept of Delinquency

The discussion of Cloward and Ohlin's conception of delinquency will be relatively brief, since the intent here is to show only that their interest in deviance is located in the same phenomena and processes as is Merton's. Most importantly, this means that in conceiving of deviance, they assume prior commitment on the part of the actor to the dominant system of norms. Hence, as is Merton, they are interested in the factors which lead the actor to *withdraw support* from the once-supported, dominant pattern. Their view of the delinquent is one of an actor who, once having been committed to the norms, no longer attributes legitimacy to them.

> It is our view that members of delinquent subcultures *have withdrawn* their attribution of legitimacy to certain of the norms maintained by law abiding groups of the larger society. . . [emphasis added]. (Cloward and Ohlin, 1960:19)

Cloward and Ohlin contend that behavior which fits the *legal* category, *delinquency*, may be described in the terms of the *sociological* (Mertonian) *concept of deviance*. The distinction between the legal and sociological terms is of some importance. A *delinquent* or *criminal* act (legal terms) need not be conceived as "deviant" in the terms of the theory of Anomie. In fact, one of the theories of delinquency that Cloward and Ohlin contest in their work (that of Walter Miller, 1958) suggests that delinquency should not be conceived as "deviance."

Miller argues that delinquency is an outcome of *conformity* to a long-standing cultural tradition which is distinct from, and subordinate to, the dominant culture. The cultural tradition to which he refers is associated with the lower class. From Miller's view, this tradition is separate from the dominant culture and has a history and integrity of its own which distinguish it from the patterns of the middle class. If this is the case, the dominant cultural structure has little, if anything, to do with the emergence of the delinquent act. The child who is engaged in delinquency is viewed as never having been committed to the dominant way of life. He is a child of another way of life. The delinquent act, so conceived, does not involve a prior commitment on the part of the actor to the dominant pattern. In short, from Miller's view, delinquency is an outcome of a co-existent but separate socio-cultural milieu to which

26

lower-class persons are oriented. It is only from the perspective of the middle class and the law (which is viewed as external to the lower-class tradition) that the acts are defined as delinquent. Thus *delinquent acts*, from Miller's view, are not *deviant acts*, in the terms associated with the theory of Anomie. From Miller's perspective, there is no question of "withdrawal" of support from the dominant structure, since there is no prior commitment on the part of the actor to such a structure. The delinquent, from this point of view, is in very important respects an outsider to the group which adjudges him.

In opposition to Miller, Cloward and Ohlin contend that delinquency *is* "deviant," i.e., it is an action associated with one's membership in the group. Thus, Cloward and Ohlin deny Miller's contention that the lower classes are independent from other groups of Americans.

> Miller's analysis suggests a degree of cultural independence of the two classes that has probably not prevailed since the mass immigrations of the nineteenth and early twentieth centuries. (Cloward and Ohlin, 1960:71)

Just as Cloward and Ohlin dispute Miller's "differential socialization" - "value conflict" hypothesis, they oppose "faulty socialization" explanations. They say, in relation to such explanations of delinquency: "We do not subscribe to explanations of this kind, for we do not view the delinquent as untouched or unreached by the society of which he is a part" (1960:37).

The actor of reference in Cloward and Ohlin's theory is, then, a fully socialized member of the society whose rules he violates. Two more brief quotes from their work should establish this even more clearly: "Conformity, taking cultural mandates seriously, is thus a crucial step in the process by which deviance is generated" (1960:38). And: "In summary, it is our contention that problems of adjustment [which may lead to deviance] are engendered by acts of social conformity performed under adverse circumstances" (1960:39). Hence, according to Cloward and Ohlin, deviance and conformity are closely associated with one another, and both are associated with membership in society. In sum, they argue that the situation which characterizes American society is one of relatively high consensus concerning what is "preferred conduct." The problem of deviance begins with the assumption of this consensus, and the question then becomes (as it does for Merton), "Why, given widespread mutual commitment, do some members of the society withdraw support from the patterns?" Thus, Cloward and Ohlin have characterized the "delinquent" behavior of youth in American society in terms of the conception of deviance which is here also associatd with Merton and Durkheim.

5. Summary

This section has established the particular conception of deviance associated with the theory of Anomie. It has been shown that the category of "crime" developed in the work of Emile Durkheim is associated with consensual societies. Crime, according to Durkheim, is a product of such consensus. Further, within the framework of Durkheim's thought, it is not necessary to leave the bounds of the consensual group in order to locate the "criminal" actor. The "criminal" is associated with the established consensus as a member of the group. There is no need to look outside the bounds of the consensual group to locate the sources of deviance. Just as consensus creates conformity, it also gives rise to deviation. Crime is a violation of the institutions of the group which is carried out by members of the group.

Merton, as has been shown, was influenced by Durkheim. In employing the concept of deviance, he, too, focused upon a phenomenon of society defined as a consensual group. Merton's actor engaged in deviance is not an alien in relation to the group whose institutions are violated. Merton is even more explicit than Durkheim in suggesting that the deviant actor in whose behavior he is interested is one who has been inducted into the group--one who shares the deposit of values--one who is a member of the society. The deviant actor, to Merton, is one who has been committed to the norms, but who has become uncommitted (alienated).

Cloward and Ohlin's work represents an attempt to appropriate this conception of deviance in the conceptualization and explanation of patterns of delinquency. They argue that the actor involved in such conduct is not isolated from the influences of the dominant society, but, rather, is attached to society. Delinquent behavior is viewed, then, as requiring explanation in the terms of the sociological concept of deviance. He, too, although an alienated member, is a member of the group whose norms his behavior flouts, and it is this membership which has influenced his behavior.

D. The Specification of the Fundamental Anchoring Points Within the Systemic Variant of the Functionalist Matrix

1. Introduction

This chapter will conclude with a discussion of the "systemic variant" of the Functionalist matrix. This wing of the matrix is represented by the work of Parsons (1951) and Cohen (1955). The decision to isolate this statement from the preceding section on the "Anomie variant" was not made because the two operate as separate matrices, but because of some differences in emphasis between the two. Parsons and Cohen are much more systematic and elaborate in dealing with the psychological element, heretofore vague, within the approach. Also, they are more self-conscious about the conceptual contours of their theorizing than are other representatives of the Functionalist approach. As a result, the outline of the exemplary conception of deviance is more pronounced in their work than it is within the Anomie variant of the approach.

2. The Setting and Specification of Deviance

a. Parsons

Parsons' analysis of deviance begins with an explicit statement which establishes his point of view on the subject. Consistent with the Anomie approach (but more explicit), Parsons proposes a model of consensual interaction which he refers to as "the fundamental paradigm of social interaction." The following statement outlines the model in terms of which the problem of deviance is framed.

> . . . assume that ego and alter have, in their interaction, developed mutual cathectic attachments to each other, so that they are sensitive to each other's attitudes, i.e., attitudes are fundamental as sanctions, and that the interaction is integrated with a normative pattern of value orientation, both ego and alter, that is, have internalized the value pattern. . .

> This paradigm provides the setting for the analysis of the genesis of motivation to deviance. (Parsons, 1951:251-252)

There are two aspects of this statement that deserve emphasis: (1) deviance takes place within a setting characterized by a *shared institutional complex*, and (2) all actors have *internalized* the relevant patterns. The statement makes it clear that the problem of deviance does not exist, nor is it resolvable, in relation to persons who are: (1) outside the institutional complex which is the point of reference, or (2) "incompletely socialized," although nominally within the institutional system. Parsons, then, leaves no doubt that the behavioral contraventions of norms which are "deviant" involve commitments to the pattern violated. It is this element that makes the behavior deviant rather than simply different. As previously noted, the other scholars within this tradition have employed a similar concept of deviance involving commitments to the patterns ultimately violated. However, they have not devoted much attention to the psychodynamics which accompany such violation. Parsons devotes considerable attention to this problem in the development of his category of "deviant motivation."[3]

Keeping this paradigm in mind, a brief review of Parsons' statement concerning the development of deviance will exhibit the psychological processes which are, for Parsons, definitive of deviance. Deviance, defined at the individual level,[4] is "a motivated tendency for the actor to behave in contravention of one or more institutionalized normative patterns." When a disturbance is introduced into the system, deviance is the result. Further, ego (the actor who is the point of reference) is

---

[3]This does not imply that the other scholars within this tradition would necessarily accept Parsons' solution. Rather, it suggests, given the way deviance is conceived by these scholars, that they would agree that deviance involves a *change* in one's commitments, and this suggests the occurrence of particular psychological dynamics.

[4]Parsons defines deviance at the social system level as, in essence, that behavior which disequilibrates the social system. It should be noted that behavior which is conformative may also have such a consequence. This level of analysis is not the focus of the work within this matrix, nor does Parsons devote much attention to it in his work. Primarily, the explanation of deviance, from this perspective, has focused on the individual point of reference.

frustrated by the deviance of his interactional partner, alter. When ego is frustrated by alter's behavior, he is, in Parsons' terms, faced with a "problem of adjustment." Alter's deviance from ego's expectations may be frustrating to ego in one or more of the following ways. Ego's expectations in relation to alter are part of his "need-dispositions." This is the case since ego cathects (cares about) alter so that *what alter does matters to ego*, and ego cannot easily end the relationship, i.e., *alter matters to ego*. Ego is frustrated because the internalized value pattern is violated. That is, for Parsons, if the actor has internalized the value or normative pattern, he is then viewed as disposed to follow it; hence, he is disturbed by not being able to do so. The "strain" in such a situation can be relieved in one or more of the following ways: (1) ego may inhibit his need-disposition to conform to the norm being violated; (2) he may cathect a new alter, i.e., reject the old attachment and seek out alters who conform to the norm; (3) he may renounce or change the value pattern, substituting a new pattern in its place. However, each one of these adjustments leads to an *ambivalent motivational structure*.

From Parsons' view, any time strain is introduced into a system, the result is ambivalence. To conform to a pattern under strain involves some costs, and, in turn, results in a negative component in the orientation to the relevant pattern. In short, one might wish he could "do it another way." At the same time, deserting the pattern to which one is committed involves the inhibition of strong and persistent need-dispositions to follow the normative patterns. However, to desert the pattern also involves some "costs." That is, "doing it a new way" requires one to repress the desire to "do it the old way." The result in either case is dual and opposing orientations toward persons and/or norms.

The analysis will now focus upon the orientation of persons to each other. If alter's behavior has changed such that ego's need-dispositions are frustrated, and ego does not cathect a new alter, ego's cathexis is disturbed, i.e., his attitude toward alter is likely to become ambivalent. At the same time that ego conforms to alter's new attitudes or behavior (or "tolerates" alter's deviance), ego likely will develop hostility toward alter because of the frustration he experiences in doing so. In Parsonian terms, there is, then, the development of a *negative* component in ego's attitude toward alter which parallels the *positive* component. Ambivalence is a problem in that, regardless of which side of the ambivalent motivational structure is expressed, there is the internal problem of managing the opposite side. The actor has the problem of defending against the repressed component's breaking through and disturbing his adjustment even further. It is at this point that Parsons adds to the Freudian concept of ambivalence the associated concept of reaction-formation. It is a defense mechanism in which the actor tends to behave *compulsively* in an attempt to control the repressed component of his ambivalent attitude. *This is always the case of the actor who is described as motivated to deviate*.

It is equally possible (and of more interest here) that the actor (ego) may develop an ambivalent motivational orientation toward norms and/or values, i.e., the institutionalized patterns. For example, if ego continues to conform to norms from which a cathected alter has deviated, and if alter negatively sanctions ego's conformity to the norms of

30

the larger system, ego's conformity to the norms becomes "costly." In such a situation, it is likely that ego will develop some *alienative* feelings toward the norm. More generally, any time conformity or attempts to conform are costly, in that they inhibit other needs, *alienation* from the norm will develop. Simply put, in such a situation, ego begins to chafe under the regime that the norm imposes. As ego's alienation from the norm grows, he may attempt to subordinate the alienative component of his motivational structure by accentuating the conformative component. This will give rise to what Parsons describes as *compulsive over-conformity*. An example might be chauvinism in its original sense, i.e., an overzealous patriotism. The obverse case, which finds ego "seduced" away from the norm (i.e., the case wherein the alienative component of motivation is built up so that it becomes dominant) by whatever rewards there may be, is also costly. This is so in that ego's "need-dispositions" which were satisfied by his former conformity are now frustrated. Thus the conformative component remains operative and troublesome, although alienation dominates, giving rise to the necessity to subordinate it *via* reaction-formation. The situation in this case is described as "compulsive alienation." Parsons (1951:257) dichotomizes the two primary directions of deviant motivation just described (compulsive over-conformity and compulsive alienation) by distinguishing active and passive forms. In so doing, he arrives at the following classification of types of deviant motivation (Figure 2, from Parsons).

	Active Orientation	Passive Orientation
Conformative Dominance	Compulsive Performance Orientation	Compulsive Acquiescence
Alienative Dominance	Rebellion	Withdrawal

Figure 2

According to Parsons, all deviance is associated with ambivalence. Each motivational orientation described above contains both (a) a conformative component (an element of orientation to the norm connecting the actor to the relevant system) and (b) an alienative component (suggesting a negative component of attitude toward the system to which the actor is oriented). In order for the behavioral outcomes to be described in the terms of deviance, both components must be present. As to the possibility that an actor may behaviorally contravene norms toward which he is not oriented via positive commitment (a possibility that Parsons, of course, readily grants), Parsons states: "Where there is no longer *any* attachment to the object and/or internalization of the normative pattern, the attitude is not alienation but *indifference*" (Parsons, 1951: 254). If the actor is indifferent, he is, in the terms employed thus far, simply not a member of the "society" which is the point of reference. In

31

this case, the actor, being no longer (or perhaps never having been) oriented to the institutions, cannot be described in relation to them as deviant or alienated. Of course an actor may, over time, change his commitments. When the conformative orientation to a system of norms to which an actor was originally oriented has dissipated, the actor (no longer being so oriented) is not deviant; having changd, he is simply "different." Thus, from Parsons' perspective, all deviance is associated with ambivalence. It follows that all deviant behavior is, at least to a degree, compulsive behavior.

Parsons has supplied a psychological foundation for a conception of deviance that associates the phenomenon with membership in a societal group. In Parsons' work, the intrinsic relation between deviance and membership in the group stands in clear relief, such that the deviant actor, in order to be so described, must be a full-fledged member of the group. The psychological phenomena which Parsons describes are an outcome of the fact of this membership.

b. Cohen: Gang Delinquency as Deviance

The category of delinquent acts is a legal category. This category of acts or any particular delinquent act may or may not fit the definition of, or be explicable by reference to, the Functional Theory of deviance. In a plural social situation, an act which violates the law may well be the outcome of socialization into a subordinate culture and be comprehended solely in such terms. The act, then, is not deviant but conformative, although only to the norms of a subculture. Such conformity may get one in trouble with the law. However, even if it does, the act need not be referred to as deviant, but simply illegal.

Cohen's thesis in *Delinquent Boys* (1955) is, at the most general level, similar to the thesis of Cloward and Ohlin (1960). In essence, Cohen's argument is that delinquency can be understood as "deviance." Furthermore, he suggests that positing the existence of a subculture of delinquency in order to explain the phenomenon of delinquency is not an adequate explanation. It does not address the question of the source of the subculture. It is in answering this question that Cohen employs the conception of deviance developed by Parsons. It is in regard to his use of Parsons' systematic psychology that Cohen is distinguished from Cloward and Ohlin and Merton. Cohen begins his analysis as do the other Functional Theorists, not with a subculture, but with elements of shared culture--with persons who are members of the same society, oriented to the same complex of institutions. With his usual clarity, he states the major task of his work.

> How is it possible for cultural innovations to emerge while each
> of the participants in the culture is so powerfully motivated to
> conform to what is already established? This is the central theo-
> retical problem of this book. (Cohen, 1955:59)

Clearly, then, the problem of deviance from his perspective (emergence of cultural innovations) begins with and focuses upon members of the "society" (i.e., persons powerfully motivated to conform to what is already established). To deny that persons are so motivated in order to explain their failure to live up to institutional expectations is not to supply an answer to the problem but to deny the problem.

Cohen's use of the concept of reaction-formation to explain aspects of delinquent behavior amplifies Parsons' suggestion that the actors defined as. "deviant" have internalized the patterns which their behavior contravenes. What is important to us at the moment is not what reaction-formation explains, but that it indicates that internalization has taken place. In developing his primary interest, the explanation of working-class male delinquency, Cohen suggests that working-class youth are oriented to the dominant institutions of American society.

> Indeed, it seems probable that most children in American society, of whatever class, assimilate to some degree the middle-class value system. Some assimilate it in almost "pure" form, others in various attenuated versions and various uneasy combinations with the working-class value system, sometimes submerged by the working-class system but rarely altogether stifled. (Cohen, 1955:104)

Such being the case, Cohen argues that at least some lower- and working-class youth seek to conform to the dominent "middle-class" pattern. But, as will be evidenced by reviewing Cohen's explanation, the situation in which these youth are placed makes conformity with the dominant system of institutions difficult for them to accomplish. Cohen's approach does not focus on working-class culture, but rather implicates the dominent American cultural patterns which extend into the "working-class" milieu. In fact, the child of the working class who is not heavily influenced by middle-class culture, according to Cohen, is much less likely to engage in delinquent behavior than are those who are strongly affected by the middle-class way of life. As Cohen points out, drawing upon Whyte's (1937) typology of lower-class youth, there is a stable, law-abiding pattern among working-class youth. Working-class culture need not be viewed as "delinquent culture."

The delinquent boy, unlike the "nondelinquent corner boy," is oriented in important respects to the dominant cultural patterns. However, his attempts at conformity do not succeed and are, therefore, "costly." Such frustrated attempts at conformity lead to the development of an alienative component in the attitude of these youth toward the dominant system of norms and values. If the alienative component should become the stronger of the two, reaction-formation will take the form of the accentuation of the alienative component which will accomplish the suppression of any lingering conformative orientation to the norm. This motivational set, combined with an active orientation, fits Parsons' "rebellion" category and is Cohen's description of the delinquent boy. The following remark by Cohen exhibits the sense in which the actor viewed as deviant is attached to the institutions from which he ultimately departs.

> We have made much of the corner-boy's basic ambivalence, his uneasy acknowledgement, while he lives by the standards of his corner-boy culture, of the legitimacy of college-boy standards. May we assume that when the delinquent seeks to obtain unequivocal status by repudiating, once and for all, the norms of

the college-boy culture, these norms really undergo total extinction? Or do they, perhaps, linger on, underground, as it were, repressed, unacknowledged but an ever-present threat to the adjustment which has been achieved at no small cost?. . . [W]e would expect the delinquent boy who, after all, has been socialized in a society dominated by a middle-class morality and who can never quite escape the blandishments of middle-class society, to seek to maintain his safeguards against seduction. Reaction-formation, in his case, should take the form of an "irrational," "malicious," "unaccountable" hostility to the enemy within the gates as well as without: the norms of the respectable middle-class society. (Cohen, 1955:132-133)

Delinquent boys, then, are youth who are originally oriented to the middle-class way of life. However, since they often fail in terms of middle-class standards (for structural reasons which will be reviewed in the next section), they develop negative feelings toward the middle-class way of life. When these negative feelings become dominant, a likely result is delinquency in the form of an attack on the middle-class way of life. The delinquent subculture, from Cohen's view, is middle-class culture "turned upside down." As such, it can only be explained as a reaction to the dominant culture by persons who are or have been oriented to it.

CHAPTER IV

ETIOLOGICAL-FUNCTIONALISM:
THE EXEMPLARY SOLUTION

A. Introduction

Through the examination of the work of major theoretical contributors, the previous chapter established the conception of deviance which is employed within the Functionalist matrix. In this chapter, the task is the consideration of the mode of the explanation of deviance. In general, the form of explanation developed is social-structural. In the terms of this approach, this means that the explanations refer to the existence of institutionalized norms and values which are viewed as influencing the conduct of persons.

B. The Exemplary Solution Within the Anomic Variant

The following analysis will be organized around six social-structural concepts which are associated with four scholars. Each concept bears upon the explanation of deviance. As in the previous section, the analysis will begin with Durkheim, whose work represents the "exemplar" as a "concrete scientific achievement" giving rise to this mode of explanation. Others have elaborated, modified, and reappropriated his structural concepts so that the "exemplar" of the perspective has a dynamic quality. But what remains, after all the elaborations and modifications in each case, is a social-structural concept which is employed in the development of an explanation. The four structural concepts which Durkheim developed in *Suicide* (1951) and which have been appropriated to the study of deviance are Egoism, Altruism, Anomie, and Fatalism. After focusing on Durkheim's work, Merton's modification of the concept of Anomie in "Social Structure and Anomie" (1967) will be considered. Last, the work will focus on the structural explanation of the directions of deviant behavior, i.e., on the form the explanation takes, through the concept of "illicit opportunity structure" as developed by Cloward and Ohlin (1960).

1. Durkheim

Perhaps more clearly than any other figure of Sociology's classical period, Durkheim established and employed the concept of social structure as an element of the explanation of human conduct. Commenting upon the mode of explanation employed in Durkheim's work, *Suicide* (1951), Nisbet remarks:

> How do we account for the variable rates of suicide in human society? In precisely the same way we account for variable rates of deviance in general and, for that matter, for all types of human behavior: through inquiry into the variable social structures we find in history and in any complex society and into the variable relationships of such structures to individual human beings. (Nisbet, 1974:228)

Durkheim makes it quite clear that he believes that the key to social behavior is always the social structure, when he states the following principle: "The determining cause of a social fact should be sought among the social facts preceding it and not among the states of individual consciousness" (1938:110).

Although the principle stated above may not be strictly adhered to by modern Anomie theorists, there is no doubt that social-structural explanation is at the core of their theory. The task in this section is to indicate the development and major components of social-structural explanation as it has been applied to deviance.

a. Social Structure and Crime

The description of these conditions will begin with a primitive typology of structural conditions related to "crime rates," which is implied in *The Rules of Sociological Method* (Durkheim, 1938: Chapter 4).

Although Durkheim takes the position that the existence of crime is normal, he notes that the rate of crime may be either abnormally high or low. Either case indicates a "pathological" state of society, and each is related to a specific condition of the social structure. Crime, as noted in the previous discussion, is always related to states of the "collective conscience." Hence, if the crime rate is too high or too low, it must be an outcome of some quality or condition of the shared beliefs and sentiments of the group. In the case in which the rate of crime is excessively high, the collective conscience is relatively weak (i.e., the strength of commitment of group members to the set of beliefs and sentiments which govern conduct is low).[1] As a result, widespread violation is likely. In the case in which the collective commitment is high, the corresponding rate of crime is low. Note, just as the crime rate may be excessively high (indicating social dissolution), it may also be excessively low (indicating that the power of the collective commitment is too strong). This latter condition is as much a sign of pathology as the former.

The collective sentiments at the basis of morality must not be hostile to change, and consequently must have but moderate

---

[1] If these sentiments are so weak as to not be shared at all, then, in Durkheim's terms, there is not a "collective conscience." Therefore, there is no "violation"--there being nothing to violate--hence, no "crime."

energy. If they were too strong, they would no longer be plastic. (Durkheim, 1938:70)

As a result, "Crime is then necessary; it is bound up with the fundamental conditions of all social life and by that fact is useful" (1938:72). And, in one of Durkheim's most important statements, he says:

> There is no occasion for self-congratulation when the crime rate drops noticeably below the average level, for we may be certain that this apparent progress is associated with some social disorder. (Durkheim, 1938:72)

From the discussion of crime in *The Rules*, one can discern at least three states of the collective conscience (varieties of the structure of mechanical solidarity) that may be related to the rates of deviance. In the first social state, the crime rate is abnormally high as a result of a low level of collective commitment (which seems to be the germ, at least, of the social state of "Egoism" as developed in *Suicide*). The second is a state of moderate collective commitment in which the crime rate is normal, neither excessively high nor low. The third state is one in which the crime rate is abnormally low as a result of a high level of collective commitment (which is the germ of the social state of "Altruism" as developed in *Suicide*).

The treatment of crime in *The Rules* is consistent with Durkheim's discussion of the category in *The Division of Labor*. In both works, crime relates to the collective conscience, that is, the elements of mechanical solidarity.

b. Social Structure and Suicide

(1) Suicide and Deviance

Shifting the focus from Durkheim's discussion of the general category of crime to the category of a specific act—suicide—takes the discussion out of the bounds of the concept of deviant behavior. His study of suicide was not necessarily a study of deviance, but was, rather, a study of a particular act. Whether or not the act was, to employ Durkheim's conception of crime, one offensive to strongly held collective sentiments is left without specification. In some of the cases of interest to Durkheim, the suicide act is deviant. In fact, in modern society, it usually is, hence, "Egoistic" and "Anomic" suicide, which are characteristically modern, are generally considered to be deviant. However, in the case of at least one variety of Altruistic suicide—"obligatory-altruistic suicide"—the act is, by definition, normative. In this case, suicide is clearly in line with the society's shared beliefs and sentiments.

> Now, when a person kills himself, in all these cases, it is not because he assumes the right to do so but, on the contrary, *because it is his duty*. If he fails in this obligation, he is dishonored and also punished, usually, by religious sanctions. (Durkheim, 1951:219)

Thus, Durkheim's study of suicide was not only a study within the sociology of deviant behavior, but was, more generally, a study of the impact of social relations on individual behavior. Nevertheless, a primary concept employed in this work--"Anomie"--has influenced the study of deviant behavior perhaps as much as any other theoretical concept.

(2) Suicide and Social Integration

Integration refers to a condition of the collective conscience. A group is well integrated if it possesses "a common conscience of shared beliefs and sentiments, [and] its members interact with one another . . . and have a sense of devotion to common goals" (Johnson, 1965:876). Durkheim related the variable of integration to two types of suicide: (1) low integration--the social condition of Egoism, which gives rise to "Egoistic suicide," and (2) high integration--the social condition of Altruism, which gives rise to "Altruistic suicide."

(a) Egoistic Society

Since some have challenged the suggestion that the social condition which Egoism describes can be meaningfully distinguished from Anomic society, it will be given considerable attention here.

In the case of Egoism, the collective conscience is relatively weak, and it is, thus, possible for the individual to be deprived of its effects, i.e., the individual may "escape" the influence of collectively held beliefs.

> . . . society cannot disintegrate without the individual's simultaneously detaching himself from social life, without his own goals becoming preponderant over those of the community, in a word without his personality tending to surmount the collective personality. The more weakened the groups to which he belongs, the less he depends on them, the more he depends only on himself and recognizes no other rules of conduct than what are founded on his private interests. (Durkheim, 1951:209)

Such is the description of the social state of Egoism and the resulting condition of the individual. In what sense, however, is the actor who is thus relieved of collective influence perhaps inclined to suicide? As Durkheim put the question, "What is there in individualism which explains this [the suicidal] result?" (Durkheim, 1951:210). In essence, the weakness of the collective sentiments deprives the actor of a context of meaning in terms of which his action makes sense and has consequence.

> . . . the more the believer doubts, that is, the less he feels himself a real participant in the religious faith to which he belongs, and from which he is freeing himself; the more the family and community become foreign to the individual, so much the more does he become a mystery to himself, unable to escape the exasperating and agonizing question: to what purpose? (Durkheim, 1951:212)

Egoism, then, involves a weakening of the collective sentiments (their disintegration), a loosening of the bond between the individual and society, and, as a result, the deprivation of the individual of truly collective activity. Hence, as Durkheim says, the individual is denied "object and meaning."

38

Durkheim illustrates this state of the breakdown of collective sentiments by reference to religious groups, familial groups, and political
communities. In so doing, he emphasizes that it is not the substance of
the beliefs, but their existence--as strongly held, shared beliefs--which is
important. Among both Protestants and Catholics, there are clear prohi-
bitions within the sacred texts against self-annihilation, but Protestants
commit suicide at a higher rate than do Catholics. Further, among Jews,
whose creed does not so strongly prohibit suicide, the suicide rate is
noticeably lower than that of Catholics or Protestants. In the European
Jewish community of Durkheim's day (due to its historic isolation), the
collective sentiments within the community were most strongly felt. The
explanation lies, then, not in the substance of the sentiments, but,
rather, in the strength of shared sentiments regardless of their content.

As in weak religious communities, weak familial groups are also
subject to a higher rate of suicide. Among the widowed, divorced, and
childless, whose community of shared sentiment is either disrupted or too
narrow, suicide is more likely to occur than among families that include
children or remain intact.

(b) Altruistic Society

While it is necessary that the social group be well integrated in
order to protect the individual from tendencies to self-destruction, it is
also possible for a society to be "overintegrated."

> In the order of existence, no good is measureless. . . If, as we
> have just seen, excessive individuation leads to suicide, insuffi-
> cient individuation has the same effects. When man has become
> detached from society, he encounters less resistance to suicide
> in himself, and he does so likewise when social integration is too
> strong. (Durkheim, 1951:217)

Thus, the social condition of overintegration, which Durkheim called "Altruistic," also generates suicide, but a type quite distinct from Egoistic
suicide. The milieu of Altruistic suicide is not like that of the Egoist
who is cut off from the context of meaning provided by the social group.
Rather, it takes place within a powerful (in fact overpowering) context
of meaning. Altruism is best represented by such acts as the "obligatory
altruistic suicide" of bereaved widows in India (i.e., the practice of
"suttee" required the Hindu wife to take her own life following the death
of her husband). The act, in this case, is filled with meaning; the individual is, in fact, driven to it by the significance attached to it by the
group.

A note of caution is in order concerning the representation of
obligatory suicide as the archetype of Altruistic suicide. It would be inappropriate to conclude that all Altruistic suicide is based upon a norm
which specifies suicide as appropriate under certain conditions. If this
were the case, it would be the *substance* of collective commitment that
brought about the act. However, as has been pointed out, it is the existence of powerful sentiments, regardless of their substance, which is the
focus of the dimension of integration. In brief, if the actor is enveloped
in a powerful context of meaning, he may be overcome by the influence
of the group, even to the extent of giving up his life. It is not necessary

that he feel "obliged" to do so in order for him to become willing to do so. An example provided by Durkheim from the military setting may serve to illustrate this point. Imagine the soldier who gives up his life to protect his compatriots, e.g., a soldier who leaps upon an exploding hand grenade. He is not obliged to do so, but, under the influence of powerful sentiments, he is willing to make such a sacrifice. In this case, the individual is definitely under the control of the group and, thus, is clearly different from the Egoist. Durkheim distinguishes further between Altruism and Egoism in the following remark:

> While the egoist is unhappy because he sees nothing real in the world but the individual, the intemperate altruist's sadness, on the contrary, springs from the individual seeming wholly unreal to him. One is detached from life because, seeing no goal to which he may attach himself, he feels himself useless and purposeless; the other because he has a goal but one outside this life, which henceforth seems an obstacle to him. (Durkheim, 1951:225)

(3) Suicide and Social Regulation

"Regulation" refers to the ability of the social structure to control what Durkheim called man's "appetites." Durkheim explains that Man, unlike other organisms, does not possess physiological mechanisms that control all of his desires and provide a point of satiation. The human individual has a range of appetites beyond that of lower organisms. This range is given in Man's social nature. For example, Man's sexual desires are not just physiological, just as his need for comfort does *not* simply refer to the comfort of the organism. How, asks Durkheim, may one:

> . . . determine the quantity of well-being, comfort or luxury legitimately to be craved by a human being?. . . It is not human nature which can assign the variable limits necessary to our needs. They are thus unlimited so far as they depend on the individual alone. Irrespective of any external regulatory force, our capacity for feeling is in itself an insatiable and bottomless abyss. (Durkheim, 1951:247)

The dimension of "regulation," then, is distinct from that of social integration, i.e., the strength of collective sentiments. It refers to the ability of social institutions to limit Man's appetites. This concern involves not only the strength of collective life, but also its substance.

(a) Anomic Society

The concept of Anomic society has to do with the tendency of some social institutions to "de-regulate" persons. It is important for Man's appetites to be controlled, for, as Durkheim states, "No living being can be happy or even exist unless his needs are sufficiently proportioned to his means" (Durkheim, 1951:246). In order for needs to be fulfilled, it is important that they be attached to a goal. Desires do not of themselves suggest the object of their satisfaction. It is precisely in this sense-- Man's social appetites as a "diffuse craving"--that Durkheim means human beings' feelings are an abyss. How are the limits to Man's appetites to be established and the individual to be brought under control? The answer is in terms of the moral force which is, of course, provided by society.

The degree to which Man's appetites are successfully regulated, then, is an outcome of the character of the social structure:

> Men would never consent to restrict their desires if they felt justified in passing the assigned limit. . . They must receive it [the limit] from an authority which they respect . . . society alone can play this moderating role; for it is the only moral power superior to the individual, the authority of which he accepts. (Durkheim, 1951:249)

When this regulatory force provided by society breaks down, Man's appetites are loosened, and it becomes impossible for them to be fulfilled. As a result, persons are disappointed, unhappy, and prone to suicide. The essence of the condition of Anomie is that the social structure has failed to provide a milieu in which goals are established such that persons can reasonably expect fulfillment. Normally, societies provide such a context. However, some social situations include institutions that de-regulate the individual. Durkheim provides us with two major illustrations: one from the institutional sphere of the family--divorce--and the second from the institutional sphere of the economy--the unregulated Capitalist market.

In the case of "familial anomie," Durkheim refers to the existence in society of the institution of divorce. He notes that in those societies where this institution is strongest (as indicated by the rate of divorce), the suicide rate is high, and this is partially due to the increased rate of suicide among divorced males. Marriage, according to Durkheim, is an institution that regulates Man's sexual appetites, which, as we have indicated, are not viewed as strictly biological. When marriage is weakened--and it is weakened by the existence of the institution of divorce-- Man's sexual appetites are no longer limited. Of the unmarried man, Durkheim states: "As he has the right to form attachment wherever inclination leads him, he aspires to everything and is satisfied with nothing" (Durkheim, 1951:271).

A second example of Anomie is drawn from the economy. In modern societies, the institutional structures of the economy, specifically, *the market*, are a perpetual source of Anomie. Whereas at one time the sphere of economic activity was under the control of either religious or governmental authority, in modern society:

> . . . religion has lost most of its power. And government, instead of regulating economic life, has become its tool and servant. [And] . . . economic progress has mainly consisted in freeing industrial relations from all regulation. (Durkheim, 1951:255)

The institution of the market, believed by some to be a source of regulation in itself, fails to limit the desires of persons. At the same time, it overwhelms those institutions that might accomplish such regulation.

Although the market is a continual source of "over-weening ambition," the character of its impact on Man is best exemplified by alternating periods of great prosperity and economic depression. In either case, Durkheim expects the suicide rate to increase. In periods of depression, the reason appears to be obvious. Persons in a position to expect a certain level of reward have their means for attainment reduced and cannot adjust. Their former goals are no longer realistic, and, as a result, these persons are left without established objects of pursuit. The outcome is their despair. On the other hand, those who are propelled by periods of prosperity to levels beyond their former means become, in a sense, disoriented by their success. They, too, are now outside the range of aspirations attached to concrete goals. Having received what they sought and more, how are they to establish new, realistic aspirations? This disorientation, according to Durkheim, is likely to lead to a state in which "Reality seems valueless by comparison with the dreams of fevered imagination. . ." (1951:256). The problem is not only one of having goals that one cannot reach, but the failure of society to provide established goals at all.

(b) Fatalistic Society

In his brief mention of this type of suicide, which he views as an outcome of over-regulation, Durkheim again refers to the familial sphere. The first of his illustrations refers to marriage which, as previously noted, is an institution which regulates the sexual appetite, among its other functions. The institution of marriage may over-regulate, leading to a fatalistic situation. The example which Durkheim provides is that of the young husband who perceives the avenues for fulfillment of his diffuse sexual cravings to be blocked by a rigid but unfulfilling institutional arrangement. One may assume in this case that, although the object of satisfaction (the goal of sexual fulfillment) is established, the institutional limits are so constraining that satisfaction of the appetite cannot be achieved. The other illustration which Durkheim provides is that of the married woman who is unwillingly childless. Again, in this case, the goal (to have children) is established, but there is no possibility of fulfillment. Hence, the individuals' aspirations in these cases are crushed--they are "over-regulated."

(c) Excursus: Egoism and Anomie

There has been some dialogue in the literature as to the difference between Anomie and Egoism. Barclay Johnson, in an article entitled "Durkheim's One Cause of Suicide" (1965), argues that there is no difference between the two. Durkheim seems to be aware of the possibility of confounding the two when he states: "Certainly this [anomic] and egoistic suicide have kindred ties. Both spring from society's insufficient presence in individuals. But the sphere of absence is not the same in both cases" (1951:258).

As has been indicated in the discussion here of the two concepts--Egoism and Anomie--they can easily be analytically distinguished.

Egoism refers to the relative weakness of collective sentiments, regardless of their substance. For Durkheim, any set of collective sentiments may provide the individual with a context of meaning. In Egoism, the collective sentiments are lacking, and, in turn, the individual lacks a socially provided answer to the question, "To what purpose?"

In the case of Anomie, the actor may be well within the context of meaning which society provides. However, this social context involves the existence of institutions (such as the market or divorce) which, by their very nature, de-regulate the individual by undermining the establishment of concrete goals. The market and divorce foster pursuits which may be well within the social context of meaning, but, being "endless," they lead to suicide. Anomie is associated not with a lack of commitment, as is Egoism, but with a societal commitment to certain institutions. Anomie involves the *institutionalization* of *de-regulative patterns* of life. However, these patterns, although de-regulative, are primary constituents of the context of meaning.

2. Merton: The "Modern" Theory of Anomie

Merton does not simply adopt Durkheim's conception of Anomie and appropriate it to a new set of problems. In employing the term in his explanation of deviance in American society ("Social Structure and Anomie," 1967), Merton modifies the concept in a number of ways. However, he does follow Durkheim in conceiving of Anomie as a condition of the social structure. The Mertonian concept of Anomie refers to a structural configuration. As for Durkheim, the condition involves societal members' commitment to institutions which eventually results in a loss of institutional influence over the behavior of persons.

In the article, "Social Structure and Anomie," Merton refers to a continuum upon which types of social structures can be placed. The continuum describes societies in terms of the degree of strength of two structural elements basic in regulating conduct: culturally favored goals and regulatory means. On the one hand, there is "anomic society":

> There may develop a very heavy, at times a virtually exclusive, stress upon the value of particular goals, involving comparatively little concern with the institutionally prescribed means of striving toward these goals. The limiting case of this type is reached when the range of alternative procedures is governed only by technical rather than by institutional norms. (Merton, 1967:133)

At the other end of the continuum there is "inflexible society":

> A second polar type is found in groups where activities originally conceived as instrumental are transmutted into self-contained practices, lacking further objectives. The original purposes are forgotten and close adherence to institutionally prescribed conduct becomes a matter of ritual. (Merton, 1967:133-134)

In suggesting that in the anomic case the *stress* is on the goals, Merton intends that the mechanisms that establish commitment in these societies attach a relatively greater priority to the establishment of commitment to goals than to the legitimate *means* of goal attainment. However, Anomie is not given only in successful institutionalization of relatively greater stress on goals than on means. Just as importantly, the condition of the social structure must be such that there is pressure on some actors to give up their commitment to the use of legitimate means. The structural configuration which leads to the withdrawal of commitment from culturally prescribed means includes a "malintegration" between the culture (the pattern of goal orientation) and the social

43

structure (the pattern of access to the legitimate means). The situation of Anomic society is one in which commitment to culturally favored goals is diffused throughout the society. At the same time, the level of access to the legitimate channels of pursuit of such goals is not distributed equitably throughout the class structure. The situation is further aggravated by the character of those institutions which foster the very nearly universal commitment of members of society to the same goals. This diffusion of commitment is accomplished by the institutionalization of the ideology of equality (see Merton, *Social Theory and Social Structure*, 1967:137-139, 170-176). Insofar as persons become committed to an ideology which suggests that all have an equal chance to attain "success" (defined in the same terms for all), it is possible to motivate almost all of them to "realistically" aspire to the same goals. The fact is, of course, that all do *not* have an equal opportunity to succeed. The combination of an equalitarian ideology and a positive moral obligation to strive (with the stress on goals) places certain actors under strain (those with limited access to legitimate means) and makes them prone to withdraw their commitment from the culturally prescribed means in favor of more efficient (although illicit) procedures in the pursuit of the goals. This withdrawal of support from the institutionalized means is the heart of Merton's concept of Anomie. It is a state in which the institutionalized means no longer effectively regulate the pursuit of culturally favored goals.

Thus, Merton's description of American society as an Anomic society involves a number of central tenets. First, it involves a widespread, nearly universal commitment on the part of the population to the same pattern of success goals. Second, this widely diffused pattern of commitment to goals has been accomplished with the aid of an institutionalized ideology which suggests the existence of equality of opportunity and the importance of achievement. Third, some sectors of the population do not have high access to the culturally prescribed means to attain the goals to which they have become committed. That is, they do not have an equal opportunity to succeed. Finally, and as a result, those who are "cut off" from the legitimate means withdraw their support from those prescriptions in favor of alternate means which offer a more efficient pursuit of goals.

3. Excursus: The Concept of Anomie in the Work of Durkheim and Merton

The distinctiveness of the respective concepts of Anomie in the work of Durkheim and Merton has been obscured by the prominence of Merton's work among contemporary sociologists. However, there are some basic differences in the approach of the two theorists that deserve consideration. The differences primarily derive from the distinct assumptions concerning the basic nature of Man held by the two.

Man, according to Durkheim, has appetites beyond those established by organic being, i.e., Man has needs that are not in any direct sense organic (although rooted in the organism), but are the result of the fact that he is a social creature. Since these appetites are associated with the social nature of persons, they are not necessarily subject to regulation at the physiological level. Thus, insofar as they depend on the organism alone, they have no established limits. Since the source of Man's appetites is given in his nature as a social being, there is no need for concern with their variable social sources. It is social existence itself, no matter what its form, which generates these appetites. Thus, they exist wherever Man is found. As a result, there is no need for Durkheim (as there is for Merton) to be concerned with the variable impact of social structure on Man in relation to the source of his striving. That is, from Durkheim's view, it is not necessary to be concerned with the *substance* of Man's institutional commitments in order to explain that which leads him to pursue the satisfaction of diffuse and insatiable appetites. To be specific, Durkheim does not describe Anomie as an outcome of an institutionalized commitment to goals themselves, as is the case in Merton's approach. For Durkheim, rather, it is the fact that persons are not given goals by society--limits to their appetites--which leads to the problem of Anomie. It is the *character* of Man's institutional commitments which leads to the *lack of regulation* of these appetites. However, the *source* of the appetites is not found in any specific institutional arrangement. Anomie, for Durkheim, involves a commitment to certain types of institutions--"de-regulative" institutions (e.g., the market). These institutions overcome the limits on Man's appetites established in the "normal" social situation. Hence, they lead to unregulated pursuits and, ultimately, to a high rate of suicide.

Merton's description of Anomie is based upon a view of Man which is distinct from that of Durkheim. From Merton's perspective, social appetites (Man's nonbiological needs) vary from one social context to the next. The degree to which "high aspiration" is induced by the social structure is not a constant (i.e., it is not given in the social), as it is in Durkheim, but is a variable. Persons do not share (by the mere fact of their humanity) a set of "diffuse and insatiable appetites" according to Merton. Rather, needs are an outcome of particular social arrangements. We may say, then, that whereas Merton and Durkheim agree as to the social character of needs, they disagree as to their pan-cultural scope. Merton does not hold that needs are the same everywhere. Rather, they vary from one social structure to the next. From Merton's point of view, there are structural conditions which, rather than allowing "over-weening ambition," produce persons who aspire to little. In this case, there is no a priori "insatiable appetite" for society to control. The appetite, not having been induced, need not be controlled. For Merton, the appetite is established by the institutionalization of the goal.

The primary difference between the two descriptions of Anomie is that Merton begins with the existence of commitment to common goals. This commitment, combined with a lack of access for some persons to the legitimate means, is the "problem" which leads to deviant behavior. In Durkheim, it is the absence of such commitment, the lack of specification of goals, which leads to the "de-regulated search for satisfaction." If Man's goals are not established via collective commitment, he cannot be happy. In short, from Durkheim's view, Man in Anomic society "craves," but does not know what he wants--he has diffuse appetites, but no specified and attainable objects of satisfaction. From Merton's view, Man in Anomic society knows precisely what he is looking for, but he is deprived of access, through legitimate processes, to its attainment.

4. Cloward and Ohlin: Illicit Opportunity and the Organization of the Slum

Cloward and Ohlin seek to explain three patterns of juvenile delinquency: (1) the "criminal pattern"--the emulation by juveniles of adult criminality (e.g., professional theft and racketeering), (2) the "conflict pattern"--gang fighting activity between warring groups of juveniles, and (3) retreatism--the privatized, but nonetheless subcultural, search for sensuousness (e.g., the use of drugs). They agree with Merton that the pressure to deviance is an outcome of a "malintegrated" structural configuration which finds persons with high aspirations "cut off" from the legitimate means of goal attainment. However, Cloward and Ohlin seek to extend structural analysis to account not only for the pressure to deviate, but also for the type of deviance which emerges. In so doing, they bring into the theory of Anomie aspects of other theoretical orientations. The theories of crime proposed by Sutherland (Differential Association) and Shaw and McKay (Cultural Transmission) have stressed the way that criminal behavior is learned (see Sutherland, 1947; Shaw and McKay, 1942). Cloward and Ohlin incorporate these statements into the theory of Anomie by conceiving of the milieu which fosters the learning of such behavior as not only a learning structure, but also an "opportunity structure."

Cloward and Ohlin emphasize that, just as there is an institutionalized structure of opportunity in relation to access to legitimate means, there is also such a pattern in relation to illegitimate means. Furthermore, just as legitimate opportunities to success goals are not readily available to all members of the society, neither are illegitimate opportunities always "there for the taking." Cloward and Ohlin point out that some earlier works on delinquency implied that illegitimate means are freely available, "as if the individual, having decided 'you cannot make it legitimately' then simply turns to illegitimate means which are readily at hand whatever his position in the social structure" (Cloward and Ohlin, 1960:162). Rather, they point out, there is not only an "inequitable distribution of legitimate means," but an inequitable (differential) distribution of _illicit means_ as well. In short, not all members of the society have an equal opportunity to become a professional thief, an associate of the rackets, etc.:

> Roles, whether conforming or deviant in content, are not necessarily freely available; access to them depends upon a variety of factors, such as one's socioeconomic position, age, sex, ethnic affiliation, personality characteristics, and the like. The potential thief, like the potential physician, finds that access to his goal is governed by many criteria other than merit and motivation. (Cloward and Ohlin, 1960:147)

Cloward and Ohlin are not concerned with the lack of access to deviant roles of those in the population who are not subject to the "pressure to deviate," in the Mertonian sense. Rather, they are concerned with those sectors of the society which are "cut off" from legitimate opportunities. Within these sectors of the population, they focus upon the differential access to illegitimate opportunity. As a result, an analysis of the social organization of lower- and working-class communities is required.

Illicit opportunity in the United States takes two major forms: professional theft and organized rackets. The emergence of patterns of delinquency which emulate these forms depends upon a community organized in a particular way. As Cloward and Ohlin point out, "The criminal subculture, like the conflict and retreatist adaptations, requires a specialized environment if it is to flourish" (Cloward and Ohlin, 1960:161). In order that illicit opportunity be available in the lower-class sphere, two basic "social-organizational"[2] requisites must be met. First, within the community, there must be integration between the carriers of conventional and illegitimate values. And, second, there must be integration of various age levels of offenders within the community.

The first of these conditions, the integration of conventional and illegitimate value carriers, refers to the necessity of interdependence within the slum between the "straight" and the criminal world. In order for professional theft to flourish, there must be shopkeepers who are willing to sell stolen goods (the fence), bondsmen who will extend credit, lawyers who will cooperate, and policemen who will "turn their heads." The level of "reciprocal cooperation" necessary to maintain the "rackets" within an area may well be even greater. The establishment of such relations may not only involve shopkeepers, bondsmen, lawyers, and police, but the establishment of close relations with political machines, office holders, and judges as well (see Daniel Bell's, "Crime as an American Way of Life," 1953). If integration between these realms does not exist (i.e., if the community is not organized in this way), these illicit opportunity routes will not be available for alienated youth to employ. Quoting Tannenbaum, Cloward and Ohlin argue that:

". . . to develop the [criminal] career requires the support of middlemen . . . fences, lawyers, bondsmen, 'backers,' as they are called." The intricate systems of relationship between these legitimate and illegitimate persons constitute the type of environment in which the juvenile criminal subculture can come into being. (Cloward and Ohlin, 1960:165)

The second structural requisite for the existence of illicit opportunity in an area demands, just as does the passing on of any item of culture, institutionalized contact between those who "know" and those not yet initiated: that is, the integration of age levels must be ongoing. In those neighborhoods where a stable adult criminal subculture exists, in order for it to influence the emergence of a delinquent pattern, the adult criminal values must penetrate the world of youth. As a result, the "criminal" subculture of youth emerges and is sustained only in those

---

[2]Cloward and Ohlin intend to indicate very specifically here that the slum must be *organized*. In so doing, they are reacting to the suggestion that "crime" is found in disorganized areas of the society.

areas in which the norms and values governing adult criminal performance "filter down" to younger age groups. This process of "filtering down" is contingent upon the existence of an "age-graded structure"[3] which links the youthful offender to older criminals. By an age-graded structure, Cloward and Ohlin intend a situation which finds twelve- to fourteen-year-old delinquents in contact with sixteen- to eighteen-year-old delinquents who are in contact with adult criminals. In this way, the adult values may filter down through the age ranks, ultimately influencing very youthful offenders who have no direct contact with adult criminals.

In those neighborhoods where these structural requisites are met (i.e., where there is an institutionalized pattern of integration between the carriers of deviant and conventional values and an institutionalized pattern of age-integration), the criminal pattern as an "opportunity structure" can emerge. Thus, in these areas, it is possible for those who are denied access to legitimate opportunity to take on the criminal adaptation (i.e., they are in a position to learn the rules associated with adult criminality). Thus, the "criminal" subculture is seen as an institutionalized learning and opportunity structure, which, when available, affords frustrated youth an opportunity to learn the techniques associated with an illicit channel to culturally favored goals.

The other "deviant adaptations" to which Cloward and Ohlin refer (conflict and retreatism) also emerge in areas of the society in which the legitimate means are not available. However, these two are more likely to emerge when the structural requirements associated with illicit opportunities are absent.

C. The Exemplary Solution Within the Systemic Variant of the Functionalist Matrix

The attention given by Parsons and Cohen to the psychodynamics associated with deviance has led to the suggestion that their analysis is at the motivational level. There is no doubt that, in a sense, this is true. One of the components of their description and explanation of deviant behavior is psychological--the process of reaction-formation. However, reaction-formation and the associated ambivalence of the actor are at best secondary explanations of behavior. That is, ambivalence and reaction-formation are treated, for the most part, as simply indicative of the phenomenon and are seen as requiring explanations themselves. As with the Anomic variant of Functionalism, the primary explanation of deviance (and of the associated motivational orientation--ambivalence) is to be found in the institutional structure of social relations.

---

[3]The family is a similar institution linking up different age levels and, hence, accomplishing socialization, i.e., the transmission of adult values to the young.

1. Parsons

Parsons' task in *The Social System* is not to develop an explanatory theory but, rather, a paradigm or conceptual scheme to orient sociological research. He suggests that this task must precede the development of systems of explanation, although his scheme does indicate, in a very general way, the direction that that explanation will take. Due to the abstract nature of his analysis, the treatment here will be brief and limited to the general type of explanation suggested in his scheme.

Parsons makes it clear that the explanation of motivational processes in general, as well as deviant motivation in particular, is to be found in the structure of social relations:

> It is a cardinal principle of the present analysis that all motivational processes are processes in the personalities of individual actors. The processes by which the motivational structure of an individual personality gets to be what it is are, however, mainly social processes. . . . Thus the sectors of the motivation of the individual which are concerned with his motivation to deviant behavior, are the outcome of his processes of social interaction in the past and the whole problem must therefore be approached in social interaction terms. (Parsons, 1951:249-250)

Parsons suggests several ways in which the structure of social relations may impose strain on the actor in such a way that an ambivalent, hence deviant, motivational orientation might emerge. First, some patterns which are institutionalized are simply more difficult to live up to than others. Parsons remarks, "in spite of socio-cultural variations [in the process of becoming committed to patterns] some types of value-patterns impose inherently greater strains on most human beings than others" (Parsons, 1951:267). This being the case, actors face special problems when such patterns become institutionalized. Attempts to live up to these patterns may present the actor with difficulties or hardship, resulting in the development of some alienation from the pattern. As with other scholars within this tradition, Parsons begins with actors who take cultural mandates seriously, and this commitment must be taken into account in any attempt to explain an actor's deviant behavior. As indicated previously, this view of "deviance within membership" requires that deviance be analyzed in terms of a system of norms and values to which the actor is oriented and from which he can be meaningfully described as "departing." The alienation from cultural mandates is a result of "hardship" which can only be experienced as such when the actor is expending effort to live up to some set of expectations.

The second general source of strain also refers to the nature of the normative pattern. In some situations, although the value is internalized, the specific normative expectations are vague. This situation may be filled with anxiety, especially for some personality types. Furthermore, persons who are trying to decipher and live up to expectations may get "burned" a few times in the process. If this is the case, it is likely that some negative or alienative feelings will emerge in the situation and possibly be directed toward the value itself. Parsons states:

> We know that this factor [indefiniteness] is particularly difficult

to tolerate for some types of personalities, especially we may surmise, the compulsive conformists. By increasing anxiety, the impact of indefiniteness of expectations in this sense may be a factor in deepening the vicious circle of the progressive motivation to deviance. (Parsons, 1951:270)

The third source of the development of deviant motivation to which Parsons points is that created by role conflict. The actor is exposed to conflicting role expectations such that the fulfillment of all the expectations is realistically impossible. The most important form of role conflict is the one in which the source of such conflict lies in the malintegration of the social system. "[T]he source of the conflict may not be ego-made. It may be imposed upon the actor from the malintegration of the social system itself" (Parsons, 1951:281). The explanations provided by Merton and Cohen represent explanations that fall within this type, i.e., explanations which posit role conflict generated by a malintegrated structural pattern which gives rise to deviance.

2. Cohen

The basic structure of Cohen's explanation of deviance is much the same as Merton's theory of Anomie.[4] However, Cohen does add some dimensions to Merton's scheme which result in a more complete consideration of the emergence of deviant behavior. Of these additions, two which stand out as particularly important are (a) the general theory of subcultures and (b) the explicit attention to the psychological concomitants of deviance (Cohen, 1955). However, despite Cohen's elaborations, he describes a malintegrated structural constellation similar to that developed by Merton. Furthermore, just as in Merton's theory, the outcome of such malintegration is the actor's withdrawal of support from dominant institutions, leading ultimately to deviant behavior.

Cohen begins his discussion with the premise that there is a standard of performance or success which is institutionalized throughout the class structure of American society. He refers to the set of criteria which constitutes this performance standard as the "middle-class measuring rod." Important traits which make for success in terms of this standard are: ambition, the ability to defer gratification, the development and possession of certain economically salable skills and/or academic abilities, and the rational cultivation of manners ("courtesy and personableness"). The last of these traits, of course, involves the ability to control emotional expression, physical aggression, and violence. Although this standard of "middle-class achievement" is institutionalized throughout the class structure of the society (i.e., it is operative in other sectors of the population, such as the working class), Cohen views the ability to perform in relation to this standard as not being so equitably distributed. This differential performance ability is class-linked, i.e., the character of the socialization of children in the working class is not as

---

[4]This is not to suggest that the *substance* of the explanation or the *object* of explanation contained in the two theories refer to the same behaviors.

likely to produce the requisite performance capacity as is the socialization of children in the middle class.[5] The brute fact is that, as a result of differences in the substance and style of their socialization, working- and lower-class children do not stand much chance to succeed.

These socialization differences become problematic for many children because of the institutionalization of the ideology of the "democratic ethos" which suggests that "we all have an equal chance, and we all must try." Hence, the working-class child (just as are all other children in American society) is taught that he is to compete against all comers. It is much the same as the case of the peasant's child in feudal times being urged to compete in terms of the same standards of success as a nobleman's son. Whether or not we have all had the same training (i.e., an equal opportunity to learn to handle the criteria) is not taken into account in the evaluation of individuals in American society. A loser is a loser, and he is seen as inferior to the winner, even if the winner had a ten-mile head start in an eleven-mile race.

Cohen argues that of working-class children those most likely to become delinquent are those who accept the dominant performance standards of American society (i.e., they are taught and are at least somewhat committed to the norm: "One should perform well in school") and are also committed to the "democratic ethos." However, since the working-class child is often ill-equipped by his upbringing (a fact that is explained structurally) to perform well in relation to these standards, he suffers failures in their terms. Thus, working- and lower-class children often come out "at the bottom of the heap" in the competition (i.e., in the middle-class value-dominated school). Insofar as the performance standards are institutionalized in groups in which these children are placed (even if, in the language previously used, they are only "expedient members" of the groups--see Chapter II), the youths will suffer from a status problem. In addition to being subject to evaluation in terms of middle-class expectations, Cohen argues that these children also *accept* the middle-class standards; hence they are, in relevant respects, "genuine members" of the society whose norms they come to violate. Thus, they not only suffer from a "status problem," but, insofar as they accept the standards, they develop an additional problem of "self-esteem" (i.e., they view themselves as failures).

It is Cohen's contention that failure to meet these middle-class standards, combined with the fact that these standards have been internalized, produces the ambivalence (hence, the motivation to deviance) toward the dominant institutional structure.

The situation, then, is that of a child successfully socialized into a commitment to a way of life, but one with which he has not been adequately prepared to cope. These children have a "problem" because they

---

[5]The way of life of working- and lower-class persons in the United States is viewed as an adjustment to the problems which their status presents. The adjustment involves practices and values that, although adaptive, in that they foster adjustment to the situation, they do not foster the characteristics which make for success in terms of the dominant performance standards of American society.

lack the ability to live up to the normative demands which they accept as valid. Repeated failure in relation to those demands (for example, in the middle-class milieu provided by the school) gives rise to the alienative component of orientation toward the norm and, therefore, creates the ambivalence. When these alienative feelings become dominant, the result is the delinquency of lower- and working-class youth.

3. Merton and Cohen

As suggested, the basic structure of Cohen's theory is much like Merton's, although the substance is distinct. Whereas Merton focuses upon the institutionalization throughout the society of "culturally favored goals," Cohen focuses upon the institutionalization throughout the society of a single standard of performance. Also, whereas Merton focuses upon the differential distribution of legitimate means to culturally favored goals, Cohen focuses upon structurally caused and class-associated differences in child-rearing practices which result in the differential distribution of the ability to achieve in relation to dominant performance standards. However, both Merton and Cohen view the diffusion of the dominant values (Merton's "success goals"--Cohen's "performance standards") as being accomplished *via* the institutionalization of a democratic ideology. In short, Cohen and Merton both attach importance to the institutionalized belief in "equality of opportunity," although they focus upon different objects of pursuit that are associated with the ideology.

Although the basic structure of the two theories is similar, one further point of contrast should be mentioned. Cohen, following Parsons, is more explicit than is Merton concerning the psychological concomitants of behavioral contravention of norms. In so doing, Cohen more clearly illuminates the sense in which the actor whose behavior is described as "deviant" is oriented to the dominant system of norms and how this orientation is implicated in the actor's deviation.

CHAPTER V

THE SETTING FOR THE LABELISTS' APPROACH TO DEVIANCE

A. Introduction

The Labeling approach to deviance, just as the "Etiological-Functionalist" approach, derives from a more general theoretical perspective. As in the preceding discussion of Functionalism, the analysis of Labeling Theory will begin with a focus upon some of the general theoretical elements which have influenced this approach to deviance.

The Labeling approach is not as "theoretically pure" as that of the Functionalists. This indicates only that it has been influenced by several general sociological orientations which are by no means synthesized at a general level. Among the influences which have been important are conflict sociology and phenomenological sociology. However, the most important of the general theories influencing Labeling Theory has been that of Symbolic Interactionism. Accordingly, it is Symbolic Interactionism upon which this chapter will focus. The Marxist elements of explanation enter the Labeling approach at later stages of its development, and they will be considered as they enter the perspective. For the most part, the integration of these conflict elements with the Symbolic Interactionists' basis of the theory is accomplished through the work of Richard Quinney. In the later examination of Quinney's work, considerable attention will be given to the role of Marxist thought and its relation to this theory of deviance. Further, for the purposes of this section, it is unnecessary to distinguish the "phenomenological theory" elements from the Symbolic Interactionist influence, since these elements can be drawn from the Interactionist perspective.

For the most part, the theoretical basis of Symbolic Interactionism consists of contemporary interpretations of, and elaborations upon, the thought of G. H. Mead. Some aspects of Mead's thought, as well as the perspective of his influential interpreter and student, Herbert Blumer, will be reviewed in this section. The intention is not to isolate the major elements of the general theory in its entirety, but rather to elaborate those components of the theory which bear directly upon the theory of deviance.

Perhaps the most central concept of the Interactionist approach is that of *self*.[1] Related to self, and also of prime importance, is the Meadian concept of *mind*. Both of these elements of theory, as well as other major concepts within the perspective, can be viewed as "organizations of meaning." In reviewing these concepts, it is important that at least minimal consideration be given to the processes Mead discussed as giving rise to meaning, mind, and self. In so doing, consideration will be given to his social behaviorist account of: (1) the emergence of the significant symbol (meaningful symbol) and mind, (2) the emergence of self, (3) the components of self, and (4) the relation of mind and self to meaningfully organized conduct (acts).

B. Social Behavior and the Emergence of Symbol and Mind

The significance of the symbol is that it establishes meaning, the basis of action in the human world. Meaning forms the constituents of the processes that are mind and self as they are conceived within Symbolic Interactionist thought. Such being the case, the development of the symbol is a precondition of the emergence of the individual. This fundamental element of the constitution of mind and self, the symbol, emerges in social behavior. Hence, social behavior--interaction between members of the species--precedes the development of symbol, mind, and self.

Within the context of social behavior, the development of the "vocal gesture" is particularly important. It is a peculiar gesture in that, when the word is spoken, it is presented with the same force to all parties within the behavioral context. The individual who utters the word can hear what he says, as can the other(s). Unlike other gestures (e.g., facial gestures which are not presented to the individual initiating them in the same form in which they are received), the vocal gesture is more likely to act as a similar "stimulus" to both parties of the interaction. As he hears what he is saying, the same attitude may be evoked in the speaker as is "called out" in the recipient.

> This ability to stimulate oneself as one stimulates another, and to respond to oneself as another does, Mead ascribes largely to man's vocal-auditory mechanism. (The ability to hear oneself implies at least the potentiality for responding to oneself.) (Meltzer, in Manis and Meltzer, 1972:7-8)

The shared nature of the response, the establishment of the meaning of the gesture, is originally given through the reaction of the other to the gesture as incipient symbol. "In the very beginning the other person's gesture means what you are going to do about it. It does not mean what he is thinking about or even his emotion" (Mead, 1934:49). The symbol, then, is *not* established by following the intention of the actor who emits it, but rather in noting the behavioral response of the other to the

---

[1]The concept of "self" may be viewed as central to the Symbolic Interactionist approach in the same sense as "institution" is in the Functionalist tradition.

invocation of the gesture.[2] It is in this sense that shared meaning, the symbol, is established behavioristically. The establishment of such symbols, then, depends upon one's capacity to take "the role of the other;" it is necessary to view and understand the meaning which the other attaches to one's gestures. Understanding the response of the other allows adjustment of the incipient phases of the act (as gesture) so as to eventually, through the establishment of symbols, convey intentions. This whole process is accomplished through the observation of the other within the context of behavior. When the role of the other is successfully taken, the significant symbol--e.g., language, the most important--is established. Mead summarizes the process by suggesting that when the individual emits a gesture:

> . . . the meaning of his gesture appears in his own experience-- insofar as he takes the attitude of the second individual toward that gesture, and tends to respond to it implicitly in the same way that the second individual responds to it explicitly. . . In this way every gesture comes within a given social group or community to stand for a particular act or response, namely, the act or response which it calls forth explicitly in the individual to whom it is addressed, and implicitly in the individual who makes it; and this particular act or response for which it stands is its meaning as a significant symbol. (Mead, 1934:47)

The importance of the symbol is that it is through the existence of a system of such symbols--language--that mind is literally constituted. "Looked at from one standpoint, it is mind; from another, it is communication. Functioning within the organismic processes and social activities of the specific individual, communication is mind" (Troyer, 1972:324). It is through the association of mind with the significant symbol that the all-important capacity of human reflection emerges. Through the employment of symbols, humans can consider various possibilities for action prior to the completion of the act. This is what is meant by reflective intelligence. As such, human mind stands between stimulus and response:

> Not only does the human organism select its stimuli on the basis of attitudes, but it may also test out implicitly the various possible completions of an already initiated act in advance of the actual completion of that act. This it does through the employment of significant symbols. There is thus interposed between stimulus and response a process of selection. Mead referred to this phenomenon as "delayed reaction." To him this seemed to be the basis upon which it is legitimate to speak of choice and conscious control of behavior. (Troyer, 1972:322-323)

Mind stands between stimulus and response in at least three important respects. First, as the statement above suggests, mind allows selection among stimuli (or mind endows stimuli with *significance*) by enabling the

---

[2]The time sequence implied here between the gesture and the establishment of meaning is endemic to, and heavily influences, the Labeling approach to deviance.

individual to direct attention. Second, and perhaps even more fundamental, mind endows "stimuli" with *meaning*. That is, in Mead's view, "objects (anything which man selectively attends) are constructed through an interplay of mind and the "natural environment." Mead remarks:

> Although external objects are there independent of the experiencing individual, nevertheless they possess certain characteristics by virtue of their relations to his experiencing or to his mind, which they would not possess otherwise or apart from those relations. These characteristics are their meanings for him, or in general, for us. The distinction between physical objects or physical reality and the mental or self-conscious experience of those objects or that reality--the distinction between external and internal experience--lies in the fact that the latter is concerned with or constituted by meanings. Experienced objects have definite meanings for the individuals thinking about them. (Mead, 1934:ftn.131)

Third, in that mind allows reflection, it permits the actor to consider the role that objects play in the construction of his acts. Certain objects, although attended and given meaning, may come to lose their significance. When reflected upon, the object may appear irrelevant to the actor; hence, its role in the construction of the act is eliminated.

C. Self

As is mind, self is formed within the context of a social process. As in the creation of significant symbols, persons begin to develop a self by "taking the role of the other." In this case, rather than ascertaining the meaning of our gestures in a general sense, we are more specifically concerned with the attitude of the other toward us (i.e., what he thinks of us, what his intentions are as his act is directed toward us) and our conduct. In a sense, the concern is with the other's orientation to us and our actions (i.e., what meaning the other attached to us and to our acts). Mead described the basic process that is involved here as a kind of "play." What is "played at" is "being" the other. In this process, persons come to view themselves in the terms in which they are regarded by the other. Through "play," one comes to comprehend the way he is viewed by others and to develop a conception of self. In this way, one develops a self. At the same time, one grasps what others expect in terms of conduct (e.g., what kind of conduct the other will approve or disapprove and what kind of conduct makes sense in relation to the other). Importantly, insofar as one has apprehended and taken seriously the attitude of the other, the formerly external attitude now becomes an element of the person, or a constituency of the self--"the me." The "me" is the social component of self based upon the apprehension of the attitude of the other. As such, "the me" acts as a controlling influence upon conduct. At the same time, the self has an "impulsive" side, which can be thought of as the "disposition" to act in a specific direction prior to reflection. The "I," as Mead called this aspect of self, may be regarded as the source of action as, in fact, *constituted by the incipient stages of an act.* It is the act prior to consideration and reflection. The developed human self, then, constructs acts out of the interaction of these two components-- the "I" and the "me."

It is with respect to the two components of the self that the self makes its contribution to human reflectivity. When combined with mind, these aspects of the self can carry on what is best described as an internal conversation. The conversation is, of course, implicit (i.e., it takes place within consciousness) and may occur prior to or during action. It is in terms of this conversation that the actor may reflect upon his action, assess the attitude and intention of the other, hold up alternatives, and consider his options. In so doing, the actor can arrive at conclusions as to the direction of his conduct and control his action. Important in this "control" of action is the capacity to take the role of the other. Insofar as the actor does this, he can adjust his own acts and intentions to the perceived acts and intentions of the other. This does not necessarily imply a cooperative relation between the two, but it does allow "joint action" (i.e., a "meaningful" altercation implies a consensual element, an "understanding" of the other). This joint action may take the form of cooperative efforts or, at the other extreme, war (see Blumer, 1969:70).[3] Persons, ascertaining each others' intentions, may act accordingly--the adequately apprehended act of the other may be joined.

D. Human Acts

The "act" has been alluded to a number of times in this brief discussion of Symbolic Interactionist thought. This section will more systematically review the character of the act as it developed within this tradition. First, consistent with the above, all elements of an act represent components within a constellation of meaning. With regard to the "I," if the impulse simply comes into play (translates into action) without having been reflected upon (i.e., without having been given significance or meaning), it does not represent an act. Such an event is more like the behavior of the lower animals or reflex action and is not characteristic of human action. The act, however, does emerge as an "I"--a disposition to act. The source of this disposition, the ultimate derivation of the act as "I," is left vague in Mead. Most likely, it is viewed as rooted in multiple sources--biological, social, etc. Meltzer comments:

> The concept of the "I" . . . represents a vaguely-defined residual category. Mead clearly specifies the nature of the "Me," but in effect, labels the "I" as simply the not-Me aspect of the self. As in the case of the very closely related concept of "impulse," Mead does not indicate the limits of the "I." From his discussion, the "I" would seem, however--and this is an inference--to include

---

[3]It is with regard to "joint action" (Mead's "social act") that the Symbolic Interactionist concept of society is established. Society is, essentially, people orienting themselves to each others' intentions and, hence, acting together.

everything from biological urges to the effects of individual variation in life-history patterns. Still . . . the "I" serves the very useful purpose of evading a complete collective, or socio-logical, determinism of human conduct. (Meltzer, 1972:19)

The act begins with the impulse that emerges as an "I." The actor, notic-ing the impulse and indicating it to himself (assigning it significance and meaning), begins to shape and control the impulse. In so doing, he is cre-ating the act. He shapes the act in terms of the "objects" in his environ-ment, both social and nonsocial. It must be recalled that *object* here refers to all things in the environment to which the actor attends. This includes, as Meltzer indicates, all of the elements traditionally seen as "forcing" human action which have been developed by orthodox psychol-ogies--the actor's emotions, perceptions, cognitions, his orientations to others, norms, values, etc. The divergence of Symbolic Interactionism from these traditional psychologies (and sociologies for that matter) is that, from the Meadian view, these elements are brought into the act *by the actor* in his creation of the act. They are not there independent of him, forcing the act. He brings them in selectively, shaping them as "ob-jects" and attending them, indicating them to himself. The act is viewed as the *process* by which it is constructed. It is in this sense that the actor is viewed as active rather than simply reactive. The act is his con-struct.

As Blumer emphasizes, it is the capacity of human beings to indi-cate to self in a process of self-interaction which is crucial for the understanding of human acts:

> To indicate something is to stand over against it and to put one-self in the position of acting toward it instead of automatically responding to it. . . With the mechanism of self-interaction the human being ceases to be a responding organism whose behavior is a product of what plays upon him from the outside, the inside, or both. Instead he acts toward his world, interpreting what con-fronts him and organizing his action on the basis of the interpre-tation. (Blumer, 1969:63)

Since it is the actor's selecting and shaping of the "environment" from which his intentions are formed (and through this process the act con-structed and given direction), it is of utmost importance that the actor's point of view be taken. This is the only point of view from which the observer can understand the direction and meaning of the actor's con-duct.

> Since action is forged by the actor out of what he perceives, interprets, and judges, one would have to see the operating situ-ation as the actor sees it, perceive objects as the actor per-ceives them, ascertain their meaning in terms of the meaning they have for the actor, and follow the actor's line of conduct as the actor organizes it--in short, one would have to take the role of the actor and see his world from his standpoint. (Blumer, 1969:73-74)

The elements of Symbolic Interactionist Theory discussed above

58

have greatly influenced the Labeling approach. First, many Labelists explain the emergence of "deviant acts" in a way consistent with the work of Mead and Blumer. Second, Labeling Theory focuses upon conduct which is meaningfully organized by the actor. Third, Labelists focus upon issues associated with the formation and transformation of the self, identity, and mind. Attention will now turn to an examination of the development of the Labeling approach itself.

CHAPTER VI

LABELING THEORY

A. Introduction

The object of this chapter is to examine the fundamental anchoring points of the disciplinary matrix associated with the Labeling approach to deviant behavior. As in the previous section, the focus will be upon the nature of the concept of deviance as it is employed by Labelists and the basic explanations proposed within the matrix.

The group of sociologists whose work will be examined in this section are designated by a number of different titles, the three most prominent being Neo-Chicagoans, Interactionists, and Labelists. Throughout this chapter, the term "Labelists" will be employed, as it is the most widespread designation currently in vogue. This is appropriate, since the emphasis will be upon the elements of the theory of deviance itself, rather than on an examination of the historical influence of earlier approaches to deviance (Neo-Chicagoan) or the general theoretical underpinning of the approach (Interactionist).

There are numerous scholars who have made important contributions to Labeling Theory. Of these, there are five major theorists whose work represents the fundamental elements of the Labeling school. These five will be focused upon in the discussion and analysis of the Labeling perspective: Howard Becker, Edwin Lemert, Thomas Scheff, David Matza, and Richard Quinney.

B. The Conception of Deviance Within the Labeling Approach

In this section, the work of Howard Becker will be analyzed first. Although Becker was not the earliest Labeling Theorist, he was the first to articulate the Labelist conception of deviance in such a way as to expose its radical divergence from previous modes of conceptualizing the phenomenon and, consequently, the first to rivet scholarly attention on Labeling as a new and viable means of analyzing deviance and control. After examining Becker's formulation, the discussion will turn to the major divergencies from, and elaborations of, this formulation as represented in the works of the other four scholars.

1. Howard Becker: The Nature of Deviance

The fundamental aspects of the conception of deviance which characterize the Labeling approach were set forth by Howard Becker in his work, *Outsiders* (1963). His most often quoted statement conceptualizing deviance is as follows:

> . . . *social groups create deviance by making rules whose infraction constitutes deviance*, and by applying those rules to particular people and labeling them as outsiders. From this point of view, deviance is *not* a quality of the act the person commits, but rather a consequence of the application by others of rules and sanctions to an "offender." The deviant is one to whom the label has successfully been applied; deviant behavior is behavior that people so label. (Becker, 1963:9)

In order to fully understand this conceptualization and the extent to which it represents a departure from other sociologies, one must focus upon its two major related components. First, consideration must be given to the sense in which Becker intends that "*social groups create deviance by making rules whose infraction constitutes deviance*." Second, the foregoing must be related to the sense in which he means that "deviance is not a quality of the act the person commits. . ."

Commenting on the first of these components of the definition of deviance, Merton remarks:

> The first theoretical claim is blatantly true and trivial: namely the statement that behavior cannot be considered "deviant" unless there are social norms from which that behavior departs. It seems banal and safe to stipulate: no rule, no rule-violating behavior. (Merton and Nisbet, 1971:827)

On its face, it may seem that Merton's sharp statement is warranted. However, in making such a statement, he misses the essential aspects of the point of view Becker is trying to communicate. A central feature of the distinction between Merton's perspective on deviance and Becker's is the time sequence or time relation between *rule existence* and "*behavioral violation*." Merton's entire approach rests on the assumption that the *rule* comes *first* (or, for Merton, the norm), *then* the *violation*. As was discussed in the previous section, from the Functionalist perspective, the deviant is one who is oriented to a norm; in fact, the actor is, at first, motivated to conform to it. Thus, from a Functionalist's point of view, the norm (or rule) must be viewed as existing prior to violation. From Becker's point of view, this certainly need not be the case. From his standpoint, the situation is reversed--action which *eventually* comes to be viewed as violative may well precede the existence of rules which eventually come to prohibit it.[1] Further, whether the behavior will be

---

[1] The difference as to the time sequence between the act and the pattern violated, which is associated with the occurrence of deviance, does not raise an empirical question and, therefore, cannot be resolved by empirical research. Rather, it is a matter of definition--a primary theoretical matter.

reacted to as "rule violative" (giving rise to the question of deviance) cannot be known prior to a reaction's having taken place (an occurrence which is problematic, not given).

This differential time sequence between act and application of a rule is deeply embedded in the two perspectives. In the first place, the difference derives from the meanings of "rule" and "norm" as these terms are employed by the two schools of thought. The concept of norm, as was seen in the review of the Functionalist literature, implies some element of "shared meaning" in human relations, which further implies a degree of stability in such relationships. It is difficult to imagine people sharing something unless it is *relatively* fixed (i.e., stable), and when people do share something, *we imagine* that it relatively "fixes" it. Hence, the suggestion of "sharedness" implies that a belief, a value, or rule is, at least momentarily, "fixed." When such stability is implied, as it is by Merton's use of the concept of norm, it is possible to discuss violation of previously existing patterns, i.e., the violation of norms. Given such a conception, it is possible to specify when normative violation has occurred, independently of societal reaction. Thus, both the actor and the sociological observer can predict with certainty that, given discovery, a response to the act as "deviant" will occur on the part of those who share the norm.

The concept of rule, as it is employed by Becker, does not imply the normative element of "sharedness" between interacting parties. That is, I may have a rule to which you do not share a commitment. As such, even if you are subject to it, it is still my rule. Obviously then, the substitution of the concept of "rule" as opposed to "norm" has a number of ramifications for the conceptualization of deviance. For one thing, the actor not sharing a rule may not even know of its existence; hence, the behavior he engages is not, *from his perspective*, rule violation (see Becker, "Whose Rules?", *Outsiders*, 1963:15). Second, unlike a norm, a rule need not be viewed as existing prior to the "violative" pattern of action. A *rule* may be applied *ex post facto* (this is Becker's archetype); the notion of an *ex post facto* application of *norms* is, of course, a contradiction in terms. The final implication, the one which really lies at the heart of the theoretical matter, is that rules, since they are not shared, need not be taken as stable elements which guide human relations. As a result, the whole interaction process is regarded as at least in flux, and perhaps even as totally unspecified as to behavioral expectations for one or both of the parties to the interaction. In a world populated by *rules* rather than norms, the reaction to an act is not so eminently predictable as imagined above. Hence, in a situation of "rules-in-flux," deviance can be established only in reaction.

The Labelists' world-in-flux, perhaps containing rules but not norms, extends even into what are conceived by other sociologies to be the central regions of powerful norms, e.g., the governing of sexual relations in the clan/family. Whether or not some group's rule/taboo against incest can, in the first place, be said to exist or, given that it exists, whether or not it will be brought to bear upon the "incestuous ones" is problematic. "Recall Malinowski's example of the Trobriand islander who had committed clan incest. Everyone knew what he was doing, but no one did anything about it" (Becker, 1963:122). In this situation, deviance does not exist.[2]

No doubt Becker's view on the time-sequence relationship between act and assignment of deviant status to the act has its theoretical roots in Mead's formulation discussed briefly above--the establishment of meaning is given *in response*. We do not know the significance of our gestures except *via* the behavioral response of others. Hence, the significance of an act in terms of its deviant or non-deviant status is contingent upon the interpretation given it by an audience of reactors who, in their reaction, establish its meaning. As Becker states:

> . . . deviance is not a simple quality, present in some kind of behaviors and absent in others. Rather, it is the product of a process which involves responses of other people to the behavior. (Becker, 1963:14)

Considerable attention has been given to the distinction between such concepts as rule-violation and norm-violation in attempting to convey Becker's conceptualization of deviance. Giving the matter such attention may leave the reader with the false impression that rule-violation is, in Becker's view, essential to the making of deviance. This is simply not the case, as the definitional statement from Becker, quoted at the beginning of this chapter, should make clear. Rule violations need not occur for deviance to exist, rather deviance is the application of rules and sanctions to an "offender." The *application* of the rules and sanctions can take place without actual rule-violation having occurred (e.g., "witches" in Salem), that is, with or without a "real offender." The rules have only to be applied to someone and the presumed conduct, in order for "deviance" and a "deviant" to be created.

Becker, then, is making a distinction between behavior that violates rules--"rule-breaking behavior"--and deviance, which is the application of the rule and the deviant label to some behavior or person. It is possible that the two (rule-breaking behavior and deviance) coincide, but it is also possible, and theoretically just as significant, that they do not. In the making of deviance, rule-violation is somewhat irrelevant--it may or may not set off the reaction which creates deviance.

Becker's typology of "deviant behavior" includes some actors who have violated rules, and others who have not. (See Figure 3 below.) The chart suffers from a number of problems, given Becker's conception of deviance, but it does exhibit a distinction between rule-breaking behavior and deviance. Clearly, "secret deviance" would be better entitled "unapprehended rule-violation" rather than "deviance," since the emergence of deviance as conceived by Becker requires reaction and application of the rules. It should also be emphasized that the "falsely accused" are deviant only insofar as the definition has been successfully applied to them.

---

[2]As Becker reports, someone did ultimately react. But Becker's point, emphasized here, is that whether or not such reaction will occur is problematic. And from Becker's point of view, since reaction is problematic, one cannot specify what is or is not deviant until after a reaction has occurred.

Becker's Typology of Deviant Behavior
(From *Outsiders*, 1963:20)

	Obedient Behavior	Rule-Breaking Behavior
Perceived as Deviant	Falsely Accused	Pure Deviant
Not Perceived as Deviant	Conforming	Secret Deviant

Figure 3

a. The Case of Marijuana

The general theoretical orientation developed by Becker and discussed above becomes clear in his discussion of "Rules and Their Enforcement" and "Moral Entrepreneurs" (1963:121-162, Chapters 7 and 8). The archetypal case provided by Becker is the reaction to marijuana use as deviant by the Federal Bureau of Narcotics. In this case, deviance is created by the social group, in that a rule is formulated and enforced which defines a pattern of *previously ongoing, "legitimate"* behavior as "deviant." Becker's major point is that marijuana smoking preceded, as an ongoing pattern of action, the response to it as an illegal activity, i.e., it preceded the establishment of a rule prohibiting such action. This being the case, the use of marijuana in order to get "high" is deviant only when it is responded to as such, and whether or not it will receive such response cannot be known prior to reaction. Prior to the response, the activity had gone on for years and was not regarded as "rule violative," but rather was ignored by almost everyone. Perhaps it should be pointed out that the Federal Bureau of Narcotics was among those who simply did not attend the action.

This brings us to the second major element of Becker's conceptualization--his suggestion that there is no qualitative difference between deviant and nondeviant acts. From this perspective, it should be clear that the construction of the act of marijuana smoking by the actor has not, in any sense, undergone modification because of a change in response to it. The act is still an outcome of the same processes as it was before the emergence of the response to it as "deviant." There is no basis upon which to suggest that the quality of the act changes, although the situation of the act does. Hence, the sense is established in which the act is viewed as qualitatively the same both before and after rule construction and enforcement. The *act* is the same, only the *reaction* to the act is changed. Being reacted to as deviant is, then, the only sense in which the act is deviant--it has nothing to do with the character of the act itself.

b. The Relative Insignificance of the Etiological Question

The bearing of the above on the importance of the question of the etiology of deviant acts should be obvious. If deviant acts are not qualitatively different from other acts, there is no question of the "special etiology" of deviant behavior. This does not suggest that one should not attend the question of the etiology of acts at all, but it does imply that one's conclusions will specify nothing distinctive about the emergence of acts which violate rules as opposed to those which conform to the rules. In short, there is no need for sociologists interested in deviance to develop a special theory of the etiology of deviant acts. Partially as a result of this conclusion, Labeling Theorists have not been particularly interested in etiological questions, preferring instead to concentrate their efforts on the interaction among "rule violators" and "rule enforcers."[3]

Secondly, the importance of the question of the etiology of rule-breaking acts is diminished in significance simply because, as deviance is defined, it does not necessitate the existence of such behavior. Hence, violations are relatively insignificant to this perspective.

There is one other aspect of Becker's perspective on deviance which has been implied above but deserves further emphasis. Unlike the approach of the "Etiological-Functionalists," deviance is not defined by Becker with the individual as the point of reference. For Becker, deviance is always defined from the point of reference of some "other" group or individual, and those others may be far removed from the "deviant actors." As Becker remarks, concerning "unintended acts of deviance":

> They imply an ignorance of the existence of the rule, or the fact that it was applicable in this case, or to this particular person. . . How does it happen that the person does not know his act is improper? Persons deeply involved in a particular subculture (such as a religious or ethnic subculture) may simply be unaware that everyone does not act "that way" and thereby commit an impropriety. (Becker, 1963:25)

As implied in the previous discussion of the character of "rule" versus "norm," the "others" who do the defining are not, from the Labeling perspective, necessarily related to the individual whose action is responded to as deviant (in the sense of sharing his world-view or culture). The "others" are, in important respects, *aliens* from the world in which the deviant action is ongoing, i.e., the rule-enforcer is an intruder. As Lemert puts it, commenting (critically) on this view which he only nominally shares:

> "Others" vis-à-vis the deviant initiate interaction: for the most part they are instigators who intentionally or inadvertently degrade, discredit, or invade the privacy and territories of deviants. (Lemert, 1972:17)

---

[3]There are other factors which lead to this lack of interest in etiological questions which will be considered later. One is the Labelists' interest in "stabilized" patterns of deviance rather than episodic rule-breaking, another is their view of an appropriate "science" of human conduct.

The "deviant actor" (if one can use such a term), then, is not viewed as necessarily related to, by way of his own commitments, a way of life which he comes to violate. If his action may be described as violative, it is of someone else's prescriptions as to how one should live.

2. Edwin Lemert: Primary and Secondary Deviance

Edwin Lemert is credited by many as having been the first to set forth a number of the aspects of the Labeling approach. However, Lemert is of another generation of sociologists than are the others associated with this group and, as a result, does not share some aspects of their orientation. Nevertheless, some of the elements of the perspective he provides are central to that of Labeling and necessitate his inclusion.

In relation to the conception of deviance associated with the Labeling perspective, Lemert's major contribution is to make a clear distinction between what he calls "primary" and "secondary" deviance. In specifying this distinction (*Social Pathology*, 1951), Lemert first comments upon the fallacy of confusing "original causes" with "effective causes." He associates original causes with primary deviance, effective causes with secondary deviance. Lemert does not believe that it is possible to develop a general theory of "original causes," nor does he see his task as the development of a sociological theory of such causes. In short, Lemert, like Becker, is not interested in developing a sociological theory of the etiology of the deviant act. The proper focus of a sociological theory of deviance is suggested by Lemert in the following statement:

> From a narrower sociological viewpoint, the deviations [primary deviations] are not significant until they are organized subjectively and transformed into active roles and become the social criteria for assigning status. The deviant individuals must react symbolically to their own behavior aberrations and fix them in their sociopsychological patterns. (Lemert, 1951:75)

In other words, the sociologically significant questions are not concerned with the sources of what Lemert calls "primary deviation," but rather with "secondary deviation"--behavior transformed into active roles.

"Secondary deviation" is an outcome of "societal reaction" for Lemert, just as it is in Becker's conception of deviance, and involves transformations in the actor's identity and behavior that are a consequence of his having been reacted to as deviant.

> When a person begins to employ his deviant behavior or a role based upon it as a means of defense, attack, or adjustment to the overt and covert problems created by the *consequent societal reaction* to him, his deviation is secondary. (Lemert, 1951: 76)

After the actor has been reacted to as deviant, the conditions of his action are changed, resulting in the need for some type of adjustment on his part. One possible adjustment involves the employment of further deviant behavior, i.e., secondary deviance may emerge. Comparing primary deviation with secondary deviation, Lemert states that "Primary deviation, as contrasted with secondary, is polygenetic, arising out of a variety of social, cultural, psychological, and physiological factors, either in adventitious or recurring combinations" (Lemert, 1972:62). On the other hand, he says, "Secondary deviance refers to a special class of socially defined responses which people make to problems created by the societal reaction to their deviance" (Lemert, 1972:63).

The relationship between Lemert's concept of secondary deviance and Becker's definition of deviance becomes more clear when it is realized that the initiation of reactions generating secondary deviance need not involve primary deviance. Hence, concern with primary deviance and its sources is diminished in importance. Further, even if primary deviance precedes the reaction which generates secondary deviance, the primary deviation need not be an incipient form of the pattern of secondary deviance which finally emerges as a stable pattern. Lemert's discussion of two of his major interests, stuttering and paranoia, presents these two possibilities. In relation to stuttering, he suggests:

> [It] represents the "pure case" of secondary deviance. I say this because stuttering thus far has defied efforts at causative explanation. It appears to be exclusively a process product in which, to pursue the metaphor, *normal speech variations* [emphasis added], or at most, minor abnormalities of speech (primary stuttering) can be fed into an interactional or evaluational process and come out as secondary stuttering. (Lemert, 1972:87)

Thus, no primary deviance is necessary in order for the secondary pattern to arise.

A similar situation exists in the case of the emergence of paranoia. In this situation, "normal events" and bona fide or "recognizable issues" introduce strain into the relational system of the person. Although these strains may give rise to primary deviance, it need not necessarily be a type of deviance that is associated with paranoia, i.e., the strain does not give rise to the incipient stages of paranoia. Rather, paranoia is an outcome of a reaction to the individual by others which leads to his exclusion from normal patterns of interaction. In the process leading to exclusion, the person's primary deviations may at first be tolerated as "a variation of normal behavior." However, in the eventual emergence of paranoia, the primary deviations cease to be tolerated. The assessment of normality is withdrawn and, "From a normal variant the person becomes 'unreliable,' 'untrustworthy,' 'dangerous,' or someone with whom others 'do not wish to be involved'" (Lemert, 1972:253). It is this particular reactive interpretation of primary deviance which fosters a certain type of exclusion of the person and eventually leads to the emergence of the pattern of secondary deviation which is described as "paranoia." Other possible reactions to the primary deviations would not have the same consequence.

In short, paranoia as a pattern of conduct emerges only as a result of a certain pattern of reaction to the person. This reaction may or may not be provoked by deviance. Although, according to Lemert, a pattern of deviance may be given prior to reaction, this pattern is not referred to as paranoia. Rather, paranoia is associated with a specific pattern of reaction--exclusion--and, as such, is a classic form of secondary deviance.

deviance.

In establishing his major conclusion that the "reactive community" of the paranoic is real, not pseudo, Lemert remarks: "members of communities and organizations do unite in common effort against the paranoid person prior to or apart from any vindictive behavior on his part" (Lemert, 1972:263). This community of reactors participates in the shaping of paranoic patterns of action.

In short, Lemert's concept of *secondary deviance* contains the essential element of Becker's conceptualization of deviance. Its central core involves the "*application* of rules and sanctions to an offender" by some "reactor-other." The behavior or characteristics of the person reacted to are relatively unimportant (e.g., as in the case of stuttering), in that they do not necessarily determine the quality of reaction to the person.

3. Becker and Lemert: Conceptions of Deviance

We have already noted two basic distinctions associated with the conception of deviance in the works of Becker and Lemert. In Becker, the primary distinction is between "rule-breaking behavior" and deviant behavior; in Lemert, it is between primary and secondary deviance. It appears that for most applications within this paradigm the concepts need not be distinguished. What is rule-violating to Becker is primary deviance to Lemert, and what is deviance to Becker is similar to secondary deviance in Lemert's terminology. These two latter concepts focus on interactive processes--the processes of reaction--and represent the central concern of the Labeling approach.

There are, no doubt, sound theoretical reasons for Becker's choice not to employ the concept of deviance in relation to what he calls "rule-breaking behavior." Some of these reasons draw attention to the theoretical divisions between Becker and Lemert and are directly relevant to the concerns of this work. Hence, a brief consideration is in order. Becker's position assumes a lack of sharing of the relevant patterns and the further lack of rule stability; these assumptions force a fundamental reformulation of the concept of deviance. However, Lemert's perspective does not preclude a conception of deviance that implies some stability and sharing of the rules, i.e., it recognizes norms.

Divergence on this point between Becker and Lemert represents an important distinction with respect to the general conceptualizations of deviance. Further, it bears upon the concept which Lemert contributes to the Labeling perspective--secondary deviance. The fact that Lemert acknowledges stable patterns qualifies his association with the Labeling perspective to the extent that it involves a rejection of the "time sequence" between act and rule which is implicit in Becker's work. Insofar as this is the case, the relationship between rule-breaker and rule-enforcer is not, from Lemert's view, one between aliens. The deviant--whether primary or secondary--is related to the norms which he violates in ways other than that of merely being present in the milieu in which they are operative. However, the specific relationship between the actor and the rule he violates is only vaguely expressed in Lemert's concept of deviation. As a result, its nature cannot be specified with greater precision. It is never quite clear whether or not the actor must have internalized the norms, been cognizant of them, etc. prior to his failure to live up to them, in order to fit Lemert's category of deviance. However, it appears that the analysis of deviance for Lemert, unlike Becker, involves behavioral departures from norms by an actor who is more than simply in the milieu where the rules are operative. That is, the patterns are more than just "conditions of his action." The actor is in some sense related to them; in what respect remains unclear. Although there are these important differences between Lemert and Becker, in one fundamental sense, they must be seen as sharing a perspective: they both conceive of deviance as a category of acts which violate others' expectations and which are an outcome of societal reaction.

4. Thomas Scheff: Labeling and Mental Illness

Thomas Scheff, in *Being Mentally Ill* (1966), is concerned with the development of a sociological theory of mental illness. In conceiving a category of deviance in which mental illness fits, Scheff explicitly follows Becker in making a distinction between "rule-breaking behavior" and "deviance." He suggests:

> . . . deviance can be most usefully considered as a quality of people's response to an act, rather than as a characteristic of the act itself. . . By this definition, deviants are not a group of people who have committed the same act, but are a group of people who have been stigmatized as deviants. (Scheff, 1966:32)

Scheff's interest in deviance then, like Becker's, is in a phenomenon that includes a *reaction* by an audience to a presumed rule-violation.

While explicitly following Becker in making the distinction between rule-breaking and deviance, it does not appear that Scheff is concerned with making a distinction between rules and norms and, hence, "rule-breaking behavior" as opposed to "primary deviance" (associated respectively with Becker and Lemert). As previously indicated, there is no great difference between the substance of the two concepts; the divergence lies in the theoretical issues from which they are derived. It appears that Scheff is more closely in agreement with Lemert than with Becker on the issue of institutionalized norms. Rather than following Becker in relation to the absence of sharedness with regard to the pattern violated, it appears that the violations of concern to Scheff are of widely shared, deeply internalized *norms* (i.e., they are part of our assumptive world--"goes without saying," "taken for granted"). Scheff indicates his disregard for the issue by using the terms norms and rules interchangeably, but it is clear that he is concerned with the violations of widely shared patterns. In answer to the question which Becker poses, "Whose rules are violated?" Scheff's response is, "Everybody's." In fact, it is this widely shared quality of the normative pattern which leads to the charge of "mental illness" when violations of the world-taken-for-granted occur.

> There are innumerable norms, however, over which consensus is so complete that the members of the group appear to take them

for granted. . . A person who regularly violated these expectations probably would not be thought to be merely ill-bred, but as
strange, bizarre, and frightening, because his behavior violates
the assumptive world of the group, the world that is construed
to be the only one that is natural, decent and possible. (Scheff,
1966:32)

Scheff, unlike Becker, operates with a conception of the social world
which contains entities such as norms as well as "rules." As a result,
Scheff's perspective is more in line with Lemert's concept of "primary
deviance" than with Becker's "rule-violating behavior."

In any case, it is not the "primary deviant episode" with which
Scheff's sociological theory of mental illness is concerned. Scheff suggests, as does Lemert, that the sources of primary episodes are of a
wide variety and thus of little concern. Aside from this, there are other
reasons why Scheff is not particularly interested in episodic deviance.
Primary episodes of such behavior are often just that, i.e., *episodic*. Primary deviance is often transitory, passing, relative to secondary deviance, i.e., it is behavior of the moment. Furthermore, it is widespread,
with virtually everyone engaging in conduct which could fit the category
of mental illness from time to time. Most often such episodes are simply
not considered important. "The high rates of total prevalence suggest
that most residual deviance [read "mental illness"] is unrecognized or
rationalized away" (Scheff, 1966:51).

The experience of battlefield psychiatrists can be interpreted to
support the hypothesis that residual deviance is usually transitory . . . most children go through periods in which at least
several of the following kinds of rule breaking may occur: tem-
per tantrums, head banging, scratching, pinching, biting, fantasy
playmates or pets, illusory physical complaints, and fears of
sounds, shapes, colors, persons, animals, darkness, weather,
ghosts and so on. In the vast majority of instances, however,
these behavior patterns do not become stable. (Scheff, 1966:52)

Rather than focus on the variable sources of such widespread but episodic behavior, Scheff is interested in those cases in which these behavior
patterns which violate assumptive norms become stable. That is, in
Lemert's (and his own) terms, Scheff is interested in secondary deviance.
Whereas primary deviance is "amorphous and uncrystallized," secondary
deviance is patterned and stable. Scheff uses several phrases to refer to
this stage of deviance which he seeks to explain--among them are "organized illness," "deviant careers" and the "*stabilization* of rule-breaking."
All of these terms make it clear that Scheff is concerned with that
stage of deviation which Lemert calls secondary deviance.

Scheff's statement of his basic theoretical question indicates the
distinction developed by Lemert between the stages of deviance—
episodic and stable--and Scheff's interest in the latter:

If residual rule-breaking is highly prevalent among ostensibly
"normal" persons and is usually transitory . . . what accounts for
the small percentage of residual rule-breakers who go on to
deviant careers? To put the question another way, under what

conditions is residual rule-breaking stabilized? (Scheff, 1966:53)

5. Matza: Becoming Deviant

Matza, in *Becoming Deviant* (1969), begins his discussion of the conception of deviance with a nominal definition, although later in the book, he develops something closer to a "real" definition. Matza first suggests that, nominally, "to deviate is to stray, as from a path or standard" (Matza, 1969:10). As he, himself, indicates, this does not say much about his conception of deviance. And although the promise is made to return to the problem of conceptualization in the last chapter of the book, the issue is never directly addressed again. Despite the lack of explicit attention to the matter, it is possible to extract aspects of Matza's view of deviance implicit in this work, especially from his last chapter (Chapter 7).

In order to understand Matza's conception of deviance, and the relationship between his views and those of Becker, Scheff, and others, it is important to examine four major concepts around which this discussion is organized: "ban," "bedevilment," "transparency," and "apprehension." Prior to this, however, it is essential to consider the concept of "guilt"--a concept of which Matza makes little, explicitly, but which forms the primary underpinning of the remainder of his treatise. For Matza, "guilt" is at the heart of the process of "becoming deviant." Only through an understanding of the means by which both the activity in which the actor is engaged and the actor himself are "made guilty" can one grasp the concept of deviance which Matza employs.

a. The Concept of Guilt

There are at least two ways in which the concept of guilt is widely employed. The first will be referred to as *legal guilt*, the second as *psychological guilt*. In the first case, it is possible to speak of the actor's being *found* guilty (by others) and being, therefore, in a sense, *made* guilty. In the second case, it may be said that the actor simply *is* guilty or *feels* guilty in the sense that *he* is disturbed by his action.

These two conceptualizations of guilt imply, of course, two wholly separate circumstances concerning the relation of the actor to his action and the patterns which he violates. In the first case, "legal guilt," the actor and the rule may be completely removed from one another. That is, at a point in time, the actor may not even know of the rule, nor has the rule been applied to the actor. However, these separate entities (rule and actor) may be brought together when, perhaps with no change on the actor's part, he is placed under the jurisdiction of the rule. In such a case, the actor's association with the behavior in question originally may have been "innocent" (i.e., the actor may not have been cognizant of rules prohibiting the behavior), but the behavior can be "made guilty" through being brought under the jurisdiction of the rule.

Bringing the actor under the jurisdiction of the rule does not imply that the actor in any sense "absorbs" the rule, i.e., believes in it or in its validity. The suggestion is only that the rule now exists in the actor's milieu. Now the rule is, in Parson's terms (discussed above), a *condition* of the actor's action. Such is the significance of being under the jurisdiction of ban.

The second conception of guilt, "psychological guilt," implies, of course, a wholly different relationship between the actor and the patterns violated. In this case, the actor and the rules are "together" (i.e., as in the Freudian and Parsonian sense, the rules are literally constituents of the actor's personality). The actor is not necessarily "made guilty" in that he is brought under the jurisdiction of the rules, but he "feels guilty" in that he has done something he thinks he should not have done. In Parsonian terms, the rules, rather than being part of the conditions of action (in the situation), are part of the actor's *orientation* to the situation. The actor carries the rules into the situation--they are not imposed by his simply being within their jurisdiction. The actor is not "made guilty" after the fact; rather he, himself, attaches significance to his action and *feels* guilty.

b. Ban: The Moral Transformation of Activity

When Matza suggests the existence of guilt, it is clear that he intends something similar to what is referred to above as "legal guilt." This stands out in his discussion of ban (as in his discussion of bedevilment, transparency, and apprehension which will be considered in the section on explanation). It is via these processes that the actor is *made guilty* and eventually becomes deviant, i.e., develops a deviant identity. Matza leaves little doubt as to the importance of the illegality of an act in the eventual ability to establish "guilt" and "deviance." Action is "made guilty" and "made deviant" by the fact that it is banned.

> . . . marijuana use as described there [earlier in the text] was more or less *innocent*. Before considering anything else, I must elaborate, for in truth the marijuana user is already guilty, though only in a certain sense. To make that correction we turn to the first element of signification--ban--and its meaning. (Matza, 1969:145)

It is ban and simply ban that first makes activity guilty. And, as Matza says, this should come as no surprise, for this is widely known to be the purpose and consequence of ban.

> The moral transformation of activity is the purpose of ban; the simplest way of summarizing the legislative and purportedly public intention is to predict that with time the activity will exist in guilt. (Matza, 1969:146)

This statement is consistent with the conception of deviance held by other Labelists. It suggests the same time sequence between the act and the relevance of the rule as is seen in Becker's work. It also implies the same relation of the actor to the rules as is present in the works of the other theorists. The actor is, at first, innocent. Something then intrudes--The State--which has the power to morally transform his activity, i.e., to "change" him. Further, the relation between activity and guilt occurs in the same time sequence. First there is innocent activity; later the actor is made to feel guilty: "with time the activity will exist in guilt" (Matza, 1969:146).

In sum, Matza's use of the concept of "legal guilt" suggests that he

73

conceives of "deviance" in basically the same terms as the other theorists treated in this section. Legal guilt implies that it is others (those represented by and representing The State) who, through ban and reaction, bring the actor and rule together. By initiating the interaction with the rule-violator, the reactor "transforms" innocent activity, i.e., he "makes" the activity "guilty." In the process of interaction, initiated and controlled by The State, deviance is created.

6. Richard Quinney: Conflict, Law, and Crime

Unlike the other Labeling Theorists which have been discussed, Quinney self-consciously incorporates elements of conflict or Marxian Theory into his approach to crime. Although the influence of a conflict perspective is evident in Becker and Matza, it is Quinney who develops these themes and makes their relationship to Labeling explicit (see especially, *The Social Reality of Crime*, 1970, and *Critique of Legal Order*, 1973). Another difference in emphasis between Quinney and the others is his explicit concern with crime, rather than other patterns of deviance. Certainly, illegal behavior is important for Matza (evident in the stress he places on "ban") as well as for Becker, who often draws on types of criminal behavior for his illustrations. However, unlike the others, Quinney does not employ a sociological conception of deviation, but rather a strictly legal concept of crime. The focus on legal definition of behavior eliminates some confusion in conceptualization, as well as serving to direct attention away from criminal behavior and toward the nature and development of legal systems--Quinney's major interest.

Like the other Labeling Theorists, Quinney is only incidentally concerned with the question of why a particular *act*, which is called crime, is committed, i.e., he is only incidentally concerned with the etiological question. Rather, his primary interest is in why a particular act comes to be called "crime" or is placed in the category of criminal acts.

a. The Law

Quinney presents two contrasting conceptions of law. The first he asociates with Roscoe Pound (1943), although it could just as well be associated with Durkheim's conception of the role of restitutive law in organic society. Quinney's second view of the law is presented as an alternative to, and fundamental reformulation of, Pound's perspective.

Pound sees law in terms of a "pluralistic-consensual" model of society. That is, while he recognizes individual and segmented group interests in society (heterogeneous society), he sees a consensually held law as regulating the conflict of interests and relations among plural groups. This law is viewed as operating in the whole public's interest. Elaborating on this conception of law, Quinney states:

> Jurisprudence has generally utilized a *pluralistic* model with respect to law as a social force in society. Accordingly, law regulates social behavior and establishes social organization. . . In recent juristic language, law functions "first, to establish the general framework, the rules of the game so to speak, within and by which individual and group life shall be carried on, and

secondly, to adjust the conflicting claims which different individuals and groups of individuals seek to satisfy in society." (Quinney, 1970:33)[4]

The similarity between the above and Durkheim's conception of restitutive law, especially regarding the specification of its functions, is obvious. Law, from this point of view, is something that is shared and is in the common interest of otherwise diverse groups. In Pound's terms, *law is in the category of social interests.* In the language which has been employed in this work, Pound's conception of the law is normative—it is something shared in the relation between interacting parties. Hence, plural society is viewed as consensual with respect to the nature of the law.

Quinney's alternative conception of criminal law, which exposes his conception of crime, is quite distinct from the above in three respects. First, society is *not* viewed as consensual, i.e., the relevant relations among members of society giving rise to law are not viewed as normative. Second, society is viewed as segmented in most respects, i.e., there is little in society toward which all groups share an orientation, and society is particularly segmented with respect to commitments to criminal law. Third, the segments of society are often in conflict, at times involving a fundamental conflict of basic interests. The character of the law can be understood only in this setting of conflict among segmented groups; the law represents the victory of one set of interests over another.

To further clarify the issues involved between these alternative conceptions of law, we can return to the distinction made between norms and rules. First, Quinney suggests that each segmented group within society can be viewed as having a common institutional framework, i.e., as having its own way of life, which distinguishes it from others. "Each segment of society has its own values, its own norms and its own ideological orientation" (Quinney, 1970:38). Such segments, however, are *not* characterized by the internal existence of law. Rather, law emerges in the relations *between* segments of society, i.e., it emerges to govern (or control) relations where no norms are operative. Law, as opposed to norms, is intersegmental. As such, law exists as a body of *rules* conjured and applied by some groups in relation to the intragroup normative behavior of others. Law is an attempt to constrain or eliminate that behavior which conflicts with the interests of the dominant group. Laws are *rules* which govern intergroup relations.

Hence, although Quinney recognizes the existence of consensual groups who share norms and values, these are not the source of either law or crime. It will, for a moment, be useful to contrast his view with Durkheim's. It appears that the *segments* of society which share norms and values are similar to Durkheim's mechanical solidarity groups. As has been seen in the analysis of Durkheim's work, such groups are characterized by repressive law, i.e., criminal law. However, such societies do not

---

[4]Quinney quotes from Carl A. Auerback in "Law and Social Change in the United States," *U.C.L.A. Law Review* (July, 1959), 6:516-532.

possess what Quinney would term "law," i.e., rules which must be articulated and codified in one way or another. The very existence of such law indicates (to Quinney) the emergence of segmentation and conflict in society. That is, codified law, as a necessary body of rules, indicates the existence of tension and disorder in society, of intergroup conflict.

Crime is found then in society, when one goes *outside* the consensual group to the relations between segments of society. It emerges in a clash between somewhat alien and opposing ways of life. "Rather than representing the institutional concerns of all segments of society, law secures the interests of particular segments, supporting one point of view at the expense of others" (Quinney, 1970:40).

In sum, when a group imposes its own normative pattern of conduct on others outside the group (e.g., those with a different culture), the norm for the first group becomes, from the alien group's perspective, a rule. That is, the *imposed* norm is not something which is part of the alien group's orientation to the world, but, rather, now becomes a condition of their action. Given Quinney's conception of law, crime is created in an under-institutionalized relationship between conflicting groups.

b. Colonization, Crime, and Labeling

The Labeling perspective on crime/deviance can perhaps best be appreciated when it is cast in the light of an ideal-typical relationship between the colonized and colonizers, i.e., the emergence and administration of criminal law is best typified by a colonial relationship.[5] Such a focus on colonial relations clarifies the relationship between offenders and rule-enforcers, for colonization presents all the ingredients which, from the model which forms the Labeling perspective, give rise to "deviance." Although such a model is implicit elsewhere (e.g., in the works of Becker and Matza), it is only Quinney who explicitly uses historical examples of colonial relations to illustrate how the application of rules creates a category of offenses and offenders. In so doing, Quinney points to three colonial relations, specifying how criminal law is imposed on subjugated populations. The three cases Quinney cites are: (1) English Common Law in the American colonies, (2) British law in India and Africa, (3) American frontier law (see Quinney, 1970:49-56). In each case, but particularly in the last two, there is the imposition of wholly alien law upon indigenous populations whose territory has been invaded. In the American frontier case, this refers to, of course, the imposition of Anglo-American law upon Native American tribal groups. When a colonial power imposes its law upon a subjugated people, crime is created.

This section of the paper will close with a short summary of aspects of the colonial relationship. The sense will be shown in which the relations between colonized and colonizer illustrate the processes with which the Labelists in general, and Quinney in particular, are concerned.

---

[5] The notion of "ideal-type" is used advisedly. It is employed here, as Weber used it, in terms of a model—a construct of the scientist—that highlights the qualities involved by exaggeration. The model does not exist in pure form in the world, i.e., the "ideal-type" is not construed to be the "pure-type."

In order to clarify the utility of a colonial analogy, it is necessary to emphasize that the colonial relation is not dissimilar to the "intra-societal" (i.e., intersegmental) situation described above with respect to the relation between violators and rule-enforcers (i.e., the relation which gives rise to the Labelists' categories of crime and deviance).

The colonial relationship begins with different or, in Quinney's terms, segmented groups. They may share nothing in terms of a similar culture. That is, the two groups' beliefs, values, norms, ideology, etc. may be radically opposed. A second characteristic of such a relationship is conflict--at least latent conflict--between the radically distinct cultural groups.

A third feature is, of course, domination. In all colonial relations, one group has successfully imposed itself on another and subjugated it; the relations are of super- and subordination. Fourthly, in imposing itself on another group, the victorious group imposes its law (and/or a system of colonial law derived from the native system of law) on the other. Further, in so doing, the dominant group *creates* categories of crime out of behaviors which may have been part of long-standing cultural traditions of the now-subjugated people. For example, Quinney points out that "the British made bigamy a criminal offense in Ghana. Ghanian customary law, however, allowed polygamy" (Quinney, 1970:53). In such a case, the law is easily seen as an imposed body of rules, alien to the subjected peoples' way of life. The sixth relevant feature of the colonial relationship is that the time sequence between violative act and rule is the same as is intrinsic to Becker's and Matza's perspectives. The action brought under the jurisdiction of ban may be one of long-standing tradition. This aspect of the colonial relationship should serve to further clarify why the Labelists do not view the "deviant act" as qualitatively different from the "conformative act." The action is viewed as being consistent with a cultural tradition and is made deviant only by alien law. This imposition of law, of course, has nothing to do with the source or quality of the act. The final point of the analogy is that, in the colonial relation, the subjugated population most certainly does *not* feel guilty in acting out its way of life; the "offenders" must be taught the "error of their ways." Hence, the colonial offender is *only* "legally guilty" and must be *made* guilty. Since the colonized person is "innocent" in the first place, it is necessary that the colonizer teach him the significance of his actions, i.e., that the colonizer teach him to *feel* guilt.

7. Conclusion

All five of the scholars reviewed in this section--Becker, Matza, Scheff, Lemert, and Quinney--share certain basic elements in their conception of deviance. These elements, despite the scholars' differences, bind them within a single tradition, while differentiating them in important respects from the Functionalists. The most fundamental similarity among these scholars is their conception of deviance which involves a reaction establishing a process of interaction between two parties: rule-enforcers and presumed rule-violators.

CHAPTER VII

THE EXEMPLARY SOLUTION: EXPLANATION WITHIN THE LABELING PERSPECTIVE

A. Introduction

The immediately preceding section established the conception of deviance which characterizes the Labeling perspective. Of necessity that section touched upon the basis of explanation within the matrix. Most importantly, it was determined that, from the Labelists' point of view, it is in the emergence of the conception of deviance and its application to persons' behavior through which deviance is created. Further, the central authors of the approach (e.g., Becker) conceive deviance in such a way that it can in no way exist independent of this process. That is, deviance does not exist save by way of reaction to an act as such. This process of "deviance creation" occurs within a context of interaction between presumed rule-violators and rule-enforcers. Accordingly, in order to explain the process by which deviance arises, the Labelists focus upon this interaction. In examining this aspect of the matrix, attention will continue to be upon the same five scholars whose conception of deviance has just been reviewed.

One component of the explanation of deviance has to do with how and why the interaction between "offender" and enforcer emerges. Given its emergence, another area of interest is the consequence of the process of interaction between the parties such that deviance is created. Thirdly, Labeling analysis is concerned with explaining the effect of the development of deviant identity on the labeled person's future behavior.

In relation to the first concern, how and why the interaction between presumed offender and rule-enforcer emerges, three questions need to be examined: (1) What is the nature of rule-breaking activity-- what is its context, and how does it emerge? (2) what is the process by which rules prohibiting certain behavior emerge, and (3) in what context are such rules applied? Becker and Matza focus on the first of these issues; Becker and Quinney both devote considerable attention to the latter two.

The second area of interest, having to do with the consequences of the interaction between "rule-violators" and enforcers, focuses upon the impact of the interaction on the actor's "public identity" and self-concept. In relation to this component of the approach, there are two associated processes which occur simultaneously and are given emphasis by one or the other of the theorists. Both Scheff and Lemert are concerned with processes occurring in the interaction setting, as these processes shape identity and self-concept. Matza, on the other hand, while interested in the interaction process, takes as his major subject the processes occurring *within* individual consciousness as they are related to the development of the self.

The final emergent from the interaction context is the behavioral consequences of the formation of deviant identity and self-concept. For the most part, this involves the explanation of the way in which attempts at control result in the continuance of "rule-breaking behavior" or give rise to "secondary deviance."

While each of the theorists under review in this section touches upon practically all of the elements of explanation embodied in the matrix, each tends to focus more attention on one or the other aspect of the approach. The strategy employed here will be to draw out each aspect of the explanation by focusing upon the theorist(s) who develops it most fully.

B. Becker

1. Rule-Breaking Behavior: Becoming a Marijuana User

The importance of the rule-breaking act from the Labeling perspective is summed up nicely by Becker when he states: "The first step in most deviant careers is the commission of a nonconforming act, an act that breaks some particular set of rules. How are we to account for that first step?" (Becker, 1963:25).

The first step may be easily explained (as was indicated in the previous chapter) if the actor is simply ignorant of the rules. Being of another life-style, he simply does not know how he is expected to act. As a result, it can easily be imagined (given the complexity of social life) that he may break another's "important rule." If the rule is being enforced (i.e., if it is applied to him), the creation of deviance begins.

The more complex case is the one that Becker calls "intended nonconformity." In this case, the actor knows the rules but does not abide by them. Why not? First, Becker comments on theories which explain deviance by reference to the actor's "motivation" to commit rule-breaking acts. He suggests that such theories are inadequate, because they do not take into account the fact that more people are *motivated* to do the deviant thing than actually *do* it.

> In analyzing cases of intended nonconformity, people usually ask about motivation: why does the person want to do the deviant thing he does? The question assumes that the basic difference between deviants and those who conform lies in the character of their motivation. . . But the assumption upon which these approaches are based may be entirely false. There is no reason to assume that only those who finally commit a deviant act actually

80

have the impulse to do so. It is much more likely that most people experience deviant impulses frequently. (Becker, 1963:26)

From these observations, Becker moves to what he considers a better starting point. Rather than asking how such motives arise, he queries, "Why don't more people act on their deviant motives?" The answer, in short, is that those who restrain their impulse to deviate are "caught up in" (committed to) the dominant way of life. Their commitments are to things which they could lose (a job, a spouse, money, prestige, etc.). Out of their commitment comes restraint.

> What happens is that the individual, as a consequence of action he has taken in the past or the operation of various institutional routines, finds he must adhere to certain lines of behavior, because many other activities than the one he is immediately engaged in will be adversely affected if he does not.

Further,

> . . . the normal development of people in our society (and probably in any society) can be seen as a series of progressively increasing commitments to conventional norms and institutions. The "normal" person when he discovers a deviant impulse in himself, is able to check that impulse by thinking of the manifold consequences acting on it would produce for him. (Becker, 1963:27)

So, as Becker suggests, the focus on the explanation of rule-breaking activity must have to do with how people avoid commitments to the "institutional system." Caution must be exercised not to misconstrue the way in which the concept of "commitment" is being employed here. Becker does not refer to the actor's *moral* commitment in opposition to the deviant activity in question. The actor may be motivated to do the "deviant" act, and he may think that it *would not be wrong* to do so, but, because of what he might lose with respect to other *things* to which he is committed, he restrains himself. Hence, the actor is not necessarily restrained by his morality in relation to the activity (such that he would feel guilty if he did it), but, rather, he is deterred by the fear of loss.

However, as Becker recognizes, to simply point to a lack of commitment to the dominant way of life (a lack of commitment to the things which one might lose) is not sufficient to explain rule-breaking behavior, much less the specific direction of conduct that emerges. Absence of commitment does not automatically give rise to rule-violation. The uncommitted person may be "law abiding," even though his chance of running afoul of the law is perhaps greater due to his not having anything to lose by its violation. In short, lack of commitment does not really explain either rule-violation itself or the innumerable variations on it (e.g., why should lack of commitment lead to marijuana use?). Clearly, marijuana use as a specific pattern of activity does not inevitably flow from a lack of commitment to the things most Americans value, although the likelihood of its use may be increased by such a lack of commitment. Moreover, Becker's interests do not lie in "one-shot" behavior, i.e., single acts or random impulses which involve rule-violation. As are other

Labeling Theorists, he is interested in more stable patterns of rule-violating activity:

> . . . we are not so interested in the person who commits a deviant act once as in the person who sustains a pattern of deviance over a long period of time, who makes of deviance a way of life, who organizes his identity around a pattern of deviant behavior. (Becker, 1963:30)

The first stage in the development of such patterned activity, and the explanation of the direction of deviant motives (explaining the specific direction that deviance takes, given the lack of commitment which may allow it to be expressed) involves the *learning* of deviant motives. In short, the actor must have experience with someone or some group that "teaches" him the activity. In a concise summary of his theory of the development of the deviant motive, Becker states:

> . . . many kinds of deviant activity spring from motives which are socially learned. Before engaging in the activity on a more or less regular basis, the person has no notion of the pleasures to be derived from it; he learns these in the course of interaction with more experienced deviants. . . What may well have been a random impulse to try something new becomes a settled taste for something already known and experienced. The vocabularies in which deviant motivations are phrased reveal that their users acquire them in interaction with other deviants. The individual *learns*, in short, to participate in a sub-culture organized around the particular deviant activity. (Becker, 1963:30-31)

So, while Becker's theory is no "ordinary learning theory" (a psychological reinforcement theory), it is, nevertheless, a theory which emphasizes the learning process in the development of "deviant motives." The actor learns the motives associated with doing the deviant behavior through affiliation with those who do it.

Becker's illustrative case is provided in "Becoming a Marijuana User" (Becker, 1963). He begins with an actor who has an *opportunity* to learn how to use marijuana--an actor who is in association with a deviant peer group and who has "arrived at the point of willingness" to try marijuana.[1] Becker then establishes the steps or "sequences" involved in the development of the continuing use of marijuana, each being a necessary component in the establishment of its recurrent use. The steps must be completed in order for the actor to define such use as pleasurable--the basic prerequisite for continuation of the activity. Summarizing the sequences, the actor must (a) learn the technique of smoking marijuana, (b) learn to perceive the effects, and (c) learn to enjoy the effects. Each step is an outcome of a learning process.

To digress for a moment, how does the actor become "willing" to

---

[1] Those theorists who ask etiological questions would stop, rather than begin, at this point. Seeking out the source of the actor's "willingness" to try marijuana and having located it, such theorists would consider the activity explained.

use marijuana when presented with the opportunity to do so? Through affiliation with the deviant group, the actor develops a (vague) conception of use which he defines as, at least to some degree, attractive. A little apprehensive, perhaps, the actor is still willing to try.

> He knows others use marijuana to "get high," but he does not know what this means in any concrete way. He is curious about the experience, ignorant of what it may turn out to be, and afraid it may be more than he bargained for. (Becker, 1963:46)

At the same time, affiliation with the deviant group leads to the decline of the effectiveness of social control, through the influence and use of the group's knowledge, ideology, and rationalizations.

It is now necessary to focus more systematically upon the element of social control within Becker's framework. One possibility for Becker is that society's controls may be lacking, in that the individual may not be committed to conventional values in the first place, i.e., (1) he may be ignorant of the rules which prohibit the activity and, hence, not be aware that his behavior may put him in jeopardy, or (2) he may simply have escaped the commitment process (e.g., he may not be concerned with losing what most people are afraid of losing, that is, he is not enmeshed in the conventional value complex). But what is the character of the controls when they do operate? These controls, it appears, are something which, in a sense, are outside the individual, i.e., they are "conditions of his action." Becker does not view the actor as controlled by his orientation to the situation, i.e., it is not necessarily the actor's morality which prohibits the conduct, but an *external morality* with which he must contend. So, as Becker indicates, a primary instrument of social control is power. "Social controls affect individual behavior, in the first instance, through the use of power, the application of sanctions. Valued behavior is rewarded and negatively valued behavior punished" (Becker, 1963:60).

An examination of some of the general features of social control as Becker relates them specifically to marijuana use will show how these controls may be overcome and the possibility of recurrent marijuana use maintained. Although lack of commitment on the part of the rule-breaker may operate so that the potency of controls on marijuana use is diminished (as it does in relation to any other deviant activity), there are still obstacles to be overcome. When an actor is to some degree committed to a conventional way of life, the obstacles presented by social control are even more effective in influencing his behavior. The basic social controls which Becker describes as relevant to marijuana use are: (1) limitations on access to the substance, (2) the necessity of keeping one's activity secret, and (3) society's definition of the act as immoral. The processes by which the first two controls are overcome are easily enough understood. First, participation in the subculture of marijuana users leads one to "safe" sources of supply. As a result, one can come to feel relatively secure in efforts to obtain the marijuana, and one can begin to perceive the danger of loss of conventional commitments and "things" as sufficiently reduced to allow continuation of the activity. Secondly, the secrecy criterion may be met by learning from others how to "handle" the use of the substance without giving oneself away. The neophyte learns under what circumstances he can be detected as being "high" and by whom, and he learns how to avoid detection and how to recognize "safe" situations. In short, he learns techniques which make him secure in his activity and which, consequently, weaken society's controls.

The third aspect of control involves the question of conventional morality in relation to marijuana use and is slightly more complicated. This is particularly so given how the "rule-violator" is perceived from the conventional perspective. The issue of the morality of the act goes beyond a strictly external, power-based notion of social control, for, in this situation, it appears that Becker's actor is committed to conventional morality. Could it be that the actor who is using marijuana shares conventional morality in such a way that he is a *morally* committed member of society who, in order to continue use, must overcome his own commitments? That is, could Becker's actor be not an "outsider" but an "insider" in this respect? The Labeling perspective begins with segmentation--with moral, ideological, or value differences with respect to the deviant activity. However, Becker's statements at times seem to indicate that, in some sense, the actor suffers from a moral dilemma in relation to marijuana use. Furthermore, this dilemma stems from what is at least a limited sharing in the conventional morality. What sense of morality which the actor shares with conventional society might marijuana use disturb? Becker states:

> The basic moral imperatives that operate here are those which require the individual to be responsible for his own welfare, and be able to control his behavior rationally. The stereotype of the dope fiend portrays a person who violates these imperatives. (Becker, 1963:72-73)

In neutralizing the controlling efficiency of this morality, Becker does not posit a process by which this morality is overcome or changed. Rather, his actor finds that he can *both* use marijuana and remain moral at the same time. He does not have to be "immoral" in his own terms or change his morality in order to get "high." Although moral questions are raised, they can be dismissed as irrelevant or inapplicable.

> If use progresses to the point of becoming regular and systematic, moral questions may again be raised for the user, for he now begins to look, to himself as well as others, like the uncontrolled "dope fiend" of popular mythology. He must convince himself again, if regular use is to continue, that he has not crossed this line. . . Tests are made--use is given up and the consequences awaited--and when nothing untoward occurs, the user is able to draw the conclusion that there is nothing to fear. (Becker, 1963:75-76)

The actor, still ascribing to conventional morality concerning self-control, finds not that the morality is wrong (and, therefore, it need not be neutralized), but rather that marijuana use simply does not interfere with such morality. As a result, the conventional pattern of morality which the actor shares with other members of the society no longer acts as an impediment to, or as a control upon, the use of marijuana. The actor can remain an *insider* with regard to this morality and still get "high." The actor, now finding marijuana use consistent with his morality, remains willing to continue its regular use.[2]

Rule-breaking activity, then, can be explained by the actor's participation in a subculture which, acting as a learning structure, fosters the behavior. At the same time, participation in the group aids the actor in overcoming the obstacles to deviance (marijuana use, in this case) presented by social controls.

2. Apprehension and the Maintenance of Rule-Breaking Activity

Deviance, as conceived from this perspective, is always an outcome of an interactive situation. The significant stage of concrete interaction between "presumed rule-violator" and rule-enforcer takes place through "apprehension." Later, the focus will be upon the processes which lead to apprehension--the sought-after outcome of rule-creation and rule-enforcement. For now, it is sufficient to note the effect of apprehension upon the maintenance of rule-breaking activity.

The major irony to which Labeling Theory directs attention is at the same time the central element in its system of explanation--through efforts to control rule-breaking behavior, the behavior is sustained. Becker remarks: "One of the most crucial steps in the process of building a stable pattern of deviant behavior is likely to be the experience of getting caught and [being] publicly labeled as a deviant" (Becker, 1963:31). But how does apprehension have this effect? First, it "criminalizes" the actor. When apprehended for presumably committing a deviant act, the actor's "public identity" is likely to undergo major transformation. The nature of *deviant* public identity is such that it takes on major significance and becomes the core or central identity of the person, forming the basis on which others react to him. It is a "master status," in that it leads to the assumption by others that the actor who is deviant in a specific regard, e.g., is homosexual, possesses a whole series of other, ancillary characteristics. In the case of deviant identity, of course, the presumed supporting traits are consistent with the central feature of identity, i.e., they are assumed to be equally unattractive. The homosexual is not only homosexual, but is "irresponsible as well." The drug addict not only "does dope," but is also "untrustworthy." These assumptions, associated with such an overriding identity, lead to treating the person as if, in having committed a rather specific act, his general

---

[2]This view of the marijuana user is not inconsistent with the argument in the preceding section concerning the separation of the rule-breaker from conventional morality. Following Becker's thinking carefully, it appears that in order for the behavior to be continued, it must not be seen by the actor as conflicting with his morality. Becker's actor does not change or overcome his commitment to conventional morality; rather, he redefines, as being in error, the public's view that marijuana smoking conflicts with that morality. It is not that conventional *morality* is wrong, but that conventional *cognition* is wrong--marijuana use does not make one lose valued self-control.

At the same time, Becker suggests that, in order to maintain the

character is exposed as being deviant. As a result, the person is treated (in Becker's terms) as "generally deviant," rather than as specifically so.

Such treatment has several consequences leading to further "rule-breaking activity." First, the actor is "cut off" from the same level of participation in the "straight world" (that sector of the population committed to the law) as that which he "enjoyed" prior to being apprehended and labeled. His environment is "de-conventionalized," which, at the same time, may lead to the "criminalization" of the environment. The significance of this is obvious. The actor is to some degree isolated from the entangling commitments which, as Becker argues, tend to keep persons from acting on their deviant impulses or motives in the first place. The actor is now in a position in which the representatives of the dominant life-style have less leverage on his behavior than was true prior to his apprehension. In short, the actor, having less to lose, is more difficult to control. Simultaneously, now that he is excluded from the company of "straights" ("law-abiding" society), he is more likely to find company in association with other deviants. This, of course, strengthens the associational milieu which originally gave rise to and supported the deviant activity--the milieu in which the activity was learned in the first place.

A second consequence of being publicly labeled as deviant may be to force those so labeled into other, new types of criminal activity. Hence, the unemployable "known homosexual" or "known drug addict" must often turn to marginal or illicit activities in order to survive or to maintain his or her life-style. In sum, being apprehended and publicly labeled as deviant may well result in a far greater involvement in an "outsider" life-style than was previously the case.

3. The Interests of Moral Entrepreneurs: The Creation and Application of Rules

The primary explanation of deviant behavior from the Labeling perspective is to be found on the other side of the coin from rule-violation--in the making and application of rules. There are two aspects of this process which are of prime importance. First, by simply making the rules and applying them to patterns of conduct, societies create deviance. Therefore, it is important to understand the processes by which the rules emerge--who makes them, why and how they are applied,

---

use of marijuana, it must be defined as pleasurable. However, as Becker is well aware, there is an institutionalized value in opposition to "illicit pleasure" in the United States (an expression, he says, which has real meaning to us). Still, the actor doesn't "test" for the pleasurability of marijuana and then back away from it when he finds it so. Rather, finding it pleasurable, although certainly illicit, the actor pursues the activity. Therefore, the actor who uses marijuana is different from other persons in American society not in that he does not accept the self-control morality, but in that he does not subscribe to the moral doctrine concerning illicit pleasure. It appears, then, that the potential user must be, as indicated in the previous chapter, an "outsider" in this regard, at the beginning of and throughout the process.

and in relation to whose behavior they are enforced. Second, when the representative of the rule-creator--the rule-enforcer--and the rule-breaker meet in the situation of apprehension, the "presumed rule-violator's" future conduct is altered. The application of rules not only defines behavior as deviant and, thus, creates deviance, but it also has behavioral consequences. As mentioned above, such consequence is to enhance the tendency on the part of the labeled actor to engage in rule-breaking activity. The current focus, however, is on the emergence and enforcement of rules which create classes of acts that are labeled as deviant.

Becker's basic question in this regard is, ". . . when are rules made and enforced?" (Becker, 1963:121). His basic answer is, when it is in someone's *interest* to have a rule exist forbidding certain conduct and to have the rule enforced. From Becker's viewpoint, new rules will not be enacted, nor existing rules enforced, unless it is in someone's interest to do so. How does this process work? Rules, as rather specific guides to conduct, are usually derived from values, i.e., broader orientations to action. But values are often so broad and vague that *effort* is required to derive rules from them. From whence does the effort come? It comes from someone (or some group) who has developed such an interest in prohibiting a pattern of conduct that he is willing to be *enterprising*, i.e., he is willing to expend the effort to relate a pattern of activity to an operative value in the milieu and to show others, who share the value, how the values and the activity are incongruous. The making of rules requires a "moral entrepreneur." The same may be said for the enforcement of rules: it is often simply the induced enforcement of previously ignored rules that, in effect, makes for "rule-creation." Again, as in rule-making, it is an enterprising, interested party who makes an effort to get the rules enforced.

The interest involved in some cases may simply be a "moral interest." That is, the entrepreneur may simply find the activity abhorrent and, therefore, seek to have it prohibited and deterred. An example of such a "moral interest" would be the activities in which the members of the Women's Christian Temperance Union engaged in their attempts to have the consumption of alcohol prohibited. On the other hand, getting a rule enforced may serve one's more general interests. In fact in some cases, the act may not be morally repugnant to the individual at all--it might simply serve his economic interest to have it banned or to have the rule enforced. In the case of "clan incest" (which Becker recalls from Malinowski's work on the Trobrian Islands), it is the incestuous female's offended betrothed who seeks to have the rule against such relations enforced and applied to his competitor. In any case, it is the interest of a person or group which stimulates rule-making and rule-enforcing enterprises.

In the effort to get a rule created or enforced, the enterprising entrepreneur must point out to other persons the effensiveness of or the difficulty presented by the activity which is the object of his attention. If he is successful in getting a sufficient number of others to go along with his concerns, it is likely that the rule will be put into play. Often this involves the development of some organization to carry out a "crusade" in opposition to the behavior. In short, what is involved at this stage is the existence or accumulation of *power*. The successful moral entrepreneur must either possess or develop political power. It is interest, enterprise, and power which result in the creation and enforcement of rules. When these factors are brought into play, a "successful" outcome is the creation of a category of deviance. When this category is applied to acts, "deviant behavior" exists.

The need for enterprise, organization, and power suggests at least some reluctance (or lack of concern) on the part of others to go along with the creation and enforcement of rules. This is most certainly the case with respect to those who are engaged in the activity in question. Indeed, there is active opposition to the creation and enforcement of certain rules in a great many cases. That is, these struggles are political. The struggle will be resolved, as such struggles are, by power. This power may be simply a result of the degree of enterprise and organization of one group over another. Or, of course, the power base may be more general than that held by a crusading organization, e.g., it may rest in wealth, property, esteem, or more general political power. In any case, the creation and enforcement of rules still depends upon the accumulation or possession of more political power in society than one's opponents are willing or able to use.

Becker's archetype of the emergence of a rule is again drawn from the situation of marijuana use in the United States. In this case, the moral entrepreneur, the enterprising party, is the Federal Bureau of Narcotics. Through the passage of a federal law opposing marijuana distribution and use, the Bureau sought to bring the activity under its jurisdiction. What were the interests of the Bureau in pursuing such action? Becker is generous in his evaluation:

> While it is, of course, difficult to know what the motives of Bureau officials were, we need assume no more than that they perceived an area of wrongdoing that properly belonged in their jurisdiction and moved to put it there. The personal interest they satisfied in pressing for marijuana legislation was one common to many officials: the interest in successfully accomplishing the task one has been assigned and in acquiring the best tools with which to accomplish it. (Becker, 1963:138)

In developing public concern about the use of the "drug," the Bureau actively fed journals and papers with negative and inflammatory information about the substance. Bolstered by public support of its own creation, the Bureau led the way in requesting that Congress pass the Bureau's draft of the Marijuana Tax Act. The Bureau further acted as prime witness in favor of the legislation in ensuing House committee meetings relevant to the bill. Anti-marijuana legislation establishing a rule which prohibited its use was, of course, passed by the Congress.

What was the character of the political struggle over the passage of such a rule? It would appear, at first, that this was not a political contest at all (but, perhaps, just a correction of an oversight). And, in a way, it wasn't a contest, the pro-legislation forces so clearly having the power and, hence, the control. However, there was some opposition to the bill as originally drafted, especially from the hempseed oil producers and the birdseed industry. Their interests and objections were met through amendments to the bill which was already assured of passage (the organized opposition being exhausted). But what of the marijuana users? Bereft of a dominant value from the Western Cultural Constellation with which to defend themselves, "unenterprising," "unorganized," and without political power, their interests were overcome. They lost a political struggle and were "made deviant" in the process.

4. Summary and Conclusion

In summary, Becker's approach to understanding deviance yields the following. First, the process of rule-making and rule-enforcement is initiated by the existence of an activity which is offensive to someone—an activity which is to become or already is a "rule-breaking" activity. How is the commencement of such activity explained? In short, the actor becomes "willing" to engage the phenomenon by the avoidance or neutralization of social controls on the behavior, combined with a group affiliation of the sort which sponsors the behavior. The individual becomes associated with a segment of society which is, in respects relevant to the activity, *outside* the dominant set of values and rules.

On the other hand, there are those who make and enforce the rules. In terms of their interests, they engage in enterprise, that is, they organize and develop the power to win a political struggle that seeks to prohibit certain kinds of conduct from being carried on by others. In so doing, they create categories of deviance which, when applied, result in apprehension and in the labeling of others or of their behavior as deviant. This making of rules and the application of them through apprehension has a number of consequences. When apprehended, the "presumed rule-violator's" public identity is usually significantly affected. His identity is criminalized, resulting in his exclusion from the societal commitments which previously led him to control his impulses. The result of this may well be the individual's greater participation in deviant activity.

In short, the "making" of deviance in society is an outcome of societies' segmentation. This segmentation, combined with interest and power differences, results in the application of rules made by the powerful and applied to the persons and behaviors of the relatively powerless.

C. Edwin Lemert: The Explanation of Secondary Deviance

In some respects, Edwin Lemert can be described as only nominally sharing the perspective under consideration here. As he himself suggests, his commitment to Symbolic Interactionism is qualified. Nevertheless, Lemert has made an important contribution to this approach to deviance, particularly with regard to the conceptualization and explanation of "secondary deviance." As previously noted, the primary sources of deviance, as conceived within this perspective, are associated with the interaction context and, specifically, with attempts to control behavior. Lemert was instrumental in establishing this aspect of the tradition and remains squarely within it. In the preface to his latest collection of articles on the subject of deviance (Lemert, 1972), he states of the articles contained in the volume:

Their common concern is with social control and its

89

consequences for deviance. This is a large turn away from older sociology that tended to rest heavily upon the idea that deviance leads to social control. I have come to believe that the reverse idea (i.e., social control leads to deviance) is equally tenable and the potentially richer premise for studying deviance in modern society. (Lemert, 1972:ix)

It is this mode of explanation which is, of course, also developed in Becker's work. Lemert directs attention to a broad range of social-control relations and their potential consequences--all of which have a bearing on the explanation of "secondary deviance," i.e., deviance which is an outcome of reacting to the actor or to his behavior as deviant.

In focusing upon the societal reaction to presumed or actual behaviors, Lemert's primary concern is with the consequences of the change in the actor's *condition* which is occasioned by reaction to his behavior as deviant. His specific interest is often in the change that such reaction effects in the actor's self-concept. Such change is associated with the reorganization of the actor's behavior into a new social role which is a result of his being reacted to as deviant. It should be emphasized that both the change in social-role behavior and the effect upon the actor's self-concept are related to this change of situation which is occasioned by his being treated as deviant, *rather* than to the labeling process *per se.* Lemert qualifies his acceptance of the explanatory power of the symbolic milieu in that he does not accept the premise that the emergence of a deviant self-concept can be due simply to the changing indications of self made to the "deviant" by others. Rather, from Lemert's view, the sources of this change are to be found within the social-organizational context in which the actor is placed. In a remark that somewhat sets Lemert apart from others within the perspective, he states:

While a considerable amount has been written on the subject of identity problems, much of it has been in a phenomenological or existential mode of thought. Searching out the referents of such problems in social situations and social structures is mandatory if the concept is to have utility for sociological studies of deviance. (Lemert, 1972:91)

The differences between, as well as the similarities among, Lemert and others within this matrix will, hopefully, become more clear in the following discussion.

In specifying what he intends by societal reaction, Lemert states that it "is a very general term summarizing both the expressive reactions of others (moral indignation) toward deviation and action directed to its control" (Lemert, 1972:64). Lemert discusses the various consequences of such societal reaction under several broad headings. The first, stigmatization, refers to "a process attaching visible signs of moral inferiority to persons, such as invidious labels, marks, brands, or publicly disseminated information" (Lemert, 1972:65). When such stigmatization is widely publicized or widely recognized, it, of course, gives rise to widespread discrimination against the person. This should not be surprising, since purposeful stigmatization by social groups has just this intent. That is, it is seen as a punishment precisely because it gives rise to such discrimination. However, stigmatization may sometimes be a consequence of other occurrences in society not associated with the intentional establishment of discrimination, but which, nevertheless, have such an effect. The stigma associated with being an ex-convict is, of course, an example of this. The contribution of such a status to secondary deviance is obvious enough. First, the person is denied the opportunities that others have. For example, his inability to get a "straight" job may drive him into "illicit activities" in order to survive. The failure to develop conventional associates can create a situation in which the actor is isolated, leading him to seek out the company of other deviants and all that this association implies for his future behavior. In addition, since stigmatization and its consequences are punitive, hostility toward and alienation from the stigmatizing and discriminating groups develop. With respect to this matter, Lemert points out that the recognition of this alienative consequence of punishment was well established by Mead,[3] forming the basis of Mead's opposition to the judicial system in the United States and his support of a "juvenile-court" system, a system oriented toward "rehabilitative," rather than punitive, reactions to criminals. As Lemert states:

> The definition of stigmatization as a collective process which necessarily misrepresents what a person has done and attacks his integrity permits the deduction that it "naturally" arouses feelings of injustice. (Lemert, 1972:67)

While accepting Mead's suggestion that the punitive and stigmatizing reaction to the criminal only alienates him further, Lemert does not see a solution to this problem in the structure or "rehabilitative orientation" of the juvenile court. In fact, following Cloward and Ohlin (*Delinquency and Opportunity*, 1960) and Matza (*Delinquency and Drift*, 1964), Lemert suggests that the "arbitrary sentences" (e.g., indeterminate sentences) may simply feed the sense of injustice that the victim feels.

> Matza holds the thesis, directly contradictory to Mead's, that juvenile court procedure amounts to inconsistent punishment, that its very precept of individualized justice, when coupled with judicial arbitrariness and shifting group pressures reflected in court decisions, becomes from a phenomenological perspective an affront to the charged youth's sense of the just. (Lemert, 1972:67)

So, in this regard, the "rehabilitative court" is not an improvement over the "punitive criminal court" in reducing the tendency to further alienate those who come before it. In any case, appearance in either court may stigmatize the individual in such a way that others react punitively toward him, increasing his alienation from them and the dominant way of life.

---

[3]See Mead, "The Psychology of Punitive Justice," *American Journal of Sociology*, 23, 1928:577-602. This position concerning the alienating consequences of punishment is also well established in the Functionalist tradition. See Parsons, *The Social System*, 1951 (Chapter 7).

1. Social-Control Organizations

Although stigma, of course, exists in modern society, it rarely is intentionally attached to persons through the formal processes of the civilian legal structure. Rather, in Lemert's (1972:68) words, "In modern societies, where generalized public opinion and interest are absent, controls over deviants tend to be administered by welfare, punitive and ameliorative agencies." In short, the deviant is placed in the charge of organizations specifically designed to deal with him. We have already suggested that such placement results in stigmatization, but independent of this effect, such institutions may actually support deviance as well. These organizations contribute to the growth of deviance in a myriad of ways. In the first place, the "deviant subject" in the custody of the organization is supposed to abide by a whole new series of rules and regulations to which the "non-deviant" members of society are not subjected. Violating these rules may be as costly to the person in terms of added punishments as were his original rule violations.

> In order to become a candidate for reinstatement in society the deviant must give his allegiance to what is often an anomalous conception of himself and the social world, and try to live by rules, often rigorous in extreme, substituted for or added to those by which normals live. (Lemert, 1972:69)

Primary illustrations of such situations are, for example, (1) the revocation of parole involving a violation of parole status but not the law (e.g., while on parole, failing to show up for work without a legitimate excuse) and (2) the failure to follow institutional routines in prison. Although often trivial, violations at this level not only bring severe penalties (e.g., reimprisonment), but may also serve to validate or support a deviant self-concept, just as a serious offense may. As a consequence, deviant identity, self-concept, and behavior may be stabilized.

Further, Lemert points out that the nature of the controls represented by such organizations may themselves directly contribute to the development and/or maintenance of new or prior patterns of deviance. Perhaps one of the better illustrations of this point is an outcome of what Gresham Sykes (*Society of Captives*, 1958) called the "pains of imprisonment"--an example of which is the deprivation of heterosexual relations within prison which leads directly to widespread "deviant" sexual behavior behind the walls.

Related to the above is the formation of inmate subcultures within the confines of the various types of institutions. It has been suggested that such subcultures inevitably form [4] and support the stabilization of deviant life-styles. This is particularly true of prisons, since:

> Administrative logistics favor this by determining that recidivists are more likely than others to be sent to such institutions [e.g., professional thieves]. There they dominate the prison world, control communication with staff and custody people, and successfully propagate an ideology that "you can't make it on the

---

[4] See Sykes and Messinger (1960:13), and Cloward (1960:28).

92

outside." (Lemert, 1972:72)

Lemert does suggest that the degree to which this effect has been demonstrated to support deviant patterns in day-to-day living once the person is back on the streets has yet to be carefully assessed.

2. Law and Control

Lemert is also concerned with the differential impact of various systems of law on types of deviant behavior (see Lemert, 1972: Chapter 5). The potential effect of the law with respect to the generation of secondary deviance is most obvious in the case of morals crimes or "crimes without victims." The most general consequence is a "criminalization" of the actor's environment far in excess of that required to simply carry out a specific deviant act. Actors who seek to procure illegal goods for consumption (drugs, alcohol, etc.) are required to move in a criminal environment in order to obtain them. If the substances were legally accessible, of course, they would not be required to move in such an environment. The effect is to increase the association of otherwise "conventional persons" with those whose life-style is generally deviant. As Lindesmith and Gagnon (1964) pointed out, the Federal prohibition on marijuana use substantially altered the mode of distribution of the drug. "Dealers," who formerly distributed only illegal "hard drugs," simply added the previously more casually distributed marijuana to their "sales package." As a result, marijuana users were brought into closer proximity and had easier access to other illicit drugs. This shift in "control" and consequent shift in distribution accounts for whatever relationship there is between marijuana use and other illegal-drug use.

Another important consequence of making an item illegal is that its price is driven up and its accessibility is decreased. Hence, in order to procure the item, the actor may be driven to "illicit" sources of income, perhaps even forced to adopt a life-style in which procurement of the goods is the central feature. As Lemert states:

> . . . problems are built up for the customer seeking a supply of goods or services; he has to participate in a criminal subculture for his purposes, and he may have to expend time and money ordinarily allocated to the established or conventional claims on his budget. If he is strongly motivated, as with persons addicted to alcohol, drugs, or gambling, he may neglect his family, alienate his friends, and beyond this, engage in outright criminal activity to finance his costly habit. (Lemert, 1972:77)

3. Deviance, Self-Concept, and Personal Contacts

As has been indicated, Lemert has some reservations in relation to the force of the labeling process *per se*. These reservations are particularly strong if the essence of the labeling process is understood as a kind of direct socialization. In short, from this vantage point, the deviant, being reacted to as such in face-to-face situations, is being taught what he is. The suggestion here is that in being reacted to solely as deviant, the actor is being influenced to take on a deviant self-concept, perhaps even independent of the other consequences of rule-enforcement (e.g., criminalization of environment). Lemert backs away from this proposition in two respects. First, he finds it questionable to assume that the imputation of characteristics to a person can, in itself, result in the formation of a deviant self-concept.

> Eric Erickson, not to be designated as an idealist, speaks of changes from positive to negative identities which result from societal diagnosis by the "balance of us." This is illustrated by the mother who constantly berates her daughter as "immoral," "no good" or "tramp." The girl in time may yield to the derogatory self-image because it is nearest and "most real" to her. Yet Erickson is careful to say that this may be only the final step in the acquisition of a negative self-image, and he also refers to the necessity of confirming changes in identity. I take this to be a way of saying that there must be some basis for validating a degrading self-conception in prior acts, to which I would add that it also needs subsequent overt acts to clothe it with social reality. (Lemert, 1972:81)

Clearly then, Lemert attaches some importance to the occurrence of actual deviant behavior before a deviant self-concept can be formed through the labeling process.

A second and quite important difference between Lemert and other theorists within the matrix is his suggestion that, in certain cases, the failure to accept the "deviant self" may contribute to deviance. This is particularly the case when the invocation of "self-control" in order to avoid the deviant episodes may itself be implicated in the source of the deviant act. Noting the work of an obscure practitioner, F. M. Alexander (1910), Lemert remarks:

> Alexander . . . concerned with the psychic aspects of disease, postural abnormalities, and speech defects, had theorized that they were aggravated or preserved by faulty theories of causation; consequently efforts of afflicted individuals to eliminate their bad habits became the very means by which they were kept alive or made worse. (Lemert, 1972:86)

Lemert cites the analysis of stuttering by Charles Van Riper (1957). Van Riper contends, and Lemert agrees, that the stutterer must accept himself as such before the problem can be alleviated. It is the stutterer's attempt to control his speech, based upon a "faulty theory of causation," which contributes to the disturbed speech. Consistent with his general approach, Lemert views the person's desire to control his speech as an outcome of the importance placed upon "articulate speech" within the culture. The control systems within the socio-cultural milieu [5] contribute to the formation of the "over-control systems" of the individual, which lead to the deviance. Of these controls, Lemert suggests:

In stuttering they are neurotic mannerisms which originate as

---

[5] See "Stuttering and Social Structure in Two Pacific Island Societies" (Lemert, 1972: Chapter 11).

defensive reactions to the penalties which our culture imposes upon those individuals whose nonfluency is excessive. It is the stutterer's efforts to avoid his own defensive actions, i.e., the stuttering self, which feed back into and maintain the disordered speech. So long as he keeps trying to be what he knows he isn't—a normal speaker—his problems continue. Only by equating the self with the stuttering symptoms can change be brought about. (Lemert, 1972:87)

This possibility concerning the individual's acceptance of the deviant self-concept as a step toward the successful control of deviance contrasts sharply with Scheff's position which will be developed in the following section—that is, that it is the development of a deviant self-concept that stabilizes the deviance.

Lemert does suggest that, in some sense, self can become so identified with its own deviance that the deviance is thereby sustained. So, rather than the indications and reactions of others leading to this development of the deviant self, it is that the activity has become so central a part of the actor's everyday life and experience that it finally becomes integral to his self-concept. The activity simply becomes part of what "he is." Speaking of the long-time, heavily involved drug addict, Lemert states:

. . . he has in the course of time introduced narcotics into all or most facets of his life; he has used them night and day, at home and at work, on foot and in automobiles, and in many toilets of the land. He has injected arms, legs, knees, and other parts of his body, and he has sniffed and swallowed drugs. When this has gone on for years in countless social situations, the administration of narcotics, their imagery, and their concomitant feeling states become . . . "second nature" . . . [They] have become bound up in complex, intermeshing ways with his physiological, psychological, and social reactions which in the large form a supplementary self. (Lemert, 1972:90)

It is by reference to the self which is "bound up" in deviant activity that Lemert explains the continued craving for the substance that is experienced by the successfully (physiologically) withdrawn addict or alcoholic. It is a craving for a lost "self" and is associated with a type of "identity crisis." The source of the maintenance of deviance, in such cases, is clearly secondary. Whatever the original sources of deviation, they have likely receded into the past, or at least have become relatively insignificant as a "cause" of the behavior. The behavior is maintained through its having become a central aspect of a way of life and of self.

D. Scheff: Labeling and Mental Illness

1. Introduction

Scheff's work is somewhat unique among the other scholars' selected, in that it focuses upon the manifestation of deviance called mental illness. Furthermore, Scheff devotes greater attention to the impact of the labeling process itself, as it relates to the taking on of the deviant role and the formation of a deviant self-concept, than have the other theorists reviewed thus far. It is one thing to suggest that being publicly labeled alters (e.g., through stigmatization) the *conditions* of one's action, resulting in "defensive reactions" which take the form of a deviant role and may contribute to the formation of a deviant self-image; it is quite another to suggest that labeling in itself may result in the formation of a deviant self, independent of such auxiliary effects. It is this latter possibility which is Scheff's concern.

In approaching Scheff's explanation of "mental illness," a brief review of his conception of "rule-breaking" or primary deviance is in order. Note that (1) in its primary form, deviance emerges from diverse sources--biological, psychological, and social--and from "volitional acts of defiance," (2) most episodes of such deviance are transitory, and (3) most such rule-breaking is denied or ignored by the rule-breaker and by others. Scheff's basic questions in relation to these early acts of rule-breaking are: (1) Why do some cases of this usually episodic behavior not pass, i.e., why does it stabilize? and (2) Why, given its emergence from diverse sources, are its stable symptoms uniform? In other words, why do certain forms of brain deterioration (a biological source) result in behavior similar to that invoked by combat fatigue (a social source of such deviance)?

Scheff's suggestion (which is consistent with the type of explanation within this theoretical mode) is summed up in the last proposition of his work, which is that the answer has to do with the character of the societal reaction: "Among residual rule-breakers, *labeling* is the single most important *cause* of residual deviance" (Scheff, 1966:93). But what is meant by "labeling"? In the first place, it is *attending* the act, i.e., not ignoring it. Labeling is the opposite of *denial.* Furthermore, labeling does not involve a simple noting of the act, but is, rather, a stronger *reaction* which suggests that the act is of some significance--that, in fact, the act is of sufficient consequence to require explanation and correctional activity. Thus, although the most frequent reaction to rule-breaking is denial,

> In a small proportion of cases the reaction goes the other way, exaggerating and at times distorting the extent and degree of violation. This pattern of exaggeration, which we will call "labeling," has been noted by Garfinkel in his discussion of the "degradation" of officially recognized criminals. (Scheff, 1966:81)

2. Learning the Role Behavior Associated with Mental Illness

In order to understand how the labeling of the actor may result in the stabilization and uniformity of "symptoms" that are associated with mental illness, earlier stages of Scheff's argument must be examined. A fundamental issue involves whether the "symptoms" of mental illness are inherent (as in disease) or whether they are learned. Scheff, of course, takes the position that they are learned. Previous supporters of this position have had difficulty, in that their arguments concerning how these "symptoms" are learned are too narrow (usually suggesting the symptoms are learned within the family and through experience with significant others who, acting as role models, display the symptoms). Scheff argues that the symptoms are learned in a wider context, most often vicariously, rather than through experience with others who display the patterns. This indirect learning structure is provided by a widely institutionalized, well-disseminated image of mental illness which is held by persons within the society. Scheff discusses two aspects of the individual's "taking on" of this institutionalized image, i.e., the way in which the individual learns of it. On the one hand, Scheff documents the suggestion that the image is learned in early childhood by virtually all persons in the society. In his words, "stereotyped imagery of mental disorder is learned in early childhood." Secondly, the childhood image is elaborated and reaffirmed in social interaction throughout one's life. As he states it, "*The stereotypes of insanity are continually reaffirmed, inadvertently, in ordinary social interaction*" (Scheff, 1966:67). The imagery associated with mental illness is transmitted through the mass media, as well as in face-to-face discourse. In short, "everyone knows" what it is to be "crazy."

3. Reaction to the Deviant Episode

When one has engaged in a "residual rule-breaking act" (violated an assumptive norm) and this behavior has been reacted to, the episode is likely to provoke a crisis. That is, when an act is difficult to comprehend, it gives rise to confusion and is generally unsettling, often resulting in a crisis situation for both parties (violator and reactor). At the very moment at which his action has been noticed and he is forced to attend it himself, the violator is likely to be seeking an explanation of his own conduct. In an excellent summary of this aspect of his theory, Scheff says:

When gross rule-breaking is publicly recognized and made an issue, the rule-breaker may be profoundly confused, anxious, and ashamed. In this crisis it seems reasonable to assume that the rule-breaker will be suggestible to the cues that he gets from the reactions of others toward him. But those around him are also in a crisis; the incomprehensible nature of the rule-breaking, and the seeming need for immediate action lead them to take collective action against the rule-breaker on the basis of the attitude which all share--the traditional stereotypes of insanity. The rule-breaker is sensitive to the cues provided by these others and begins to think of himself in terms of the stereotyped role of insanity, which is part of his own role vocabulary also, since he, like those reacting to him, learned it early in childhood. In this situation his behavior may begin to follow the pattern suggested by his own stereotypes and the reactions of others. That is, when a residual rule-breaker organizes his behavior within the framework of mental disorder, and when his organization is validated by others, particularly prestigeful others such as physicians, he is "hooked" and will proceed on a career of chronic deviance. (Scheff, 1966:88)

Reaction in terms of mental illness thus provides a classic case of the creation of a situation via "collective definition."[6]

4. Maintenance of the Role and Self-Concept

Once one has accepted the label or has been coerced into operating within its terms (e.g., through involuntary hospitalization), other mechanisms come into play which foster the further acceptance of the role and/or support its acceptance. As Scheff puts it in one of the propositions of his work, *"Labeled deviants may be rewarded for playing the stereotyped deviant role"* (Scheff, 1966:84). One of the primary rewards associated with playing the "role" associated with mental illness is contingent upon the patient's occasional displays of "insight." He is rewarded (e.g., with verbal approval, a trip home, etc.) for his recognition that he is "sick" and for his willingness to live momentarily with that fact. Further "insights" (more specific ones) into the character of his illness will also be rewarded. Providing the therapist with "evidence" of his sickness or its roots in his past (where the "symptoms" may have been displayed and denied) also often brings forth approval. This reward process not only supports the deviant role, but, even more importantly, it is part and parcel of the way in which a self-concept is constructed and solidified. Other patients may also join in the process of inviting the patient to accept the fact that he is sick and may join in his punishment when he tries to "act well." After all, what could be a greater display of a patient's deluded state than to think he is well and perhaps even to "act well" when he is, "in reality," sick.

While rewards are in play to maintain and support the acceptance of the deviant role, there are, in Scheff's terms, "systematic blockages" to the re-entry into conventional roles. These blockages, in the form of "punishments for attempts at conformity," are organized around the lingering effects of *stigma* that are associated with a status such as that of "ex-mental patient." Having earlier reviewed some of the effects of stigma (see Lemert, 1972: Chapter 8, Section 3), it is not necessary to reiterate them here, except to stress that it often gives rise to invidious discrimination which reduces the person's potential employability, marriageability, and participation in other conventional role behavior.

Scheff concludes that there is considerable pressure from professionals, hospital staff, fellow patients, relatives, friends, and the community at large which forces the patient to accept and maintain the institutionalized imagery of mental illness as an organizational basis of role behavior and self-concept long after such societal reactions to "rule-breaking" have occurred. Once the self-concept has been established and the role "taken on," the tendency to act in their terms is, of course, increased.

5. The Sources of Denial and Labeling

Scheff does not systematically delve into the conditions under

---

[6]This, of course, represents a clear application of a basic dictum of the "Symbolic Interactionist" approach: "situations defined as real are real in their consequences." See W.I. Thomas (1972).

which denial or labeling is likely to occur in response to episodes of residual deviance. However, he does make some suggestions regarding various types of possible labeling reactions. For example, there are many labels, other than "mental illness," which may be affixed to someone who displays residually deviant behavior--e.g., "eccentric," "genius," "prophet," "visionary," etc. In short, milder negative responses to the behavior are possible as well as *positive* labels (e.g., "genius").

Scheff regards *power* as the basic variable which affects differential labeling. The more power (political, personal, economic, etc.) the actor has, the greater the probability of "denial" by others; or, given societal reaction, the greater the power, the less likely the charge of "mental illness." The tendency for society to have labeled Howard Hughes "eccentric" rather than "crazy" was, in part, a function of his powerful position. The "decision" as to Galileo's genius or madness was dependent upon the power he could command, as much as it was upon the plausibility of the "world-view" which he articulated vis-à-vis the dominant (power-supported) social context of knowledge.

Scheff summarizes his remarks with respect to this issue by suggesting that,

> Other things being equal, the severity of the societal reaction is a function of, first, the degree, amount and visibility of the rule-breaking; second, the power of the rule-breaker and the social distance between him and the agents of social control; and finally, the tolerance level of the community . . . (Scheff, 1966:96)

An illustration of Scheff's point can be drawn by raising this speculative question: "Why is the 'obviously mad' professor labeled as or reacted to as being 'simply eccentric'?" First, although his "rule-breaking" may be fairly visible, it takes place within the confines of the limited and highly tolerant audience of the "university community." Second, he has high status and a certain amount of power within that community. Third, his status is such that there is little social distance between himself and the rule-enforcers (e.g., some of his best friends may be "eccentric psychiatrists").

E. Matza: Labeling in a Phenomenological Mode

In this chapter, the work of scholars within the Labeling tradition has been reviewed. This work, for the most part, focuses upon the interaction process between a "presumed rule-breaker" and "rule-enforcers." The emphasis has primarily been on the consequences of such interaction in relation to (1) changing the conditions of the subject's action, (2) the formulation of deviant self-concept, and (3) the fostering of rule-breaking activity. In addition, this work has focused upon three points associated with the societal (control) reaction to behavior: (1) the emergence of rules which "transform" behavior, thereby "making" it deviant, (2) the labeling process itself, and (3) the consequences of labeling (e.g., stigma).

The processes occurring within the subject's consciousness, although often alluded to in relation to each of the foci, have not been systematically approached. Rather, they have been subordinated in favor of an emphasis upon the interaction context. However, in the work of David Matza (*Becoming Deviant*, 1969), an elaboration can be found of the concomitant processes occurring in the subject's consciousness in relation to each aspect of Labeling Theory. Matza, like Becker, also devotes some attention to the emergence of "rule-breaking" activity; unlike Becker, though, Matza casts his analysis of this problem in subjective terms. Rather than focusing upon the context of interaction associated with the socialization process, Matza follows the actor himself through the process, concentrating upon sequences which occur in consciousness.

1. Recasting Affinity

Matza begins his considerations with a critique and reformulation of the concept of "affinity." As traditionally employed, "affinity" implies that actors are "predisposed" by something in their environment or in their constitution to commit certain kinds of actions. Matza suggests that the conceptualization of affinity employed in the social sciences is close to that developed in chemistry. That is, affinity of actors to certain kinds of conduct is viewed as though an attractive force were operating, "pulling" or otherwise predisposing the actor to a pattern of action. If one assumes the possibility of an observer's locating such predisposing attractive forces within the actor's milieu, his action ought to be *predictable*. But this conceptualization of affinity does not take account of the actor's subjectivity, i.e., it does not recognize the difference between human actors and chemical particles. Whereas forms of matter other than life forms are only "reactive," and forms of life other than human are, at best, "adaptive," human beings are capable of "transcending" their circumstances. That is, they have the capacity to shape their environment or form their circumstances. This capacity is exhibited, in part, by the fact that "humans *can* say '*no*' to stimuli."[7] Further, human capacity for "shaping" the environment hinges upon the ability to direct consciousness, to *attend* or *ignore* (i.e., to select certain aspects of the milieu over others). In so doing, one creates the "significant" elements of his milieu. The recognition of this capacity forces a reformulation of the concept of affinity--a reformulation appropriate to the understanding of human subjects.

Matza's "affinity" excludes the view of persons' being drawn, inexorably, to the commission of acts. Rather, Matza's actors select, from their available resources within experience and circumstance, components out of which an act can be constructed. Perhaps raising several alternative acts as projected, people then chose whether or not to pursue a

---

[7]For this simple and straightforward statement of the unique human capacity, I must thank my colleague David Whitney. For a more complex discussion of the capacity, including an analysis of the emergence of the "interruption of consciousness" which is its basis, see Thomas Luckmann (1965), *The Invisible Religion*, Chapter 3.

constructed course of action. Human beings build the degree of "affinity" to an act out of those aspects of experience which they attend and out of which the act is constructed.

2. Being "Willing"

Matza analyzes the processes associated with *affiliation* in light of this reconceived notion of affinity. But before analyzing the affiliative context itself, he addresses the problem of how the actor "becomes willing" to get involved in a given activity.

As discussed in a preceding section, Becker begins his documentary on "Becoming a Marijuana User" (1963) with an actor who is *willing* to try marijuana. Matza conceives such willingness in terms of his recast notion of affinity. [8] He does this within the context of retracing the steps through which Becker's marijuana user passes.

In Matza's terms, what does it mean to be willing? First, willingness is distinct from being captive. "Captivity" is more consistent with the traditional notion of affinity. To be captive is to be objectified (that is, to be an object) at the mercy of forces which have overcome one. Two general sources of such captivity are The State and the organism (the body). Either can take control, and each has taken control of persons--captured them--and, in this sense, subdued them or, in Matza's terms, "pacified the will." "Being willing," unlike "being captured," is not an outcome of forces that have determinate influence. It is not that human behavior cannot be an outcome of such forces, but that this is not the unique and natural human condition. Being captured is, rather, a situation against which humanity struggles as against political tyranny or such "tyrannies of the organism" as, for example, psychoses. The struggle is one in which the will seeks to exert itself against determinate force. Persons under the control of such forces are reduced, i.e., having been reduced to the status of an object, they are reduced to a "lower order of existence." Although under such influences human behavior is determined, it is not inevitable that humans be captured by such forces. The "will" may assert itself and the person escape such captivity.

On the other hand, "uncaptive will" is not "free." Will emerges within the context of human experience and within the subject's milieu. To say that one shapes his milieu is not to say that it is escaped. As Matza states:

> To recognize and appreciate the meaning of being willing is by no means to assert the existence of a free will. Indeed, it is the very opposite. The logic of one's past, the human agencies in one's situation are certainly real. They are the grounding for the conduct of will. Free will, as the phrase itself implies, takes will out of context, converting it inexorably into an abstraction of as little use as any other. (Matza, 1969:116)

---

[8]Matza suggests that Becker operated with a notion of willingness consistent with this "recasting" of affinity. Whether or not this was Becker's intent is open to debate, but it is not relevant here. In any case, it is Matza who elaborates the idea of willingness.

Will and acts are constructed from the resources at hand. In that sense, will is constrained by the available resources, e.g., the actor's life-experience, but the possibilities (choices) are open within the range of that experience, making it indeterminate. Consistent with Matza's naturalism, will is understood as it is being experienced by subjects. It is "a conscious foreshadowing of specific intention capable of being acted on or not" (Matza, 1969:116). The actor imagines (or, in the more precise terms of phenomenology, he projects) an act as completed. In so imagining, he is able to "evaluate" it. On the basis of his evaluation, he is then able to *decide* whether or not to do the thing. But of what do his evaluations and his imaginings of the act consist? Prior to his "concrete affiliation with the act" (actual, instead of imagined, involvement in the concrete project), such imaginings are based upon "limited resources." At this point, the project consists only of his abstract conception of what it would be like to do the thing, and, given his conception of himself doing it, how it would bear upon his other projects--the other things which he, in imagination, selects and relates to it. For example, the actor reflects upon the ways in which doing the activity might affect his health, his relationship with his mother or his wife, his ability to do his job, or anything else perceived as potentially relevant to the act and its potential consequences. On the basis of such considerations, the actor decides whether or not to engage in the activity. After taking account of "relevant" matters in this way, the actor may decide that he can do a particular act. If so, it can be said that he has become willing. This is the sense in which an affinity between the subject and the projected act is established. He has decided, based upon his selected experiences, upon the factors in his milieu which he has considered, and upon his projected image of himself, that he will do it. He then has, on these bases alone, a tentative and limited "affinity" with respect to the activity. The "causes" of the act are the actor's "selected considerations;" they have led him to the possibility of engaging in the deviant activity.

> In the natural world of the subject, *the consequence* of affinity is being willing to do a thing, no more and no less. So conceived, the ordinary consequence of affinity becomes apparent. Affinity permits self-ordination. Under proper circumstances, the self as it encounters the invitational edge of novelty experiences an option. Thus the ordinary affinity yields permission instead of compulsion . . . the ordinary consequence of having been exposed to the "causes" of deviant phenomena is not in reality *doing* the thing. Instead, it is picturing or seeing oneself, *literally*, as the kind of person who might possibly do the thing. (Matza, 1969:112)

Such "picturing" does not, of course, suggest that the actor must inevitably do the activity. He can, by "recasting" the project (by reconsidering it, by including new information or aspects of his circumstances and experience), become unwilling to do the act. The actor is not seen as *inevitably* gravitating toward the activity unless he is "naturally reduced" (i.e., captured by agents of tyranny, e.g., the organism or The State). So, as Matza suggests, "affinity's yield in explaining deviant behavior is, in the first place, 'slight'." As shall be seen, however, the "affinity" may be increased through the subject's affiliation.

3. The Affiliative Context

As first applied to deviant behavior by Sutherland (1947), affiliation was conceived in much the same terms as is the conception of contagion in the case of disease. Such a notion, which at bottom suggests that the actor can "catch" a deviation, is, of course, not consistent with Matza's view of the nature of the actor. It implies, as does the traditional conceptualization of affinity, that the actor is under the influence of forces which he cannot "fend off" (e.g., the force of peer-group pressure). This notion of contagion through affiliation does not recognize, as Matza suggests it should, that the actor exerts control over his affairs. The idea of contagion does not recognize that the affiliative context simply brings more things into the actor's milieu which he may choose to consider in constructing a projected act. He can now assess further and more accurately his affinity to the activity. The affiliative context provides new material out of which affinity can be further strengthened or undermined. It is still the actor, not his peers, who is constructing the act. However, having "advanced" to concrete affiliation, he is now building the act from a new perspective. Previously "outside" the context of affiliation with the group and the activity it sponsors, he is now "inside." Led by his tentative willingness, he is now part of the action. At this point: "The subject may now reconsider, *in light of disclosed meaning built in the course of experience*, whether his initial understanding of his own affinities--as he pictured them--was sound" (Matza, 1969:118).

The subject now affiliated will continually reassess his willingness. He could "back off" or "back out" at any moment--elements of the concrete experience being not at all as he imagined, his affinity could be destroyed. On the other hand, he *may* go on. An illustration can be found by following Becker's neophyte "marijuana user" via Matza's interpretation of the affiliative context. Discussing affinity in the affiliative context, Matza focuses upon one of the early steps in the process of becoming a marijuana user--becoming an inhaler, and "a special kind of inhaler" at that. As Becker points out, the actor must *learn* the technique. More than that, as Matza emphasizes, he must *relate* himself to the technique. This may be a small moment in the process, but it is an important one:

> American marijuana use--before anything else--is an act of smoking. The student of abstracted affinities seeking correlations outside the context of experience who neglects this "antecedent condition" does so at his own peril. (Matza, 1969:120)

The subject's "imagined affinity" for marijuana use could end if, for example, he discovers that he cannot tolerate the burning in his throat caused by inhaling the smoke of "harsh grass." But, before this can happen, the subject must agree to "take a toke," i.e., to inhale some "dope." Being willing to try some, he does this. *Now* his affinity will be reassessed. The actor is *then* able to establish his relation to marijuana through the concrete experience of having inhaled the substance. The actor does not gravitate to use--as one particle gravitates toward other particles--he assesses and evaluates the relation of himself to the activity. The actor decides whether or not to continue the activity by conceiving of himself so engaged, assessing this image of himself to other selected images of himself, and then asking himself, "Does it fit?"

> First, he pictures himself doing the thing as he is doing it. In Meadian terms, and at this early point in the process he objectifies himself as an inhaler. Second, he builds onto the meaning of affinity, which is itself being enriched in experience, the intuition of relation derived from existing in a project. The yield of this combination is correlation: the relation of himself as inhaler to himself in other projects, past, present or future, that he sees or depicts--the ones of which he is reminded. (Matza, 1969:121)

If the correlations the actor has established give rise to the decision of "fit," i.e., if they are positive, then the actor may continue the activity.

> After correlating the picture of himself as inhaler with a picture of himself in reminiscent projects, say, that of appearing graceful and competent in company, of learning to inhale cigarettes, of avoiding arrest, of being instructed, or perhaps even of avoiding cancer and other irritations of the lung, the subject makes up his mind one way or the other. (Matza, 1969:122)

What must be emphasized and taken literally in this quote from Matza is that the subject makes up his mind. The "causes" of the conduct are the "variables" he muses about.

The subject proceeds through the course of events and decisions which permit marijuana smoking. In much the same way as discussed above, he relates himself to the effects of marijuana use. While going through the process, he is continually assessing himself with respect to the various aspects of the concrete act, arriving at an evaluation of his relation to the activity. If he continues to assess the relation as one of "fit," he will continue the activity.

4. The Subject's Authority in the Affiliative Context

Given Matza's view of the relation between the subject and the activity, it is of particular importance that the subject be seen as controlling and directing the whole process. This is the case even in light of the influence of peers in the process of becoming deviant. The traditional relationship suggested between subject and peers implies that the subject is "under the influence" of peers such that, given a certain quality and quantity of interaction, the subject will inevitably take on the activity and world-view which the peers sponsor. Matza's view of the subject emphasizes that, even in the face of peers, the subject controls the process. The cajoling, daring, rationalizations, and suggestions of peers are simply something to be taken into account along with everything else the subject wants to consider. That is, his relationship to his peers may be, and likely will be, among the things that he selects as bearing upon the project at hand and, therefore, will consider in his musings. The subject takes the group and all of its resources, "the esteem of personnel, the intimidation of the dare, the appeal and sociability of expectation" (Matza, 1969:123), into account in arriving at a conclusion. However, the influences of the group are not sufficient to *determine* the outcome. The subject maintains the authority.

> All I mean by *maintaining authority* is that throughout the process of decision, the subject was the author of each key element. *He* made an object of himself. *He* intuited the idea of relation. *He* built the meaning of affinity. *He* correlated his present project with those *he* was reminded of. *He* gave birth to, or created an act. The subject made up the process, but out of material provided by the context of affiliation. (Matza, 1969:123)

5. Signification

As Matza conceives the process of signification, it is largely a process initiated and carried out by The State:

> This connection between the organized, though diversified authority of the state and becoming deviant is the broadest meaning of signification I want to consider. Persons unrelated to organized authority may signify too, but not so potently, or meaningfully. (Matza, 1969:144) [9]

Signification has three meanings that are implicated in the formation and maintenance of deviant identity. One meaning is simply to be *registered*, i.e., to be officially assigned the status of deviant. One may, in official records, be recorded and labeled a deviant, e.g., one may have records that show that one has been arrested and convicted as a thief. A second sense of signification has to do with persons' "putting down" or derogating others. This sense is exemplified as in "signifying" or "doing the dozens"--a routine used by urban Blacks (as well as other groups) which involves attempts through the use of one's wits to "out-humiliate" others. In this process of signification, "putting down" refers to assassinating aspects of a person's character, as well as specifying the inferior nature of the behavior in which the person is engaged. Third and, as Matza indicates, perhaps the most complex meaning of signification in this context is "to sign" or exemplify (stand for) something--to represent, indicate, or symbolize. With reference to the actor, his "deviant behavior" and the label attached to it may come to represent self, i.e., to be the indication to him of his "essential self"--that which stands for what he is.[10]

---

[9] In the latter portion of this statement, Matza appears to be in opposition to much of sociological theory. The "primary group" and "significant others," not "secondary agencies" such as The State, are usually seen as the most potent source of self-concept formation. See, for example, Berger (1963), *Invitation to Sociology*, Chapters 4 and 5.

[10] Matza also discusses symbolization or indication of deviance on the "collective level," i.e., the "signified thief" comes to stand for "thievery" in the eyes of the agents of control. Operating out of the

6. Ban, Bedevilment, and Transparency

The whole process of signification, of course, rests upon "ban," i.e., the outlawing or prohibition of certain activities by The State. As was indicated in the previous discussion of Matza, it is "ban" which "morally transforms" activity, and, thus, "makes" it guilty. The existence of a ban on an activity assures that the subject will not be able to "innocently affiliate" with either the activity or those who engage it. In short, the existence of ban on activity assures that the subject will become "bedeviled." Simply:

> . . . the scope or range of disaffiliation will surpass or go beyond the amount implicit in the deviation itself. The logic of ban creates the strong possibility that the subject will become even more deviant in order to deviate. (Matza, 1969:148)

Bedevilment is of primary importance, for it "prepares" the subject for what Matza terms "meaningful apprehension." It does this through *effecting* the "spread" of deviance--bringing it into wide areas of life and consciousness. Bedevilment accomplishes this in two basic ways. The first is through extending the range of deviant activity in which the actor, in order to do the thing, must engage. We have seen this illustrated throughout the discussion of this perspective, e.g., in order to smoke marijuana, one will likely engage in other deviant activities, such as its purchase. This compounding effect becomes more complex as one moves to other patterns of deviance. "High-priced" drug use, of course, may lead to other illicit activity in order to gain purchasing power. The tendency to get involved in illicit economic activity is still further enhanced by the fact that the "known drug addict" cannot find conventional employment of any sort. Continued "high-priced" drug use without an established economic base forces almost complete disaffiliation with conventional society. However, this pattern is hardly endemic to drug use itself: "addicted" physicians are not "bedeviled" in this particular way.

Secondly, ban "bedevils" by "making" activity guilty in another way which is equally important. Ban makes the actor *self-conscious* in relation to his activity, i.e., he is forced to *dwell* upon it. Being self-conscious, he feels "transparent" in the company of "straights." That is, he fears that he might be "seen through." He has a secret, and now he must struggle with it and worry about his capacity to keep it. This feeling of transparency emerges in the most mundane of circumstances. Even casual conversation concerning the activity in which the subject has secretly engaged may become discomforting. What if he blushes? What about the less obvious clues, such as showing too much knowledge or interest concerning the activity? It is easy to imagine that a knowledgeable slip of the tongue may elicit the response: "You really sound like you know what you're talking about." In such interaction situations, the primary consequence--self-consciousness--is an outcome of the fact that:

"method of suspicion," it is to the prime suspect (the symbol of theft), the signified thief, that the police turn whenever theft occurs within their jurisdiction.

. . . the subject must continue being cagey; he must persist at managing himself throughout the conversation. . . He is engaged in a remarkable project of imitation--being himself as he thinks he is ordinarily. (Matza, 1969:153)

The importance of the feeling of transparency is that, in almost any conventional context, the need to expend energy in order to deceive may emerge. Under such circumstances, it is easy to imagine the subject, continually forced to behave "deviously," moving further and further towards "being deviant." The neophyte,

. . . has devoted psychic effort to keeping his secret . . . if done well--the subject has built the meaning of duplicity, enriched the meaning of being devious, temporarily established the feasibility of being opaque; finally, he has created some distance between himself and right minded associates. (Matza, 1969:154)

In sum, the ban imposed by The State on certain activities establishes the incipient stages of the "spread" of deviance and deviant identity for those so engaged. This occurs even before The State's enforcement agents become directly involved with their "client." To reiterate, ban compounds deviance through bedevilment in three ways. First, it necessitates other illicit activities in order for the subject to participate in a singular deviant activity. Second, it fosters disaffiliation with conventional activities and persons and, thereby, affiliation with the unconventional. Third, by necessitating that the activity be kept secret, it leads to the feeling of transparency and the devious managing of the secret. Matza concludes:

By itself, ban serves to make the activity guilty--to rectify the mistaken belief in innocent affiliation. By making secrecy and security sensible, ban maneuvers the subject into a compounding of deviation. But the permeation of character implicit in such a development is slight, and not widespread. (Matza, 1969:155)

To increase the permeation, concrete contact with The State and its agents will do.

7. Apprehension

In approaching the significance that apprehension has for the subject, we must recall that, although the subject is not by nature at the whim of determinant forces, he can become so. If the force is great enough, the actor, treated as an "object," can be made an object. One general source of such objectification of persons is The State. The State need not objectify persons, but it can. In the situation of apprehension, the subject is faced with concentrated authority and, thereby, has his own authority reduced. The State is not a "peer;" it is a superior power. Hence, the subject's control over the occurrence of the processes may be reduced. However, the subject's role and power in the process of his becoming deviant are not extinguished by the power of The State. In fact, the actor is left with some crucial options.

Although The State has relatively great authority in the situation of apprehension, it need not be viewed as having foresight. What often happens to the subject in the hands of his apprehenders is the completion of the process of becoming deviant; however, this is not at all the intention associated with all that power. The completion, in the sense of transforming a person's identity, is a consequence of action based upon antithetical intentions. The State intends to deter and reform. But, for those not deterred, apprehension affects not reform but crystallization, completion, and solidification of the deviant self. How does this occur? What "mistakes" occur within the subject's consciousness which lead him to collaborate with the agents of The State in constructing his identity as deviant? Such collaboration is not inevitable. Although the subject's authority is reduced, it is still the subject who must "cooperate" in the formation of the deviant self.

Authority, through apprehension, seeks to impress the subject with the gravity of what he has done. The subject may have begun "innocently," doing little of significance from his perspective. What he did may have been "almost nothing"--"smoking a few joints," "a peek in a window," "a joyride in a neighbor's car," etc. But authority seeks to convince the subject that his action has significance; it seeks to *awaken him*. The idea that his action has significance is, after all, the basis of the justification of apprehension in the first place. The intention of The State's agents is to convince the subject of the significance of what he has done with respect to the system of meaning which The State represents. They intend to show the subject that what he did was wrong in terms of that system of meaning and to further show the threat which his conduct poses for the "unity of meaning" with which The State is associated. The reason for the production is to teach the subject why he should not do it again--that is because it has consequences for society. The intention of the agents of The State is to have the "unity of meaning" restored by the subject's submission to it. The object is to have him see "the error of his ways" and correct them. In Matza's terms, the subject is intended to project his attention outward to the society. Comprehending society and his relation to it, he is asked to bring himself into conformity with society: that in which he is included. He is asked to find "fit" with the societal unity of meaning and, presumably, at the same time to find lack of "fit" with his now reassessed deviant activity. Understanding, it is hoped, will "straighten him out," that is, make him follow the rules.

> Faced with the appearance of authoritative being, the deviant subject may join society in seeing that what he had done could not be taken lightly, that instead it was a matter of considerable gravity. And, dazzled by a display of the unity of meaning in society, he may conceive himself as included. (Matza, 1969:164)

But, as Matza indicates, this is not the only possibility. The subject may make the mistake (perhaps somewhat supported by the agents) of turning inward (to self) rather than outward (to society) in seeking the significance of his grave action. The "unity of meaning" to which he refers may be self, not society. That is, he may ask, "What does this action mean *of me*?"

. . . therein lies the irony--he may get everything confused, take all that was presented him and proceed in a direction different from that intended. Impressed by the show of authority, per-suaded of the gravity of his infraction, reminded of the unity of meaning, he may proceed inward. That is all he has to do to pre-pare himself to spread the deviant identity. (Matza, 1969:164)

The second "mistake" the actor may make is in choosing between "indication" and "consequence" with respect to self. In the case of "con-sequence," the act is grave in that its consequences for the actor may be of some importance--it may cost him dearly in terms of what he will lose: prestige, respect, money, etc. However, such a realization, although attaching gravity to the act, does not add to the building of deviant identity. That identity is more likely to be built up when the subject takes the act (for example, a theft), although perhaps insignificant in consequence, as *indicative* of self.

Quite different from consequence, indication points the subject to a consideration of himself; to the question of the unity of meaning of the various things he does and the relation of those things to what he conceivably is. To consider the possibility that the theft [for example] was important in the sense of being in-dicative of him puts the subject well into actively collaborating in the growth of deviant identity by building its very meaning. (Matza, 1969:165)

The question is now obvious to the subject and refers us to his next "mistake." Having referred to self and having chosen indication rather than consequence, the subject asks, "Am I, *essentially*, a deviant?" The question assumes the acceptance by the subject of the notion that the self contains a central core, a basic element of character. Given his acceptance of that assumption, how does he go about arriving at the conclusion that he has not only *done* theft, but *is* a thief? First, the sub-ject must assume that some relation exists between what he does and what he is, i.e., that there is a relationship between doing and being.

The meaningful issue of identity is whether this activity, or any of my activities can stand for me, or be regarded as proper indi-cations of my being. I have done a theft, been signified a thief; *Am* I a thief? To answer affirmatively, we must be able to con-ceive a special relationship between being and doing--a unity capable of being indicated. That building of meaning has a nota-ble quality. Elaborate structure notwithstanding, it may be sum-marized in a single thought--even in a single word. *Essentially*-- that is the economy. (Matza, 1969:170)

The question that is posed here, made possible by directing attention to self rather than to society, focusing on indication rather than on conse-quence, does not raise a simple question of fact, but rather a question of essence. The factual question, "Do I do theft?" may rather easily be answered one way or the other. The relevant question becomes a more profound one--one of character, of the core of self: "Is the essence of self exposed or indicated by this deviant thing that I do?" Remember

109

that the actor has been prepared by extended affiliation, by being "made" guilty, and by feeling the sense of transparency for the spread of deviant identity to occur. Further, his apprehenders have impressed upon him the gravity of his deed. He has directed attention to the self and taken the significance of his action in the direction of indication. All that remains in the process of becoming deviant is the introduction of a bit more evidence one way or the other in the case of identity and the equivocation of the terms of the question, "Am I, *essentially*, a deviant?"--i.e., the equivocation of "essence."

Identity is not yet crystallized, essence not quite established. How does the process continue? What if, despite having been impressed by the display of authority with the gravity of his action, Matza's subject does it again? What if, having been "awakened," and knowing the significance of the act, he commits still another offense? Such a repetition of the activity becomes, though not logically nor necessarily, primary data, shedding light on his essence. He is engaged in activity which is not only grave but is also recurrent. But how does action which is merely recurrent (although grave, it is "just doing") come to be taken as indicative of self, of being? The answer is, "Through the subject's equivocation of the meaning of 'essentially.'" As Matza suggests, essence is a word widely equivocated. The breadth of its possible equivocation is perhaps unsurpassed in the language. On the one hand, essence may mean "simply," i.e., what is right there on the surface of things; on the other hand, it may refer to: "One of the most profound relations man is capable of conceiving: the special relation in which an entire unity of being is indicated, revealed, apprehended wholly--by one small part of it" (Matza, 1969:172). The mistake that the subject makes is taking the *superficial*-- his doing of theft--as indicative of the profound. His doing of theft leads him very easily to the suggestion that he is simply a thief. From this simple observation, with the addition of the equivocation, character is revealed--that is, a revelation has occurred. The equivocation accomplished, the subject has, at least temporarily, become deviant.

8. The Subject and The State

This whole process is associated with the societal reaction to the subject's activity. The processes of concern to Matza are those which take place within the subject's consciousness concomitantly with societal reaction. The subject, from Matza's view, is not simply at the whim of these societal forces. He still exerts authority and influence (although this is diminished in the latter stages of the reaction process). The subject himself is heavily implicated, in that his "mistakes" result from real choices and options, i.e., collaboration with The State in the building of deviant identity is an outcome of the reflective directions which the subject takes. It is the actor who takes the "grave act" as relevant to self rather than as relevant to society. (Any help from the agents of The State is viewed as largely inadvertent.) Further, he takes it as indicative, rather than as "merely" consequential. Last, he "equivocated" the meaning of "essentially" in arriving at a conclusion concerning self. However, *Ban* (The State) is implicated in every stage of the process--in bedevilment and transparency, as well as in apprehension. Even though it

110

is neither the intention of The State nor its agents to develop deviant identity, this development is the consequence of their actions.

F. Quinney: Taking Labeling Theory to Marx

1. Introduction

All explanation which has been related to the Labelists' matrix has had associated with it the elements of power differential, conflict, and interest. In Lemert's work, these elements are only implicit, but in the other Labelists' work, these elements are raised to at least moderate levels of explicitness. Yet (although Matza sometimes calls himself a Marxist), none of the authors has, in a self-conscious way, related Labeling Theory to the theoretical model in which these elements are most pronounced: Marxian Theory. Acknowledgment of the correspondence between Conflict Theory and Labeling Theory has perhaps been slow in coming due to the latter perspective's historical roots in the Symbolic Interactionist tradition. However, Quinney has been associated to a lesser degree with the Symbolic Interactionists than have the other theorists reviewed here. Although heavily influenced by Labeling Theory, Quinney has been able to tie this approach to modern Conflict Theory, both conceptually and philosophically. Quinney's extension of Labeling Theory into Marxian Theory has left the Labelists' basic conception of deviance unchanged; Labeling Theory is simply further elaborated in an explicitly Marxian mode. Quinney's formulation maintains consistency with both the fundamental anchoring point of the Labelist matrix--the conceptualization of deviance--and with its explanatory form. Deviance in Quinney's work, as in Labeling Theory, is explained *via* societal reaction.

In Quinney's work, *The Social Reality of Crime* (1970), the explanation of "crime" (as does Becker's explanation of deviance) rests upon "the formulation and application of criminal definitions." However, Quinney elaborates Becker's approach in at least three ways. In the first place, Quinney's historical perspective is broader and more explicit. Secondly, he more directly indicates how the Labelists' perspective bears upon the central categories of deviant behavior. That is, Becker's focus on "marginal deviance" (e.g., marijuana use) is limited and has too easily led to the suggestion that the approach cannot shed light upon violations of the "core values" of social groups. (This matter will be elaborated below.) Finally, Quinney clearly ties the creation of categories of crime to the class structure of Capitalist society. In so doing, he completes the process of relating Labeling Theory to Marxian analysis.

2. Interests, The Law, and Criminal Categories

As suggested in a previous section concerning Quinney's conceptualization of crime, law is viewed as a coercive instrument governing the relations between segmental groups in society. Further, it is through law that Quinney's specific interest in deviance--criminal categories--is formulated. In explaining the emergence of crime (which, from his viewpoint, means explaining the emergence of *categories* of crime), the

111

question for Quinney is, "What is the source of the criminal law?" As in Becker, the answer to the question is *interests*. However, Quinney expands and modifies Becker's conception of interests by relating them to existing segmented groups in society. Quinney is also more specific about what he means by "interests." In addition, and perhaps most importantly, he relates the category of interests to groups in society as conceived in terms of Dahrendorf's (1959) modification of Marx's categories of "class in itself" and "class for itself," i.e., latent and manifest interest groups.

Quinney is no crude positivist. He does *not* see values and interests as, in some sense, objectively given or fixed, as part of "the nature of things." Rather, interests are associated with the values, norms, and ideologies of various segments of society. One must examine each of the societal segments in order to uncover interests--interests are defined by the group. It is those things that the group believes should be maintained or accomplished for its welfare which are definitive of its interests. When these interests are generally pursued within the segment, they may be regarded as institutionalized (at least within that segment). As Quinney says:

> Each *segment* of society has its own values, its own norms, and its own ideological orientations. When these are considered to be important for the existence and welfare of the respective segments, they may be defined as *interests*. . . Thus, interests are grounded in the segments of society and represent the institutional concerns of the segments. (Quinney, 1970:38)

Quinney considers two types of interest orientations. The first type, "formal interests," are those policies or activities which are in the group's interest, but which the group does not consciously recognize or act upon. This case, in which the group is not organized for action, represents a variant of Marx's "class in itself." Dahrendorf's reformulation of the Marxian category would classify the segment as a "latent interest group."[11] The second type of segmented interest group, in Quinney's terms, is one of "active interests." In this case, the relevant interests of the group are recognized by the membership and, therefore, these interests can be acted upon. This type of interest group is politically active and affects the formation of public policy. Such a group represents a variant of Marx's "class for itself;" in Dahrendorf's terms, it is a "manifest interest group." It is this second type of group which may influence the character of the law, i.e., involve itself in the creation of criminal categories. In so doing, it may overcome both the formal and active interests of other groups in society with which its interests conflict.

The segments of society should be conceived as not only diverse in terms of interests, but also in terms of power. In the conflict which emerges in the clash of the articulate interests of different segments of society, some groups are more often able to get their interests represented in public policy. Of specific importance is the representation of the interests in the establishment of the criminal law.

To sum up Quinney's view, society is, first, segmented. This

---

[11] See Dahrendorf (1959:173-174).

segmentation includes "active interest groups" which conflict with each other, because they define their interests in opposing ways. Further, the "interest structure" of society is differentiated with respect to the "structure of power," i.e., some segments have more power than others. Those segments which have the greatest power may protect their interests, while enhancing their power, by having their interests represented in the criminal law. Thus, in the historical process, categories of crime are formulated and applied in an attempt to eliminate or prohibit behavior that is not in the interest of the dominant power segments.

Quinney, clearly, has expanded upon Becker's moral entrepreneurial explanation of the "emergence of rules." Quinney views interests as lodged in the different segmented groups rather than as a result of the personal interest and efforts of some individual "moral entrepreneur." However, the basic ingredients of the Labeling perspective remain the same: pluralism (segmentation), interest, and power differentials. In examining some illustrations of Quinney's theoretical perspective, it will be seen that the depth of the Labeling approach is increased by the breadth of his historical interest.

3. The Emergence of the Criminal Law

Guiding Quinney's approach is his assertion that: "The creation of a particular criminal law must have its conception in some concrete setting of time and place" (Quinney, 1970:70). The criminal law itself, as a conception and body of law, arose and developed, of course, in history. In order to understand its character, the conditions of its historical emergence must be considered. Quinney's thesis suggests that, for the criminal law to emerge, it must have been in the service of interests of some powerful group within a society characterized by segmentation. The question is, in whose interest was it that the criminal law developed in the first place? Quinney's answer is that, historically, it developed in the interest of The State itself. Western criminal law first developed and was formed out of the interests of the Athenian State and Athenian "rulership." It emerged in a time when that state and its ruling elite were threatened by the prospects of political upheaval.

> Greek society was in the throes of a political crisis. The enactments of Solon, which formed the basis for the development of criminal law in Greece, were part of an attempt toward solving the crisis and rehabilitating Greek government. . . (Quinney, 1970:45)

The further development of the criminal law in Rome had much the same interest base: the protection of The State. When the capacity of "private groups" to handle "offenses" against The State faltered, a "criminal law" was initiated by The State. "[T]he criminal law which did emerge late in the Roman Republic was a device created mainly for the protection of the state itself" (Quinney, 1970:47). Much the same can be said of the conditions under which English criminal law arose. With the advent of William's conquest of England and the completion of the process of political unification, a criminal law began to develop. It, too, had its foundation in the "interest-power base" of the newly organized state.

113

To be sure, criminal law in England came about for the protection of particular interests, primarily those of the king. The criminal law placed the affairs of the king's subjects under his jurisdiction. The powerful landlords and the church could no longer freely create and administer law in their own courts. (Quinney, 1970:49)

From Quinney's view, it is fitting that what is always a political process, that is, the creation of criminality through the creation of criminal categories, is rooted historically in the interests of the polity itself. All crime is political crime or, at least, has a prime political component.

4. Specific Criminal Categories

In this section, the focus will be upon two of the illustrative cases provided by Quinney concerning the emergence of criminal categories; the establishment of the "law of theft" and "public interest law." The choice of these illustrations involves two considerations. First, they further represent the sense in which Quinney, although sharing the approach of this matrix, extends it by his broader and more explicit historical orientation. Second, as a consequence of its historical depth, Quinney's work establishes the utility of the explanatory mode employed within the Labeling matrix with respect to some critical issues raised against the perspective. As mentioned earlier, critics have suggested that the Labeling approach bears only on "marginally deviant activity." This critical position implies that only "marginal cases" can be associated with societal segmentation, that society contains a set of "core values" that cut across its segments. It is violations of the core values which represent the clear-cut cases of deviant behavior. Critics of the Labeling approach argue that it adds little to the understanding of such violations. Further, critics have implied that with regard to these "core values," the law represents and is an outcome of the whole public's interests. Hence, a common criticism is that those types of violations (of "rules" in Becker, of "the law" in Quinney) amenable to analysis within the Labeling matrix cannot be easily conceived with respect to the "central areas" of deviant behavior. Some Labelists have capitulated to this suggestion. As a noted Labelist, Edwin Schur, remarks:

The value of labeling analysis in explaining a particular form of deviance may be related to the degree of consensus on its social definition. . . From this point of view borderline forms of deviance seem to be especially good candidates for labeling analysis and those deviations on which widespread consensus exists (homicide, incest, and so on) less promising candidates. (Schur, 1971: 21)

This view is already in question considering Thomas Scheff's application of Labeling analysis to "mental illness." This is so, since mental illness involves deviation from the most taken-for-granted behavioral standards in society, so that it can hardly be considered "borderline deviance." Moreover, Quinney shows that the creation and application of criminal categories by one segment of society with respect to the behavior of others extends even into what are considered the central regions of deviant behavior. The definition of an act as a crime, even with regard to *centrally* criminal behaviors, is still a matter created by one group and imposed upon another. All criminal law, and hence all crime, is an outcome of group dissension and conflict. If there is no segmentation and conflict in society, there is no law. It follows, then, that all criminal categories are an outcome of segmentation, tension, and conflict of interest in society. This extends to even the most clear-cut cases of violation, i.e., to those acts which are most violently reacted to by The State and which are considered most heinous by wide sectors of the population, e.g., "murder," "rape," "suicides," etc. Illustrating this contention requires a brief consideration of Quinney's discussion of the historical emergence of the "Law of Theft." Theft is chosen for illustrative purposes because, in general, it is not considered as merely "marginally deviant;" i.e., almost everyone is against it, except, perhaps, thieves.

5. The Law of Theft

Prior to fifteenth-century English law, "there was no legal conception of theft as we know it today" (Quinney, 1970:70). Before this time, all larceny (coming into possession of property illegally) had involved an element of *trespass* conceived in a relatively narrow way: the taking of property from one who was in legal (generally physical) possession of it. However, the "objectionable" practice which gave rise to the conception of theft which is operative today (and which forms the basis of several categories of crime) did not involve what was readily construed as trespass. The "Carrier's Case," which established the succeeding legal doctrine regarding theft, involved the interests of the new merchant class which sought to have its goods transported from place to place. At that time, the carriers who were hired by the merchants to transport goods occasionally "diverted" the material to their own use. In the particular incident from which the new doctrine was established, "The defendant was hired to carry bales to South Hampton. Instead of fulfilling his obligation, he carried the goods to another place, broke open the bales, and took the contents" (Quinney, 1970:70). The problem in prosecuting the case when it was brought before the English court was that, under the prevailing notion of trespass (an essential component of all larceny), the defendant was not guilty. He had not "taken" property from one who was in rightful possession of it, i.e., he was "given" the property and, thus, had come into possession of it "legally." Hence, he had not trespassed, as formerly conceived. Coming into possession legally, he had committed no technical wrong. Obviously, the maintenance of such a situation would be intolerable from the point of view of the interests of the emerging merchant class--a class which, of course, sought to increase trade and was, therefore, dependent upon the development of an efficient system of transporting goods from place to place. Eventually, the case was decided in favor of the plaintiff[12] through an extension of the notion of trespass.

---

[12]There would have been a problem for the court if the thief had sold the bales to someone else without breaking them open. However, such problems of interpretation would have inevitably been overcome.

The fact that the defendant had broken the goods out of the bales was finally construed as trespass, thereby allowing a verdict of guilty by theft. As Quinney suggests, there were powerful, active interest groups behind this interpretation. The King himself was beginning to engage in trade, as were many of the English nobility of the time. As Hall (1952), who developed the history of the incident, says, the interests of the most important industry in England were involved in the case. Clearly in play here are the active interests of the English mercantile nobility versus the interests of the unorganized group of carriers and, perhaps, a few others hostile to English trading.[13] The outcome was the establishment of a legal doctrine consistent with the new interests of the emerging powers. Quinney concludes:

> The Carrier's Case of 1473 vividly demonstrates the way in which changing social conditions and emerging social interests may bring about the formulation of a criminal law. The decision of the Carrier's Case provided the framework for the further development of the law of theft. Eventually . . . the law was expanded to include the act of embezzlement by clerks, officers, and the like. . . The legal protection of property has always been in the interests of the propertied segments of society. (Quinney, 1970:73)

6. Public Interest Law

A potential source of criticism of Quinney's perspective on the law is the existence of Public Interest Law. The existence of such law, it could be argued, indicates that Quinney's reliance on segmentation and conflict in characterizing all criminal law can be called into question. However, Quinney does not deny that the creation and enforcement of a particular criminal law may be in the "public interest," such that practically everyone's interest is served by its passage. In fact, he argues that the emergence of criminal law in Greece and common law in England served the interest of the non-elite as well as The State. Nevertheless, the *interest source* of the criminal law in these cases was the ruling elite. The fact that it also served the interest of the non-elite was incidental and certainly not sufficient to explain the creation of the law. However, public-interest law is not only in the service of elite interests, but often finds its interest base in the organization of certain segments of the public who act as an active interest group on behalf of the public. Hence, the intent of public-interest law is the service of widespread, if not universal, interests. However, the existence of such law does not preclude segmentation and conflict of interest. Each case of the creation of a public-interest law involves a political struggle among diverse interest groups. The struggle over the Pure Food and Drug Act is a case in point. There is little doubt that such laws are in the public's interest, rather than (or as well as) in the interest of narrower groups. For

---

[13]Had the carriers been organized, the outcome might have been different. Imagine a contest which included the Teamster's Union representing the direct interests of its members against manufacturers.

example, it could be argued that controlling the "patent-medicine men" was probably not only in the interests of the medical profession which led the fight (seeking control over treatment), but was in the public interest as well. Nevertheless, each attempt at creating public-interest law has been resisted by manufacturers, processers (e.g., meat-packing houses), etc. For example, the first attempt to pass Pure Food and Drug legislation was defeated by interest groups with overlapping concerns. Quinney quotes from Mintz (1965:41):

'It [the attempt to pass the act] and other efforts like it were defeated by a durable alliance of quacks, ruthless crooks, pious frauds, scoundrels, high-priced lawyer-lobbyists, vested interests, liars, corrupt members of Congress, venal publishers, cowards in high office, the stupid, the apathetic, and the duped.' (Quinney, 1970:78)

The conflict here can be described as being between "private" and "public" interests. It involves the same type of political conflict as is involved in the emergence of any other category of criminal action. Public-interest law involves a political struggle out of which may come the creation of a category of criminal action. The contemporary scene, which involves a struggle between environmentalists and industrial interests (e.g., coal companies which are interested in the weak regulation of strip mining), exhibits the same type of contest which characterizes the creation of all criminal law.

7. Excursus: Core Values and Labeling Theory

For a moment, the assumption will be made that societies can be characterized by the existence of a set of "core values," i.e., values to which all persons in the society exhibit a high degree of commitment. Such an assumption, of course, is not one which is built into the Labeling approach. As was mentioned, based on such an assumption, some have criticized the Labelists by suggesting that the Labeling perspective bears only on marginal forms of deviation (e.g., moral crimes, crimes without victims, marijuana smoking, etc.). Implicit in this critical suggestion is the idea that there exist "non-marginal" forms of deviation which reflect departures from values to which the population is more clearly commited than they are to those associated with the "marginal forms." This excursus will shed some light on the notion of "marginal" versus "central" deviations.

Unlike Becker and others within the Labeling matrix, Quinney does not focus only on those forms of deviation which are easily viewed as marginal in that they are "subcultural activities" to which a portion of the population is clearly committed as part of a way of life. In Quinney, it becomes clear that the perspective can be equally well applied to such legal categories as homicide and suicide, as well as to violations of laws governing respect for property.

The criminal law may be said to derive from three general sources: (a) values involving respect for property (crimes against property), (b) values involving respect for the individual (crimes against persons), and (c) values involving respect for The State (crimes against The State). The political nature of the last category is so obvious that violation is easily recognized as "political crime." Therefore, a focus on the other two categories of criminal law is all that is required. Little controversy will be associated with the suggestion that criminal law can be derived from values involving life and property. However, as previously indicated, values are vague, diffuse, and nonspecific; in short, they are not very satisfactory guides to conduct. Values may orient the actor, but still not specifically direct his action. For example (with regard to values concerning respect of the individual in society), under some circumstances, it is "permissible" to take another human life. The institutionalization of a value influencing respect for life does not necessarily specify the situations where this respect need *not* be considered, e.g., the situations in which individuals are not to be respected, and/or where other values take priority. Just as is the case in the creation of any other legal category, the specifications of what is *murder*, as distinct from the "justified" taking of human life, is a *political* question, e.g., as in a war. At virtually any point in time (at least in the United States), there is an ongoing political struggle between groups concerning the conditions under which the taking of human life is legitimate. For example, questions concerning the conditions under which persons whose property is threatened can legitimately kill a "thief" or an "intruder" in the attempt to protect that property are constantly being revised. Under what conditions can the police "properly" shoot to kill? For example, were the Kent State and Jackson State affairs of 1970, in which unarmed students were shot down, cases of "mass murder" or of "justifiable homicide"? And was the "Boston Massacre" really a "massacre" or was it "justified police action"? Was the systematic and intentional destruction of the Native American population a case of "genocide," as was the destruction of the Jewish population in Germany? Who would have been tried, and what would the categories of crime have been, if the Germans had won the Second World War and, with it, the power to define "war crimes"? Further, twenty-seven of the states in the United States historically defined it as legitimate for a husband to kill his wife and her lover under the "proper" circumstance, while, at the same time, none granted a similar prerogative to the wife. The question of whether or not abortion is "murder" involves, of course, a whole series of crucial definitions. These definitions are being constructed in a political power struggle which is currently being waged (1984) in the United States. The same may be said concerning whether or not the assassination of a foreign head of state by an intelligence officer (e.g., an employee of the CIA) is an act of war (and, thereby, "legitimate") or an act of murder.

These same kinds of considerations must be brought to bear in relation to "violations" associated with the centrally held value of "respect for property." It is necessary to specify the conditions under which respect for the value is applicable: Whose property is to be respected? Under what circumstance can property be violated? What is "property"? Answers to these kinds of questions are worked out in the political processes and involve interests and power. For example, it is obvious that in the United States the value of "respect for property" has not been extended to the "public domain" with the same force as it has to "private property." In fact, the notion of property is so joined to the idea of "private" that it seems somewhat awkward to speak of "public property" in the context of criminal law. With respect to property, it can be argued that, as a direct result of this lack of respect for "non-private property," many of the earth's resources have practically been destroyed. That is, out of respect for "property," the privately propertied industrialists have been allowed to exploit and pollute the lands and waters of the nation (e.g., the Great Lakes). If change is to take place in this area, it will involve a re-specification and a re-interpretation of the meaning of the core value "respect for property." A political struggle over this issue also is now occurring. It remains to be seen just whose "property rights" will be respected as well as what is meant by "property," e.g., one question which might be asked is, "If nobody owns the earth, is it property?"

With regard to the issue of "marginal offenses," it may well be that categories of crime appear marginal only at the time at which these political struggles are going on, i.e., before the question has been settled by "power." For example, the power question has been resolved concerning the extermination of the Native American population and the German Jewish population. The Native American case was classified as simply an "incident," a necessary concomitant of "manifest destiny" (something like the need for *Lebensraum*). The German case has been deemed genocide— "a *crime* against humanity." The German Jewish case is a "fantastic crime" and the Native American "incident" is largely ignored. Whereas, in the not too distant past, marijuana smoking was viewed as a grave act, today it is viewed as a marginally deviant activity in that the power question has re-emerged. Marijuana smokers are now (1980's) relatively organized and powerful (and are mostly from the middle class). As such, they are in a position to raise some questions about the seriousness of the activity and, hence, the "legitimacy" of its classification as a serious form of deviance.

After the political questions are settled and the legal definitions are set by the victors, the process of "criminalizing" an activity does not simply stop. The definition of the situation must be diffused beyond the legislative, in order to be effective. That is, in Quinney's terms, the "*conception*" of the crime must be established and diffused in society. Images are painted and fixed in the public's "opinion." What is an abortionist? What is a "pusher" like? What was the character of the student militants or, on the other hand, the character of the men of the Ohio National Guard? Was Custer more or less the same as Himmler; is he to be worshiped or despised? Power resolves these issues. Once they are set, the crime and the criminal no longer appear at the margin. There is no longer a question. *The categories of crime appear marginal only during that period in which the struggle is being waged.* What horrifies us, what strikes us as a violation of a "core value," is established through the exercise of power. The ability to get one's view widely established (i.e., to get it institutionalized throughout the society, across all of its segments, "right down to the criminal himself") is what power is all about.

8. Capitalism and Crime

In *The Social Reality of Crime* (1970), from which Quinney's perspective on crime has been drawn, Quinney, like Becker, focused upon a number of "interest bases" as the source of the development of criminal definitions. In fact, from the perspective of that book, virtually any type of interest group is viewed as a potential producer of criminal categories--economic, political, moral, religious, etc. However, in Quinney's more recent work, *Critique of Legal Order* (1973), he derives the criminal law in modern American society not from a myriad of "active interest groups," but from the economic class structure of Capitalist society. In this work, Quinney deserts Dahrendorf's "conservative" reformulation of Marxian categories in favor of conceptions more in line with modern Marxian orthodoxy. It is in the interest of the Capitalist ruling class that all criminal conceptions are created and applied. It is only in concert with the interest of this class that criminal conceptions can be created at all. Rather than The State's having a central role in the emergence of criminal law, Quinney's *Critique* suggests, in an orthodox Marxian mode that "the state is created by the class that has the power to enforce its will on the rest of society. . . Contrary to conventional belief, law is a tool of the ruling class" (Quinney, 1973:52). How is the ruling class conceived? Again, the answer is in the orthodox mode:

> The ruling class is "that class which owns and controls the means of production and is able, by virtue of the economic power thus conferred upon it, to use the state as its instrument for the domination of society." (Quinney, 1973:53)[14]

But how can laws which are apparently irrelevant to the maintenance of the ruling class be, nevertheless, related to its interests? Why, for example, would the ruling class need to concern itself with "sexual psychopath laws," marijuana use, crimes without victims, etc.? It is because the ruling class has an interest in order, especially in the existing order. "Even when laws regulating morality are made and enforced, the intention is to preserve the moral and ideological basis of capitalism" (Quinney, 1973:55). Hence, a criminal law is passed and applied only if the ruling class, composed of the economic elite and others who benefit from the Capitalist rule (such as social scientists, criminologists, and other professionals), benefit.

G. Conclusion

Something of the quality of the "exemplary form of explanation" within the matrix of Labeling Theory is conveyed in this chapter, and, hopefully, the sense in which all the components of explanation are related to the character of "societal reaction" has been established. Societal reaction may be seen as: (1) establishing rule-breaking behavior by creating (out of the interests of persons and groups) the categories of

---

[14]The quotation is from Ralph Miliband (1969:23).

deviance, (2) changing the conditions of action by reacting to persons as deviant in such a way as to lead them into further rule-breaking behavior, and (3) positively socializing actors into existing deviant institutions (e.g., through socialization into the institutionalized role of the mentally ill, as well as into other deviant roles). The processes associated with the taking on of deviant identity are "bound up" with all of these aspects of societal reaction. They can be understood not only by focusing upon the interaction context, but upon the processes of individual consciousness as well.

CHAPTER VIII

GENERAL UNDERPINNINGS OF THE APPROACHES

A. Introduction

The modified conception of Kuhn's "Disciplinary Matrix" which undergirds this work contains four major cells. Two of these have now been treated with respect to both the "Etiological-Functionalist" and the "Labelist" approaches to deviance: (1) the conception of deviance and (2) the exemplary mode of explanation. In this chapter, the other two cells which are contained within this matrix will be considered: (3) domain assumptions and methods and (4) values.

These components of the Disciplinary Matrix are not to be considered of less salience than those previously discussed--quite the contrary. With respect to the most influential components within the constellation of meaning which these matrices represent, it may well be that the components to be set forth and discussed in this chapter are of greater significance than those previously presented. They may be the "melody" with which the conceptualization and explanation of deviance have been constructed to harmonize within both Etiological-Functionalism and Labeling Theory. However, the task of this work is not to establish the direction of influence or the relative import of the components of such matrices; rather, it is to distinguish different theoretical matrices in terms of the components previously set forth.

The decision to treat the remaining components in a single chapter was based upon considerations other than centrality of the components. First, this chapter can be treated with greater brevity than earlier ones. Owing to the discussion in the preceding sections, it is no longer necessary to laboriously document that these scholars share, in some fundamental sense, a perspective. As a result, each scholar's work need not be examined independently, but, instead, the approach may simply be characterized. Furthermore, this work will no longer be limited to those scholars and works within the matrices which apply strictly to deviance. In order to characterize each matrix with respect to certain issues, attention must be turned to more general theoretical statements made by other scholars who are concerned with the broad spectrum of human affairs.

The first task of this chapter will be to examine the component of the Disciplinary Matrix which is referred to as "Domain Assumptions and Method." Within this component, there are two general subjects of interest which will be considered here as they relate to the development of the respective concepts of deviance: (1) the conception of human beings and (2) the conception of the scientific method.

The last section of this chapter will be concerned with the final element of the Disciplinary Matrix, the "value orientations" associated with each approach. Two aspects of such orientations will be of particular interest: (1) those values which can be described as "intra-scientific" and (2) "extra-scientific" values. The latter, of course, refer to sociopolitical values and include both explicit values (those articulated by the practitioners) and implicit values (those which are implications of the approach, regardless of the views of the practitioners within the matrix).

B. Domain Assumptions

1. The View of Man

a. The Importance of the Social

The general systems of sociology which underpin the two approaches to deviance considered here are "Structural Functionalism" and "Symbolic Interactionism." Each of these systems contains, in the early stages of its development, a reaction to individualistic and biological conceptions of humanity. Each approach emphasizes the "frailty" of human biological endowment (organic nature) in relation to its potential to generate "human characteristics." As Lindesmith and Strauss (1968) point out:

> . . . through the 1930's both European and American sociologists were concerned with combating biological explanations of group and institutional behavior, believing that these explanations were either inappropriate or too simple. They had the same critical attitude toward psychological or individualistic explanations of social plenomena. (Lindesmith and Strauss, 1968:6)

While Mead (1934) was formulating his sociological conceptions of mind and self, Parsons, influenced by European sociological theory, sought to replace the positivistic "organism-environment" frame of reference with the "actor-situation" frame. Despite important differences in emphasis, both Mead and Parsons denigrated Reductionist conceptions of human beings and stressed the importance of humanity's social character.

b. Inadequacy of Human Biological Endowment

Kingsley Davis, a noted Functionalist, was concerned with the importance of the social environment and the socialization process. He suggested that the emergence of human characteristics cannot take place outside of the social context. Of Anna, an isolated child, he wrote:

> When finally found and removed from the room at the age of nearly six years, Anna could not talk, walk, or do anything that showed intelligence. . . She was completely apathetic, lying in a

124

limp, supine position and remaining immobile, expressionless, and indifferent to everything. . . Here, then, was a human organism which had missed nearly six years of socialization. Her conditions shows how little her purely biological resources, when acting alone, could contribute to making her a complete person. (Davis, 1968:204)

Mead, of course, would expect a similar outcome to be associated with isolation from the social. "Our contention is that mind can never find expression, and could never have come into existence at all, except in terms of a social environment . . ." (Mead, 1934:223). Both perspectives (Functionalism and Symbolic Interactionism) argue that humanity is biologically "incomplete" and becomes complete in social interaction. As Berger and Luckmann (1966:49) remark, "While it is possible to say that man has a nature, it is more significant to say that man constructs his own nature, or more simply, that man produces himself."

c. The Functionalist Emphasis

To this point, both Symbolic Interactionism and Structural Functionalism agree as to human character; both suggest that human beings are completed in a social process. However, as to what the person receives from the social, there is at least some significant difference in emphasis. The Functionalists emphasize human "plasticity," "which is simply a name for his capacity to learn alternative patterns [and his 'sensitivity,'] . . . which may be interpreted to be a name for his capacity to form attachments . . ." (Parsons, 1951:215). Given these traits of the organism, the person may engage in the creation of social existence, as well as being the recipient of its products, the latter being the primary emphasis of the Functionalists. Involved here, of course, is the process of socialization, in which man adopts the culture of the social group. Society--social life--provides, for human beings, guides to conduct (norms and other symbolic elements) which, through the process of internalization, generate his humanity. Most fundamental of the aspects of culture is, of course, language. As Davis (1968:52) put it, ". . . the unique trait in human society--the thing which transforms the private grouping into a new emergent reality--is the system of symbolic communications." Berger describes the role of institutions in a way not inconsistent with the Functionalist emphasis:

Gehlen conceives of an institution as a regulatory agency, channeling human actions in much the same way as instincts channel animal behavior. In other words, institutions provide procedures through which human conduct is patterned, compelled to go, in grooves deemed desirable by society. (Berger, 1963:87)

The primary endowment of the social which results in the formation of human character[1] is, from the Functionalist point of view, the internalization of these institutionalized patterns. These patterns act not

---

[1]Many Functionalists explicitly follow Mead with respect to important issues in this area. See Davis, 1968: Chapter VIII.

only to give rise to the human mind and personality, they also (and most importantly for the theory of deviance) provide the grooves into which human behavior is channeled.

d. The Symbolic Interactionist Emphasis

The endowment of the social which the Symbolic Interactionists *emphasize* is the emergence of "mind" and "self." Now it may well be that such emergence occurs only in relation to social institutions (language is, of course, often so conceived). However, from the Symbolic Interactionists' framework, it is not the institutions themselves which give rise to the direction of human conduct, as in the Functionalist matrix. Rather, from the Symbolic Interactionists' standpoint, it is the person, possessed of mind and self, who directs conduct. Particularly because of the reflective character of the human self, persons have the capacity to "forge" or "create" their own lines of conduct. The potential of the self to *transcend the influence* of the environment, including the social environment, is associated with two capacities of the self. The first capacity enables humans to endow objects with meaning. The meaning of an object does not reside in the object itself, nor is the meaning given a priori in some preformed category of human psychic structure. Rather, the meaning of an object is given in the way in which the person, at a particular moment in time, addresses the object. For example, a "white, soft rock" may be, at one moment, a chunk of chalk, at the next, a missile, at the next, a food supplement.

> Instead of the individual's being surrounded by an environment of pre-existing objects which play upon him and call forth his behavior, the proper picture is that he constructs his objects on the basis of his on-going activity. (Blumer, 1969:80)

The second aspect of self which allows persons to form their environment is their capacity to make "selective indications" (i.e., they choose what they will attend and what they will ignore) with respect to their milieu. That is, persons shape their environment through "attentional modifications."

> Our whole intelligent process seems to lie in the attention which is selective of certain types of stimuli. Other stimuli which are bombarding the system are in some fashion shunted off. . . Our attention enables us to organize the field in which we are going to act. Here we have the organism as acting and determining its environment. (Mead, 1934:25)

It can be seen, then, that the human act, that which establishes the direction of human conduct, always includes a creative element in its construction. Hence, rather than viewing human action as norm-following action, as it is comprehended by the Functionalists (explicable in terms of the internalization of norms and values), the Symbolic Interactionists see action as an outcome of individually forged epochs of meaning (Acts). Blumer states:

> Instead of being merely an organism that responds to the play of factors on or through it, the human being is seen as an organism

126

that has to deal with what it notes. It meets what it so notes by engaging in a process of self-indication in which it makes an object of what it notes, gives it a meaning, and uses the meaning as the basis for directing its action. (Blumer, 1969:14)

It should be borne in mind that this capacity to make selective indications emerges in a social process, i.e., both mind and self are social emergents. A precondition of this emergence is social behavior, the creation of the "significant symbol," and its use in the internal conversation of a reflective self capable of making such indications. (For a minimal discussion of the process of the emergence of self, see Chapter V. For more extended discussions, see Mead, 1934: Part One; and Blumer, 1967: Chapter 2.)

2. Conceptions of Humanity and Conceptions of Deviance

a. Etiological-Functionalism

Recalling Davis' description of Anna, and focusing upon human plasticity, it is clear that prior to the social (conceived as institutionalized norms and values), there is no basis upon which to expect any particular conduct, let alone specifically channeled conduct, from human beings. Human beings, prior to the introduction of the social, are not inherently inclined to live in accord with any pattern of social life, nor are they inclined to depart from any such pattern. Through the process of socialization, they must be brought into a relation with an institutional pattern before there is any basis for action at all. As a result, there is no basis for the appropriation of the concept of "deviance" or "conformity" to a person's behavior before this relation is established. Hence, the theoretical problem of deviation can emerge only after the successful socialization of the actor into a complex of institutionalized norms and values has been accomplished. Having been accomplished, this socialization establishes the expectation of conformity. It is this view of the plasticity of the organism and the significance of socialization into a pattern of norms and values that leads Johnson to remark:

Conformity to institutionalized norms is, of course, "normal." The actor, having internalized the norms, feels something like a need to conform. His conscience would bother him if he did not. (Johnson, 1960:22)

It is important to note here that ideas concerning "normality" ("normal" is an unfortunate term in this context, even when quotation marks are used) and conformity are appropriate only when the behavior of a *socialized* actor is in question or is being described or analyzed. As Johnson further remarks, in a statement which should be carefully considered:

"Conformity" and "Deviation," in the present context, have meaning only in relation to the fact that the actors in social systems are oriented to social norms that are internalized as part of their personality. (Johnson, 1960:552)

Notice, human beings are not viewed as inclined to engage in "disruptive patterns;" they have no "impervious biological drives" (see Merton, 1967);

127

they are not viewed as in need of control; they cannot be discussed as being "out of line," until the line (the norm) is established with respect to the formation of their commitment *via* socialization into a complex of norms and values. This is, of course, consistent with a view of humanity as being socially formed in all respects essential to social life. It is in terms of this conceptualization of humanity that the explanation of "deviance" in terms of faulty socialization, inadequate super-ego strength, and the absence of social bonds is *theoretically precluded* from the Functionalist perspective.

A brief word is in order regarding the relationship of the Functionalists' explanation of deviance to their conception of humanity. Not only is deviance conceived in terms of the relation of behavior to institutionalized norms and values, but it is also the case that departures from such patterns are explicable by reference to the institutional milieu in which a person is placed. In this case, human "sensitivity" is fundamentally associated with the explanation, in that persons are capable of becoming strongly attached to (of cathecting toward) the institutionalized norms and values. In short, these values and norms provide the goals toward which Man strives; they are the source of the "human effort" which is expended in order to overcome *conditions* in the world. It is here that Parsons (1937) finds voluntaristic action and the human capacity to shape the environment. It is in light of this commitment to values that persons are subject to strains or "pressures" imposed by the social structure. A situation which finds human beings incapable of attaining their goals is viewed as inherently frustrating. One of the best examples of this position is provided by Merton's schema in which cathexis is seen as not only part of the orientation toward the culturally favored goals, but as part of the orientation toward the regulatory means as well. That is, the means-ends distinction is analytical--the desire to use "legitimate means" is a human goal, just as is the desire to acquire material. As a result, persons in a situation such as Merton describes ("objectively," one which will not permit the maintenance of commitment to both "means" and "goals") must deviate from one or the other (see Chapter IV). That is, the situation is one in which the individual is forced to withdraw his commitment from one (or both) of the valued orientations to action.

b. Labeling

The term "deviance" rose to prominence in sociological thought primarily through the influence of Functionalist literature. Bound up as this idea was with the Functionalists' conceptions of norms, values, culture, society, etc., the meaning of the designation, "deviance," is inconsistent with the conception of man and human conduct adhered to within the Interactionist perspective. Nevertheless, as the study of deviant behavior grew in prominence as a legitimate area within sociology, it drew increasingly greater attention from many sociologists who were influenced by Symbolic Interactionist sociology. However, involvement of the Interactionists in this area of study led to a fundamental reformulation of the concept. From the Interactionists' perspective, neither Man nor Man's conduct is conceived in terms of his relationship to norms and values. Therefore, action is not viewed as either conforming or deviating from institutionalized patterns. Of "Mead's scheme," Blumer suggests that "it [the scheme] sees social actions as having variable careers and not as confined to the alternatives of conformity to or deviation from the dictates of established structure" (Blumer, 1969:75). Rather, the starting point for the Labelists is Man's possessing a "self" which permits the meaningful construction of courses of action. Importantly, the Interactionists' conception of the character of "self-constructed" human acts is devoid of any means for distinguishing deviant from non-deviant *acts*; this does not mean that the perspective cannot distinguish between *situations* in which deviance may or may not emerge. As exemplified by Becker and Matza, an *act* which is labeled as "deviant" is constituted like any other. It consists in forging, and acting in the terms of, an epoch of meaning. Hence, no distinction between deviant and non-deviant acts can be made by the sociologist. The study of deviance, then, is not the study of a category of acts at all, rather it is the study of the assignment of meaning to acts.[2]

A second influence on the Labeling approach to deviance that can be derived directly from the Interactionist conception of Man is the deemphasis (or indifference to) etiological questions. As conceived by the Interactionists, the capacity of the human self to shape its environment undermines (or at least allows for the supplementation of) the concept of "antecedent cause" in the explanation of "courses of action." Rather than action being viewed as an outcome of causal agents, it is viewed as associated with an organization of meaning which overcomes environmental influences. The act may be seen as "constructed," rather than as caused. As Matza puts it:

> Man participates in *meaningful* activity. He creates his reality, and that of the world around him, actively and strenuously. Man *naturally*--not supernaturally--transcends the existential realms in which the conceptions of cause, force, and reactivity are easily applicable. (Matza, 1969:8)

Although there are some differences among the various Labeling Theorists concerning the issue of causality and etiology with respect to the study of deviance (e.g., Lemert is most inclined to employ the concept of cause), each focuses upon a level of action that is meaningfully organized (rather than, or in addition to, being causally ordered). This issue will be discussed further in the next section with respect to the "view of science."

The third influence upon Labeling Theory's conceptualization of deviance which is directly traceable to the Symbolic Interactionists' conception of man is the focus upon "deviant identity" formation. If the definitive character of a person is the possession of a "self" (rather than the establishment of the person's relationship to institutions), then a new set of problems not addressed by the Functionalists arises. The primary concern within the Labeling perspective is with the impact which the assignment of deviant meaning to an act presumably has on "self." The

---

[2]Of course, such assignment of meaning involves acts. However, the meaning assigned to an act is independent of the "objective nature" of an act or a body of acts.

self, like the act, is bound up with an "organization of meaning," i.e., self-concept or identity is meaningfully formed. Further, since the self emerges in social interaction, reflection concerning self is necessarily influenced by the interaction process. The social process contains the very substance out of which self is composed (e.g., through taking the role of the other). Therefore, it may be of utmost significance to self if another suggests that one is "simply" (in essence) a thief. Commenting upon the maintenance of identity as a thief, Matza notes:

> Though the relation between Leviathan and the subject is objective, its method is to capitalize temporarily on the subjective capacity to see oneself in the eyes of another. But that puts it too weakly. More potent than that, the spell capitalizes on the subject's essential *incapacity*: He is *unable not to* see or glimpse himself as he appears in the eyes of another. As Mead taught, that is the way the subject is put together and thus part of the human nature. It is quite a capacity, but sometimes it is more usefully conceived as an incapacity or flaw. (Matza, 1969:174)

Of prime importance to the Labelists, then, is the possible consequence for self, i.e., the alteration of self that may occur with the assignment of deviant meaning to an action.

The conceptualization and explanation of deviance within this perspective hinge upon the suggestion that, by their very nature, human beings assign meaning to everything that they attend--inanimate objects, other individuals and their acts, their own behavior, etc. In the case of the creation of deviance, a struggle between actors occurs over the meaning to be assigned to certain acts as well as to certain people. From this approach, the source of this struggle is "interest;" the means by which it is resolved is "power." However, these elements are not so clearly derived from the assumptions about Man which are emphasized within the Interactionist approach but, rather, from Conflict Theory's assumptions about society.[3]   On the other hand, the object of the struggle--the successful assignment of meaning to an act, the issue of who will prevail in defining the situation--emerges directly from a view of Man as acting, and assessing action, in terms of the meanings he creates both individually and in interaction with others. The whole struggle, then, is associated with persons' attempts to make sense out of (or meaningfully organize) what they observe and to act in terms of this constructed meaning.

In concluding this section, it should be noted that all of the above emphases derived from the Symbolic Interactionists' concept of the

---

[3]These elements are much more clearly derived from a view of modern society as characterized by cleavages and power differentials, rather than as being formed by some fundamental characteristics of Man. This aspect of the view of society within the Labeling camp is clearly implied in the discussion of the exemplars, particularly through those of Quinney, Matza, and Becker. Hence, it is not necessary to further discuss it in this chapter. Nevertheless, it should be regarded as a relevant underpinning to the approach to deviance.

human being point toward two focal points: (1) the actor-as-subject constructing acts, assigning meaning, and organizing self-concept; and (2) the interactive process, which supplies the constituents from which self is formed, action is constructed, and meaning built.

C. Method

1. Introduction

This section will focus upon some of the philosophical positions associated with each of the matrices under consideration. The discussion of these positions will be drawn from the works of those scholars who have demonstrated the greatest concern with the philosophical and methodological implications of their respective paradigms. With respect to the Functionalists, the primary focus will be on Parsons and Merton; with regard to Labeling Theory, the focus will be on Blumer, Matza, and Quinney.

Within each matrix, there are a number of philosophical elements which logically combine and reciprocally influence one another, i.e., which form a consistent pattern. First, Functionalism is characterized by a heavy emphasis upon developing systematic *scientific theory*, as conceived in a particular way. This conception of theory and its role in the accumulation of scientific knowledge has had an influence of fundamental importance on the theories of deviance which have been examined here. Further, the "Functional Theory" with which this work has been concerned employs, at least implicitly, causal explanation. Third, Functional Theory is more or less deterministic; that is, its theories are perceived as logically determinant, moving toward closure. Labeling Theory, quite to the contrary, does not exhibit the same concern with the development of abstract theory. Rather, it is characterized, particularly in its latter development, by a more "severe" empiricism. In some cases (e.g., in Matza), this empiricism involves a very direct rejection of "abstraction." Second, the Labelist form of explanation is not usually based upon the principle of causality. Such explanation is sometimes deemed wholly inappropriate or, at least, in need of supplementation by an emphasis upon the meaningful organization of conduct. Furthermore, there is no insistence that explanation be deterministic, i.e., the system of thought remains *open* and indeterminant.

2. Functionalism: The Role of Theory

In spite of some significant disputes between leading Functionalists (e.g., Parsons and Merton)[4] concerning the level of abstraction at which theory should be developed, there is basic agreement as to the nature and role of scientific theory. Most Functionalists assign the highest priority to the development of theory both as an orienting system of

---

[4]This dispute over the value of "Grand Theory" versus "Theories of the Middle Range" is based on Merton's "The Bearing of Sociological Theory on Empirical Research" (1949).

concepts (a frame of reference) and, ultimately, as a system of scientific explanation. This view is perhaps best developed and justified by Parsons in his discussion of the nature of theory in *The Structure of Social Action* (1937). This conception of theory is consistent with Parsons' epistemological position which he refers to as "analytical realism," a position developed primarily as a response to the "objectionable" aspects of empiricism. Parsons characterizes empiricism rather narrowly as follows:

> The common characteristic of them [empiricist systems of thought] is the *identification* of the meanings of the concrete specific propositions of a given science, theoretical or empirical, with the scientifically knowable totality of the external reality to which they refer. They maintain, that is, that there is an immediate correspondence between *concrete* experienceable reality and scientific propositions, and only insofar as this exists can there be valid knowledge. In other words they deny the legitimacy of theoretical abstraction. (Parsons, 1937:23)

This empiricism has developed into three strains, all of which Parsons criticizes. He terms the first variant "positivistic empiricism," an empiricism which recognizes general concepts, yet reifies systems of theory. In its extreme form, it suggests that theoretical concepts exhaust the scientifically knowable aspects of the phenomenon to which they refer. The less extreme form of this empiricism suggests that prediction of variation of phenomenon is accomplished within the particular system of theory brought to bear upon it. That is, it demands that a particular system of theory (e.g., the theory of action) account for any and all observations of the phenomena to which it directs attention in order for it to be considered adequate. A second variant of empiricism, "particularistic empiricism," submits that *only concrete details* of phenomena can form the basis of objective knowledge. From this point of view, the only sense in which the relations between events can be established is in terms of a *temporal sequence*, but one which does not imply causation in the scientific sense. Causation, if employed within this system of thought at all, would be "historical causation," i.e., concern with the establishment of the relationships between particular, concrete events. Parsons holds that science, on the other hand, seeks the establishment of causal relations between universals--hence, it is abstract. The third form of empiricism Parsons calls "intuitionist empiricism." It allows a conceptual element but, as Parsons puts it, of an individualizing character. A primary example of this form is German "Idealistic Empiricism." In this case, focus is upon what might be called a "culture complex" or "*geist.*" The *geist* is viewed as a unique constellation in which the "sense" or "meaning" of the action of individuals is established. However, general knowledge of human behavior does not go beyond the description of the unique, individual *Zeitgeist.*

Parsons' "analytical realism" may also be seen as developing out of a reaction to a fourth view, one which cannot easily be described as empiricism, although it is concerned with the status of scientific concepts in relation to "reality." This last perspective is the one associated with Weber's methodology. Although Weber made much use of theoretical concepts, he held that such concepts, although essential in the study of history, are only "useful fictions." The utility and necessity of theory, according to Weber, is that it forms or arranges the data. The frame of reference allows the construction of the "historical individual" or of the "ideal type."

Parsons' own philosophy of science, developed in opposition to the forms of empiricism and Weber's "fictional view" of the status of scientific concepts, begins with a realist ontology. He assumes the existence of an external, empirical reality--one which is not the creation of the human mind and is not reducible to ideal elements. Further, this reality is a factual order which is, at least in a limited way, congruent with the order of human logic. However, Parsons' realism is modified by the inclusion of an "analytical element." First, it cannot be assumed that the reality external to persons can be exhausted by articulation with the *ideal systems* of the human mind in its "scientific phase" or, for that matter, any other mode of cognition. Further, it must be recognized (as it was by Weber) that all "entities" are constructed, i.e., no aspect of "reality" is ever fully grasped. Observation always exists within the terms of a limiting frame of reference. Entities are then, in a Weberian sense, "historical individuals." However, the frame of reference and the concepts of which it is composed are not, according to Parsons (as Weber suggests), simply "useful fictions." Rather, Parsons insists that some scientific concepts do grasp *aspects* of reality. In opposition to empiricism, however, Analytical Realism holds that concepts do not correspond fully (i.e., apprehend in any full sense) concrete phenomena. Rather, they correspond to elements which are analytically separable from the concrete and which have been abstracted by the "ideal" frame of reference. Systems of theory, then, are composed of abstractions (analytical concepts) which abstract from concrete reality.

From this view, the role and nature of theory (the frame of reference) is, in important respects, a product of the scientist. That is, "theoretical effort" is required of the scientist in his formulation of a logically coherent system of concepts. At the same time, this system is, of course, influenced by its reference to the "facts" to which it directs attention. However, the logical coherence which systematic theory possesses is not derived directly from observation of the empirical world. Hence, the root concepts with which the Etiological Functionalists have been concerned--deviance, conformity, norms, etc.--are "constructed entities," nevertheless viewed as corresponding to aspects of the external empirical world. The concept, "deviance," is not formed in an attempt to mimic the use of similar concepts employed in everyday life (e.g., "criminal," "delinquent," "queer," "con," "dope fiend," "pervert," etc.). Rather, it is formulated in relation to the other elements of the conceptual scheme of which it is a part. At the same time, the entire scheme is intended to be brought to bear upon the interpretation and explanation of "deviant" phenomena such as those listed above. Some may meet the requirements of the theoretical conceptualization of deviance and, hence, be treated as such within the scheme, while others may not. The important point is that "deviance" is not specified in the world but, instead, is specified within the scheme.

3. Labeling: The Diminution of Theory

Symbolic Interactionism and Labeling Theory have been much less concerned with the development of systematic theory than has Functionalism. There is the suggestion from practitioners within these camps that, at best, abstract theorizing is a sterile preoccupation. Rather than conjuring up such systems of theory and viewing the world through "fixed" frames of reference, it is suggested that the scientist is capable of, and should be engaged in, "direct observation." Blumer emphasizes this methodological position when he states:

> Symbolic Interactionism is a down-to-earth approach to the scientific study of human group life and human conduct. Its empirical world is the natural world of such group life and conduct. . . Its methodological stance, accordingly, is that of *direct examination* [emphasis added] of the empirical social world. . . (Blumer, 1969:47)

Matza similarly expresses this concern for "getting down to earth" and sees his work as an outcome of such a methodological focus. Describing his "naturalistic," rather than scientific, position, he states:

> Thus, the attitude of naturalism grew in America, matter-of-fact, concrete, and committed to the world despite its long flirtation with science. Its aim is a faithful rendition of worldly activities. (Matza, 1969:9)

Further:

> The fidelity of naturalism to the empirical world has created a certain stress on the mundane, the matter-of-fact--even the vulgar. Naturalism has therefore been an antiphilosophical philosophy in one key sense. The common view of being philosophical, of holding to a philosophy, emphasizes the precedence of abstraction, theory, or metaphysics over the world. That stereotype of philosophy has never been wholly incorrect; even naturalism, which began with a commitment to the world, turned away from the concrete and attached itself to the abstraction--science. (Matza, 1969:8)

The roots of this "distrust" of theory can be discerned from Blumer's philosophical and methodological positions. Like Parsons, Blumer is a philosophical realist; i.e., he views the empirical world as possessing an "obdurate character." Criticizing a "pure idealism," Blumer writes:

> The position [idealism] is untenable because of the fact that the empirical world can "talk back" to our pictures of it or assertions about it--talk back in the sense of challenging and resisting, or not bending to, our images or conceptions of it. (Blumer, 1969:22)

Blumer's realism is qualified by two important amendments. First, the empirical world (particularly the world of human experience) is not regarded as being forever and always fixed, as if given in some immutable form. Hence, there is no possibility for the development of general, universal concepts which will remain permanently valid. It is necessary, then, to be concerned with the development of particularized knowledge (i.e., *descriptions* of the world of the "here and now"), recognizing that such a world is constantly undergoing fundamental change.

> . . . the history of empirical science shows that the reality of the empirical world appears in the "here and now" and is continuously recast with the achievement of new discoveries. (Blumer, 1969:23)

Secondly, insofar as traditional realism implies that the character of the empirical world is such that it can only be known through the methods of the natural sciences, it must be amended. Blumer submits:

> The obdurate character of the empirical world is what it is found to be through careful and honest study. To force all of the empirical world to fit a scheme that has been devised for a given segment of that world is philosophical doctrinizing and does not represent the approach of a genuine empirical science. (Blumer, 1969:23)

Two elements, then, are influential within the methodology of Symbolic Interactionism and Labeling: (1) a concern with the particular and the concrete and (2) an approach to the world via methods other than those of the natural sciences. Concerning the latter point, one aspect is of particular importance. Unlike the natural sciences, the frame of reference of the human sciences must include a recognition of the human actor's subjectivity. That is, in order to comprehend human action, the scientist is required to focus upon the actor's intentions--the meaning he assigns to his action. It is with respect to this necessity that a number of Labeling Theorists have quoted Schutz's description of the relation of social science concepts to the "data" of the social world:

> The thought objects constructed by the social scientist refer to and are founded upon the thought objects constructed by the common-sense thought of man living his everyday life among his fellow man. Thus the constructs used by the social scientist are, so to speak, constructs of the second degree, namely constructs of the constructs, made by the actors on the social scene, whose behavior the scientist observes and tries to explain in accordance with the procedural rules of his science. (Schutz, 1953:6)

These "thought objects" (the concepts of the actors on the social scene) are continually in flux and subject to fundamental alteration from time to time and from group to group. This characteristic of the human world gives rise to the requirement for scrupulous description rather than to the development of abstract theory.

While the emphasis of Symbolic Interactionism is upon the particular and the concrete, as the quotation from Schutz indicates, this does not preclude a conceptual element in the scientific enterprise. Blumer makes it clear that the research act begins with a "picture of the world" importantly formed, of course, by concepts. It would indeed be strange if Symbolic Interactionism, which has emphasized the symbolic (the conceptual) in human affairs, excluded systematic consideration of this element in the scientific act. For the Symbolic Interactionist, the nature of the emergence of the symbolic and its involvement in science is viewed quite differently than it is from the Functionalist perspective. In fact, this element points up what is perhaps the sharpest distinction between Labeling and Etiological-Functionalism with regard to method.

From Blumer's point of view, a concept carries a content which is a direct outcome of experience with the reality to which it refers:

> . . . on the basis of given tangible perceptual experiences which were puzzling, certain individuals fashioned constructs which would give these experiences an understandable character. As far as I can see, scientific concepts come into existence in this way. . . They originate as conceptions occasioned by a series of perceptual experiences of a puzzling character which need to be bridged by a wider perspective. (Blumer, 1969:156)

The concept, then, is an outcome of a person's reflection upon perceived experience; it is an attempt to make sense out of the experience. As such, it may be "sharpened," refined, and influenced by a continuation, or re-experiencing, of the phenomenon. This view of the concept is well summed up by Bierstadt's characterization of Blumer's position:

> . . . Blumer . . . maintained . . . that clear and accurate definitions of our concepts can neither be "given" nor "constructed" at the beginning of inquiry, that in scientific procedure it is not always desirable to have exact definitions (because they may put a cloture on research), and that, in any event, a definition emerges properly only as one of the results and consequences of inquiry. Mr. Blumer contended, in short, that definitions increase in accuracy as a result of successive approximations and empirical confirmations, that they become increasingly definite as research and inquiry proceed . . . (Bierstadt, 1959:121)

The character of the concept, from Blumer's point of view, is not definitive but, rather, "sensitizing" (i.e., one does not begin an inquiry with a clear-cut definition of what he intends to study). Distinguishing a "sensitizing concept" from a definitive one, Blumer remarks:

> A sensitizing concept lacks such specification of attributes or bench marks and consequently it does not enable the user to move directly to the instance and its relevant content. Instead, it gives the user a general sense of reference and guidance in approaching empirical instances. Whereas definitive concepts provide prescriptions of what to see, sensitizing concepts merely suggest directions along which to look. (Blumer, 1969:148)

The sensitizing concept represents a "proposition" within the system of thought being employed. It is "tested" against reality in the formation of its content.

> When I declare that the content conceived in a concept can be studied separately, what I mean is that one can take an abstraction which has been made, test and specify its characters, ascertain its range, and endeavor to determine more of its

nature. (Blumer, 1969:158)

The concept's function in science, from this point of view, is that it permits the scientist to "hold onto perceptual experience," thus enabling further consideration (inspection) and observation in relation to that experience. At first, a concept may be only a crude attempt to "bridge the gaps" in the comprehension of an experience, but a continual re-experiencing (testing of the accuracy of the concept) allows its refinement.

4. Blumer and Parsons: The Source of the Concept of Deviance

In the broadest possible sense of the term, both Blumer and Parsons are empiricists. That is, both define themselves as scientists (although they conceive of science differently) and accept "the theory that experience rather than reason is the source of knowledge . . ." (Hamlyn, 1967:499). However, as was previously noted, Parsons' "empiricism" is importantly modified by an "analytical" (rational) element. Hence, it is accurate to suggest that Blumer's epistemology is (relative to Parsons') of a more radical empiricist variety. From Blumer's view, the content of the concept, the form that it should ultimately take, is derived from experience with the world. Parsons, in this respect, is much more a rationalist. For him, the concepts of scientific theory should be (using Blumer's dichotomy) "definitive." That is, one "begins" the scientific research inquiry with a clear-cut definition of the phenomenon with which one intends to be concerned. This suggests that the phenomenon has already been *described,* and its description is given in the definition. For Parsons, the scientific act is not conceived as concluded by an act of description, but, rather, the objective is to determine the relationship between those phenomena described and classified within a conceptual scheme. Of course, the description of the classes of phenomena may be elaborated in the research process, but one still begins with an "ideal type" which clearly articulates the definition of the phenomenon which is the subject of an inquiry. Hence, the first and most rudimentary stage of the development of scientific theory, according to Parsons, is the construction of an ad hoc classificatory scheme.

> The classes are quite independent of one another and any relations which may be discovered must come from *ad hoc* researches. Such common-sense classifications as that of "fish, flesh, or fowl" are illustrative of this type of classificatory system. (Parsons and Shils, 1951:50)

Given these contrary methodological dispositions, how does each theory group arrive at a conception of deviance? Two elements of Symbolic Interactionist thought must be taken into account. First, the empiricists' rendition of the emergence of the content of the concept is that it arises out of experience with the object of attention. Second, it must be asked what the object of attention is for the Symbolic Interactionist sociologist. The answer is clear in Blumer, but is more precisely specified in the quotation from Schutz above (see page 132): the objects of attention are the constructs of the actors on the social scene. A human science must focus upon these constructs--they are the "facts" of the social world. From Blumer's viewpoint, the second-order concepts of the social scientist should be used only *temporarily* as a tool with which to grasp the meanings (constructs) of the actors in the social world. Ultimately, the social scientist's objective is to interpret their world as they do--to interpret the actors' world through their conceptualizations of it. The content of the scientist's concepts should eventually be filled by the content of the concepts employed by the actors on the social scene. In trying to understand his experiences with actors within a segment of the social world, the social scientist arrives at second-order conceptualizations which, of course, these actors do not employ (e.g., the second-order concept of *deviance*). The second-order concept, "deviance," is used in the attempt to orient to the use of such first-order constructs as "queer," "punk," "nut," "criminal," "delinquent," "freak," etc. The content of the concept of deviance will be refined over time, as the social scientist has experience with actors who employ such concepts--refined in terms of capturing the sense in which these kinds of concepts are employed. Hence, homosexuality may or may not fit the category of deviance, depending upon the way in which it is specified by the actors in a particular social scene. If the actors do not specify homosexuality as "deviant," that category of act would fall outside of the category of deviance as developed by the social scientist. The second-order constructs of the observer, then, may undergo fundamental modification, because the first-order constructs of human actors may demand such modification.

A Parsonian-Functionalist specification of the substance of the concept of deviance involves quite different considerations from those of the Symbolic Interactionists. First, the concept is influenced not only by experience with the world, but also by its relationship to other concepts in a logically articulated conceptual scheme. Deviance is defined by distinguishing it from and relating it to other elements of the scheme. Second, although the scheme may well be oriented to the inclusion and comprehension of the use of first-order constructs of actors (e.g., institutions may be so conceived), since it is not based upon empiricist assumptions, it does not necessarily derive the content of the scientific concept from the first-order construct. That is, those behaviors which are negatively evaluated by the actors on the social scene may not fit the specifications of the category of deviance within the theoretical system. Hence, it is possible for homosexual acts to be regarded as "deviant" by the actors on the social scene (and, therefore, by Labeling Theorists) and yet not meet the definitive qualities of deviance as set forth within the conceptual scheme of the Functionalists. In fact, from the Functionalists' point of view, particular acts of homosexuality, assault, etc. (as has been noted in the discussion of deviance within Functionalist thought) may not only fail to fit the category of deviance, but, instead, may actually represent acts of conformity within the terms appropriate to the scheme.

A third distinguishing feature of Functionalism has been the goal of developing a theoretical system sufficiently abstract to be universally applicable. That is, although the *substantive* acts which are deviant may change from one point of reference to another, the concept of deviance within the conceptual scheme remains the same. Deviance is defined by

Parsons as, essentially, "a motivated departure from a moral norm." Thus, depending upon the time, the individual, and the group which is the point of reference, any substantive act may fall in or out of a particular category, but the category will remain constant.

It is clear that fundamental philosophical and methodological decisions effect the formulation of the basic concepts employed within these systems of thought. Furthermore, the resulting forms of basic concepts are radically disparate.

5. Ordering Principles: Causation and Meaning

Before discussing the principle which orders thought within these matrices, a few remarks are in order concerning the distinction between a "causal order" and a "meaningful order." This is a fundamental element of method and concerns the question of how scientific theory is to be ordered. What is at issue is not the establishment of a classificatory system, but, even more fundamentally, the character of the relations between elements of the system of thought. Some scientists might well suggest that the ordering of their theory corresponds to the order within their domain of interests (e.g., the social world). However, as is widely recognized, the implementation of one or the other of these principles represents an assumption which only the most naive would suggest could be demonstrated as valid through the method of observation (i.e., through the method of science itself). Even Hubert Blalock, perhaps the best representative of neo-positivism in sociology, submits:

> One admits that causal thinking belongs completely on the theoretical level and that causal laws can never be demonstrated empirically. (Blalock, 1964:6)

> . . . he [the scientist] cannot directly assess the validity of the causal principle itself. (Blalock, 1964:12)

On the other hand, there is no doubt that one can observe human beings engaged in the construction of meaning and attaching such meaning to their behavior. However, if it is suggested that what underlies such constructions is a causally ordered world which determines the emergence of specific intentions and meanings in relation to certain acts, no amount of scrutiny can dislodge the assumption. Hence, these distinctions need not be taken to refer to a reality "out there." Rather, they refer to the principle of order--the relationship between things--as it is established within a system of scientific thought. Whether or not the world is connected, as Hanson (1965) put it, "by cosmic glue" (p. 64) is not nearly so certain as is the observation that systems of theory are most certainly held together by some order-giving principles, e.g., causality, meaning, function, etc.

Quinney (1970) points out that there are a number of possibilities with respect to the ordering of scientific theories. Among them are causal statements, functional relations, probability statements, and meaning complexes. With respect to the Labeling and Etiological-Functional approaches, a general characterization of each of them in these terms would involve qualifications, since both causal statements and reference to meaning complexes as sources of action are involved within both.

However, there are basic differences in emphasis and intent between the two groups. The Functionalists are more inclined to view behavior as an outcome of antecedent cause, and the Labelists are more prone to concentrate upon conduct regarded as "meaningfully organized." Referring to Parsons' early work (1937), it is possible to suggest some general differences which the use of one or the other principle involves. Although Parsons was not commenting upon modern systems of sociology but, rather, varieties of positivism versus idealist thought, his remarks are none the less relevant. With respect to causation, he notes:

> This conception involves at least the postulate of process *in time*--for underlying every conception of causal relationship is that of variation. Two entities are causally related if, and insofar as, a change in one will result in a change in the other. Change in this context certainly implies a temporal process. (Parsons, 1937:482)

On the other hand, meaning refers to an "ideal element," and this implies:

> . . . a complex of elements mutually related to one another—constituting hence a "system"--but this mode of relationship is of a radically different character from the causal--it is a "complex of meanings". . . These meaningful relations of the elements of a system are not causal relations . . . the relation to time is fundamentally different. Logical relations are timeless as in the form of a work of art. (Parsons, 1937:482)

An example of such a complex of meaning is a symphonic composition (or any other art form). Players in the symphony orchestra do not play the correct note because they are "caused to;" rather, they are playing out the meaningful pattern established by the composition toward which they are oriented. The actor expends effort in an attempt to play the piece correctly. These complexes of meaning exist at many levels, from the meaning of a single word to an entire pattern of culture.

6. Labeling Theory: The Principle of Meaningfully Oriented Action

Symbolic Interactionism and Phenomenology, through concepts such as that of "self" and "mind," apply the principle of meaningfully oriented action to the individual level. The focus is upon how the actor constructs his action. The act, rather than being an outcome of the influence of a collectively held system of meaning (e.g., culture), takes the form of an individually constructed epoch of meaning. Speaking of conscious action, that action which is guided and carried out by reference to a system of meaning, Alfred Schutz remarks:

> An action is conscious in the sense that, before we carry it out, we have a picture in our mind of what we are going to do. This is the "projected act." Then, as we do proceed to action, we are either continuously holding the picture before our inner eye (retention), or we are from time to time recalling it to mind (reproduction). (Schutz, 1970:129)

140

The projected act, then, stands in the same relation to actions as does the composition to the member of the symphony orchestra. It is the image which the actor retains and reproduces in charting his conduct. He then engages in "map-consulting" (Schutz's term) following the act *previously* mapped out, which is cast "in the future perfect tense." It is such acts, previously cast (projected), which supply the *meaningful base* of action and which influence action in the world. Mead's conception of the act is, of course, quite similar.

> When . . . we speak of reflective conduct we very definitely refer to the presence of the future in terms of ideas. The intelligent man as distinguished from the intelligent animal presents to himself what is going to happen . . . man, however, does definitely pursue a certain course, pictures a certain situation, and directs his own conduct with reference to it. . . It is this picture . . . of what the future is to be as determining our present conduct that is characteristic of human intelligence—the future as present in terms of ideas. (Mead, 1934:119)

It is this level—the level of meaningfully organized conduct—on which the Labelists focus. They tend to at least supplement their implementation of the concept of causation by invoking the order which is imposed through the meaningful construction of acts. This is true even of Lemert, the most conservative of the Labelists in this regard. Lemert's concept of secondary deviance occurs at the level of conduct which is meaningfully organized by the self.

> . . . in a culture where a child is taught sharp distinctions between "good" women and "bad" women, a single act of questionable morality might conceivably *have a profound meaning* [emphasis added] for the girl so indulging. However, in the absence of reactions by the person's family, neighbors, or the larger community, reinforcing the tentative "bad-girl" self-definition, it is questionable whether a transition to secondary deviation would take place. (Lemert, 1951:76)

The importance of the reaction is that it supports the person's tendency to meaningfully organize deviance in terms of self. However, so as not to misconstrue Lemert's position, it is important to note that his general approach permits the application of the principle of causation. It is reasonable to ask, from his point of view, "What causes conduct to be meaningfully organized in a particular fashion?"

As Labeling Theory has developed, the principle of causation has steadily receded and been replaced by that of meaning. In Matza (1969), a method of understanding human affairs is developed which precludes the employment of the concept of cause. Matza sees human behavior as ordered solely in terms of the subject's meaning, which he (the subject) constructs and chooses to follow. In fact, the human being who is subject to causal (determinate) forces is "objectified," and, as such, he is reduced to a lower order of being--a non-human being. Matza intends quite literally that:

Being willing or unwilling is the ordinary form of affinity, the

ordinary yield of antecedent circumstance. Unless a natural reduction lurks in the biography of the subject, exposing him to
the compelling potency of the organism, unless a natural reduction is implicit in the agencies that define his current situation,
making him the kind of creature subject to gravitation, the hold
of circumstance, antecedent or contemporary, is limited. This
limited hold is *not* a result of our incomplete knowledge of the
determinants of human behavior. It is in the nature of the case--
man--that happens to be before us. (Matza, 1969:116)

The case of the human actor who is subject to the operation of antecedent causes is an extraordinary one. The application of the principle
of causality to persons is seen as dehumanizing. Following Blumer (1969),
Matza states:

Symbolic Interaction--the human recasting of the subject--could
hardly be applied in an intellectual context in which all the
other elements had already conspired to dehumanize. Fundamentally committed to the active *creation of meaning* and thus
human being, it was incompatible with an architecture whose
foundation was preordained being. (Matza, 1969:108)

Quinney also attaches great importance to the construction of
meaningful acts, and, as a result, his approach, too, diminishes the role
of causation in the organization of theory.

First, causal explanation need not be the sole interest of criminologists. The objective of any science is not to formulate and
verify theories of causation, but to construct an order among
observables. Explanations as generalized answers to the question
"why?" may be presented in other than causal form. . . A science of human social behavior is obviously possible without the
notion of causation. (Quinney, 1970:5)

Further, causal constructs, if employed, must refer to the *meaningful
constructs* of human beings. As Quinney says:

The world of social phenomena studied by the social scientist
has meaning for the human beings living within it. . . The social
scientist's *constructs* have to be founded upon the social reality
created by man. . . (Quinney, 1970:6)

The theory of the "social reality of crime," as Quinney conceives it, is a
theory of how persons meaningfully construct definitions of crime and
"the crime problem."

The "real world" is a social construction: man with the help of
others creates the world in which he lives. Social reality is thus
the world a group of people create and believe in as their own.
This reality is constructed according to the kind of "knowledge"
they develop, the ideas they are exposed to, the manner in
which they select information to fit the world they are shaping,
and the manner in which they interpret these conceptions. Man
behaves in reference to the *social meanings* he attaches to his
experiences. (Quinney, 1970:22)

142

Hence, according to Quinney, as well as others associated with this tradition, an emphasis on the meaningful order associated with human action within the theory is viewed as more fruitful than is reference to some underlying "non-human" causal order.

7. The Antideterminant Component in Labeling Theory

Since the human world is not viewed by Labelists as causally ordered, neither does it need to be viewed as a closed determinant system. Rather, as Edwin Schur remarks in his considerations on the approach:

> In stressing that deviance outcomes emerge from the continuous *inter*action between the individual's behavior and the responses of others, labeling analysts, far from treating individuals as passive objects, appear to challenge the tendency of other theorists to treat them as such and do in fact recognize significant measures of "freedom" and "personal dignity." (Schur, 1971:162)

The basis of this attribution of freedom is clear in both the conception of man developed within Symbolic Interactionist thought and the resistance to the idea of causation within that body of thought. This view allows for the existence of "real options." Human beings, via projection, can consider a series of alternate possibilities and can *decide* which action to take. The resistance of the Labeling Theorists to determinism is best developed in Matza's work. In *Delinquency and Drift* (1964), the concept of "drift" was proposed in order to avoid what Matza described as the postulate of "hard determinism."

> An alternative image of the delinquent can be developed by accepting the implications of soft rather than hard determinism . . . Some men are freer than others. Most men, including delinquents, are neither wholly free nor completely constrained but fall somewhere between. (Matza, 1964:27)

Matza goes even further in asserting the freedom of the individual from determinant forces in *Becoming Deviant* (1969). In a footnote of the opening chapter, he says, "In that discussion [*Delinquency and Drift,*] I more or less settle on a position of soft determinism. I suppose the present discussion moves even further away from an acceptance of any sort of determinism" (Matza, 1969:7).

Even Scheff and Lemert, who are most reserved about these matters, exhibit elements in their thought which suggest a lack of reliance upon the postulate of determinism. This is true of Lemert in his acceptance of Matza's concept of "drift" (see Lemert, 1968:78-80). Scheff suggests that one source of primary deviance may be found in "volitional acts of defiance." Such volitional acts are not viewed as an outcome of determinant sources, such as the organism, the character structure, and the social situation (see Scheff, 1966:45). Quinney, like Matza, explicitly includes indeterminancy in his frame of reference. Commenting upon the nature of social action, Quinney says:

> An assumption of man that is consistent with the conflict-power conception of society asserts that man's actions are purposive

143

and meaningful, that man engages in voluntary behavior. This *humanistic* conception of man contrasts with the oversocialized conception of man. Man is, after all, capable of considering alternative actions, of breaking from the established social order. (Quinney, 1970:13)

Hence, for Quinney, as for others within this matrix, human behavior is a constructive, open-ended (indeterminant) process: "By conceiving of man as able to reason and choose courses of action, we may see him as changing and becoming, rather than merely being" (Quinney, 1970:13).

8. The Causal Element in Functional Theory

In this section, the focus will be upon the principles which order Functional Theory. Functionalism contains functional explanation and, in some instances and at some levels, offers causal explanation as well. This dual orientation has been associated with the Functionalist perspective from its origins. Durkheim's first "rule of sociological explanation" not only suggests the importance of both forms of explanation, but also asserts his belief in their distinctiveness:[5] "When, then, the explanation of a social phenomenon is undertaken, we must seek separately the efficient cause which produces it and the function it fulfills" (Durkheim, 1938:95).

Most of Durkheim's work employs both of these principles. However, the work which has most influenced the theory of deviance (and which may be seen as the first which employs the exemplary mode of the explanation of deviance within this matrix), *Suicide* (1951), is almost solely etiological, although it is grounded in Functional Theory. Just as Durkheim's analysis of suicide is a search for the causal source of the phenomenon rather than for its functional origins or functional significance, so, too, is the work on deviance of Parsons, Merton, Cohen, and Cloward and Ohlin.

The procedure in this section will be to first delineate the realms of Functional Theory which are, indeed, functional and then to proceed to that level of the approach which is concerned with causal analysis. It is at the latter level that the approach to deviance examined in this work is formulated.

a. Functional Explanation

Functional Analysis is the analysis of the relationships among the components of what is seen as a systemic whole, i.e., it is the analysis of parts and their relation to one another. In the case of Sociological Functionalism, this involves an analysis of the relations among elements of social structure, i.e., norms, values, beliefs, rules, etc. Merton (1969), in exploring the core of Functional Analysis, suggests:

Though Malinowski differs in several respects from the formulations of Radcliffe-Brown, he joins him in making the core of

---

[5]Not all Functionalists accept the suggestion of the distinctiveness of the two modes of explanation (see Davis: 1959).

functional analysis the study of "the part which [social or cultural items] play in the society." "This type of theory," Malinowski explains in one of his early declarations of purpose, "aims at the explanation of anthropological facts at all levels of development by *their function, by the part which they play within the integral system of culture, by the manner in which they are related to each other within the system. . .*" (Merton, 1967:22)

Sociological Functionalists go beyond a simple description of the relationship of the parts to one another. They include assessments of the contribution of the parts to the maintenance of the system as a whole, either in maintaining equilibrium or integration among the parts or in meeting the "needs" (functional requirements) of the system. Most Functionalists argue that it is possible (at least formally) to carry on such analysis independently of questions concerning causality (i.e., independently of questions concerning the causal origin of the social structures which are being examined). In fact, Parsons is very reluctant to assert that the conceptual scheme which he has developed includes the question of cause and effect at all. Parsons was once confronted by someone who said, "If I am wrong, you will correct me, but my impression is that you could do without the concept 'cause and effect'." To which he responded (in a question-and-answer session following a speech):

Oh, I think so . . . I think Professor Aron is right. I, and probably most social scientists of my generation probably do not use this sort of term. . . The person who, like myself, has paid very special attention to 'system' probably shies away more than others. (Parsons, 1965:68)

Parsons is primarily concerned with relations of mutual *interdependence* among elements whose existence is given, rather than with the question of causal *origin* of structural forms. Just as it is not concerned with the source of structures, this perspective does not necessarily lead to a search for the causal influence of one component of the system upon another. That is, there may be no attempt to ascertain the weight of one variable in relation to another--the elements may simply be seen as mutually influential. Insofar as causal analysis demands the weighing of variables, it is not to be accomplished at this level of theory. Causal analysis implies some asymmetry in the relation between variables; Functional analysis focuses upon the symmetry of relations. Parsons concedes that although causal analysis is attractive, it is very rarely accomplished in the social field. In fact, he sees his conceptual scheme as a "lower order" of theory. "In our present state of knowledge, we are bound to a 'structural functional' level of theory" (Parsons, 1965:364).

b. Causation and the Theory of Deviance

The theory of deviance is located at a different level than is the concern with relations among components of social structure. The shift to the problem of deviance is to the relation of social structure to either motivational patterns (as in the case of Parsons and Cohen) or conduct (as in the case of Merton, Cloward and Ohlin, and Durkheim). Despite the Functionalists' reluctance in many cases to directly employ

145

the concept of causation in their approach to deviance, they do assume that a given social structure may act as a causal influence upon conduct. This reluctance to use the concept of causation is very general in modern science. But, as Nagle (1965) points out, whereas the term may have fallen into disrepute, the notion has not:

> Many influential scientists and philosophers have argued that the notion of cause plays a diminishing role in modern science . . . and that the notion is a relic of a primitive, anthropomorphic interpretation of the various changes occurring in the world. It is beyond serious doubt that the term "cause" rarely if ever appears in the research papers or treatises currently published in the natural sciences. . . Nevertheless, though the term may be absent, the idea for which it stands continues to have wide currency. (Nagle, 1965:12)

It seems that modern Sociological Functionalists have also deserted the word "cause," but they substitute in its place a number of other terms which imply the same idea. Whereas *structural* analysis within this camp is functional and not causal, *the theory of conduct* is causally ordered. However, only Durkheim persistently uses the term "cause." Other Functionalists, such as Parsons and Merton, typically substitute other terms, where "cause" might just as well be employed. Merton uses the word "pressure," and Parsons refers to "influence" or "guiding the actor." All of these terms, however, include the basic elements of a causal principle;[6] they imply (1) a temporal sequence which finds (2) a source factor antecedent to a specific outcome, and (3) the antecedent event "forces," or brings to bear some force, generating a consequence (an effect). Regardless of the term employed, then, the theory of deviance within Functionalism contains a definite shift to etiological questions. Merton's most basic question in "Social Structure and Anomie" refers to the social-structural source of conduct: "Our primary aim is to discover how some *social structures exert a definite PRESSURE* [my capitals] *upon certain persons in the society to engage in non-conforming rather than conforming conduct*" (1967:132). One would gain or lose little if "causal influence" were substituted for "definite pressure" in the above quotation.

c. The Causal "Entity" in Functionalism

The examination of the exemplary form of explanation (Chapter III) indicates that, from the Functionalist point of view, the primary causal entities implicated in the emergence of human conduct are institutionalized norms and values. In this section, the character of these entities and the sense in which they are viewed as causes of conduct will be examined.

The roots of the modern Sociological Functionalist tradition are established in *The Structure of Social Action* (Parsons, 1937). It is here that the use of causal principles is combined with a view of human

---

[6]Cohen does occasionally refer to "causal relevance," but not often--see "Multiple Factor Approaches" (1970).

action as meaningfully oriented. In the first place, the primary social entities--norms and values--exist as meaning complexes and are related to one another in a system of meaning (i.e., they are symbolic or ideal elements). Further, and of major import in *The Structure*, these meaning complexes emerge independently of the "conditions" of action (i.e., independently of "organic and environmental" factors. The result of interaction between human beings is the creation of a "human world" in which the actors are, in an important sense, removed from the influence of the world of "stimulus and response." Complexes of meaning, which compose the human world, operate in the establishment of the ends of human action, as well as providing a selective basis for the determination of means. As such, they establish the direction of effort and are essential in the comprehension of persons' attempts to change the "conditions of action." The course of human action, then, is to be understood in terms of these *symbolic elements* which the actor associates with his conduct, establishing its meaning, its intentions, and its direction. Hence, action can only be understood by taking *the point of view of the actor*, i.e., by "discovering" the actor's subjectivity. The method of *Verstahen*, then, is recommended, in order to "get at" the meaning which the actor assigns to his conduct. It is only through this method that the sociologist can "observe" the pattern of values and norms which influences conduct.

At the same time, from the point of view of the scientific observer, the system of values and norms appears related to action in a causal way. The pattern of values may be analytically distinguished from the "concrete" individuals within society and regarded as existing independently. As such, an "abstracted element," it can be viewed as a cause of action. In short, the crucial "causal entity" within Functionalist thought is a complex of meaning which is *institutionalized*. The method of *Verstahen*, then, leads not only to the discovery of individually constituted human acts, but also to the patterns of institutions which may be viewed as "external" influences on conduct.

By the time he wrote *The Social System* (1951) and *Toward a General Theory of Action* (1951), Parsons not only emphasized the functional relations among institutions and their role in fulfilling the functional prerequisites of social systems, he also emphasized their role in the emergence of motivational patterns. Patterns of meaning, when institutionalized, constitute the social system--when internalized, they constitute important aspects of a person's personality system as well, and, as such, they directly influence the direction of conduct. Commenting on the importance of culture, Parsons summarizes the relations among his primary levels of analysis:

> Analysis of the third kind of system [culture] is essential to the theory of action because systems of value standards (criteria of selection) and other patterns of culture, when *institutionalized* in social systems and *internalized* in personality systems, guide the actor with respect to both the *orientation to ends* and the *normative regulation* of means and of expressive activities, whenever the need-dispositions of the actor allow choices in these matters. (Parsons and Shils, 1951:56)

The statement indicates clearly that, regardless of the *source* of

147

cultural elements or institutions, once internalized, they are treated as determinants of action.

The relationship of the actor to the system of values, such that it may be regarded as causing his conduct, is established through reference to the process of socialization. The actor who is socialized into a milieu in which a particular pattern is institutionalized develops a commitment to that pattern. When commitment is established, the actor is said to have a "need" (need-disposition) to follow the pattern, i.e., he will expend effort in an attempt to live up to the standard. At this point, the pattern may be viewed as directly influencing or "causing" the actor's conduct.

d.   The Institutional Source of Deviant Motivation

The relationship of institutions to behavior which is alluded to above has been taken to be *the* theory of conduct associated with the Functionalists' scheme. Focusing upon this aspect of the approach has led some to conclude that deviance is accounted for within the matrix by reference to faulty socialization.[7] However, as the review of the conception of deviance associated with Functionalists indicates, they begin their analysis with an actor who is fully socialized (see Chapter III). The more important aspect of the Functionalists' theory of motivation and behavior, as far as the problem of deviance is concerned, is that in which the social structure is viewed as both an element of the actor's orientation and a condition of his action. This situation, and the theory of motivation it implies, has been illustrated in all the modern theories of deviance which have been reviewed here under the Functionalist scheme, but it is perhaps most clearly presented in Merton's and Cohen's works.[8] In these theories, the essential element of the cause of deviance finds the actor oriented to socially structured goals as well as means. However, because of his objective position within the social structure (e.g., one which denies opportunity), the actor is cut off from a real opportunity to act within the framework of his orientation. This condition, which can be fairly described as a "dialectical contradiction," subjects the actor to a "strain" which is the *cause* of the distinctive motivational pattern which is his "motivation to deviance." This *institutionally induced strain* is the source of the ambivalent or alienated quality which is definitive of the Functionalists' characterization of deviance.

---

[7] The mistaken assumption that this is the only explanation of motivation within the Functionalist matrix is an error of the work of Taylor, Walton, and Young in *The New Criminology* (1974). They compound the error by suggesting that deviance within the Functionalist approach is accounted for by "under socialization."

[8] Although Durkheim's theory is also institutional, it does not take precisely this form. However, within his thought, it is conditions of the social structure which make for deviance.

D. Values Within Deviance Matrices

1. Introduction

This section focuses upon values as a component of disciplinary matrices in sociology, and it contains two segments. The first segment is concerned with "intra-scientific values;"[9] the second focuses upon "extra-scientific values," i.e., socio-political commitments as matrix components.

2. Intra-Scientific Values

Activity within scientific theory groups, as with any other human activity, may be characterized as associated with patterns of value commitment. Some scientific values refer strictly to decisions internal to the doing of science. Commitments of this sort may exert important influences on the "science" which is produced by the members of the group.

The most general values within a matrix refer to the question, "What kind of knowledge should our efforts produce?"[10] Should it be the kind of knowledge that fosters accurate prediction? If it is oriented toward prediction, scientific activity will take a particular direction.[11] However, other scientific values may lead to only a subsidiary interest in prediction or, perhaps, to no interest in prediction at all. Depending upon *their* values, the scholars may seek to establish various types of "understanding" of phenomena or the relations between and among phenomena. For example, some scientists may emphasize the desirability of constructing a "plausible explanation" which may or may not enhance accurate prediction. They may submit that the specification of a relationship between two variables which makes prediction possible is not to be as earnestly sought after as is the explanation of a relationship which is already considered established. The discussion of intra-scientific values within this section will be limited to the primary values associated with a matrix. Hence, the focus will be on the most general values that are built into an approach.

---

[9]This conception is discussed in Kuhn's Postscript to the 1975 edition of *The Structure of Scientific Revolutions*, pp. 184-185.

[10]Certain values will be shared across all scientific theory groups, e.g., that knowledge is better than ignorance, that "theories" should be logically coherent and consistent, etc. These values are of great importance to the form that science takes. As Kuhn remarks: "Imagine what would happen in the sciences if consistency ceased to be a primary value" (Kuhn, 1970:186). However, this discussion will concentrate on those values over which scientific groups may diverge.

[11]An example of a contemporary scientific theory group which values prediction is the "New Causal Theorists," discussed by Mullins (1973: see Chapter 9).

a. Epistemology and Value

Certainly, the valued forms of knowledge of the course of human conduct associated with Labeling and Functionalist Theory are related to their respective epistemologies. However, given the limits on the production of knowledge specified by the epistemological theories, there may remain a field in which various value choices are possible. Where these choices exist, values will specify what can be done. The following discussion of the valued types of scientific production will not directly relate epistemology to values, although there is such a relation.

b. Valued Science: Symbolic Interactionism and Labeling

There is a radical split within the Labeling camp with regard to the valued form of science. Those scholars most directly influenced by the work of Herbert Blumer appear to value a rigorous "analytical description." Most clearly, Becker and Matza operate with an emphasis upon such description rather than on "scientific explanation." Accordingly, there is much vacillation and inconsistency within the Labeling matrix concerning the use of such terms as "theory" and "science." The difficulty lies in the fact that one wing of the perspective is interested in the development of an "explanation" of the scientific-theoretical type and the other is not.

Rather than "science," as that term is normally understood,[12] Becker and Matza value "description." Matza indicates of his "naturalistic" approach:

> To locate or assert an essential feature of phenomena is a basic part of naturalist analysis, as basic perhaps as posing a relationship between two variables is in more conventional sociological analysis. For the naturalist, the location of essential features is crucial because it is an attempt to cogently assert what the phenomenon *is*. (Matza, 1969:27)

This focus upon the description of the phenomenon, rather than referring to some forces underpinning and explaining its emergence and character is, at times, traced to the philosophy of Edmund Husserl. Schur (1971) sees this influence operating in the perspective: "A basic theme, emphasized over and over again in phenomenological writings, is the need to return 'to the things themselves,' as Edmund Husserl expressed it" (Schur, 1971:116). Consistent with this value, Matza complains about traditional sociologists' lack of concern with the phenomenon they purport to explain.

> When deviant phenomenon are seen and studied from the correctional perspective, the possibility of "losing the phenomenon"-- reducing it to that which it is not--is heightened. The purpose of ridding ourselves of the phenomenon manifests itself most clearly in an overwhelming contemporary concern with questions of causation or "etiology." The phenomenon itself receives only

---

[12]A fundamental element of science is the development of generalizations and abstractions; Matza and Becker seek to avoid both.

cursory attention . . . traditional studies of deviant behavior have been highly vague and shortwinded about the phenomena they presume to explain. (Matza, 1969:17)

The human sciences value more than mere "analytic-naturalistic" description; they seek description from "inside the phenomenon." This mode of description is seen as quite distinct from "objective description" by a detached observer. Rather, it is a method, like the method of *Verstahen*, which insists that the observer discover the "world-view" of those he seeks to understand, i.e., that he enter into the world of human subjectivity.

. . . if the scholar wishes to understand the action of people it is necessary for him to see their objects as they see them. Failure to see their objects as they see them, or a substitution of his meanings of the objects for their meanings, is the gravest kind of error that the social scientist can commit. It leads to the setting up of a fictitious world. (Blumer, 1969:51)

Seeing persons' objects as they see them allows the scholar to *describe* the world of his subjects. From this point of view, the subject's actions may then be comprehended. Becker makes a plea for this type of description in *Outsiders*.

Very few [studies] tell us in detail what a juvenile delinquent does in his daily round of activity and what he thinks about himself, society, and his activities. When we theorize about juvenile delinquency, we are therefore in the position of having to infer the way of life of the delinquent boy from fragmentary studies and journalistic accounts instead of being able to base our theories on adequate knowledge of the phenomenon we are trying to explain. It is as though we tried, as anthropologists once had to do, to construct a description of the initiation rites of some remote African tribe from the scattered and incomplete accounts of a few missionaries. (Becker, 1963:166)

This statement may be interpreted as simply suggesting that sociologists should gather accurate data upon which "to base theories" in the sense of "theoretical explanation." However, in the context of other remarks by Becker, such an interpretation appears to miss the point. Rather than testing theories, Becker is seeking a more inclusive and more accurate description of (as Matza [1969] puts it) "what the phenomenon *is*." Such description is, for Becker, an end in itself—sufficient for the "scientific" comprehension of human behavior. Blumer and Becker lend to the confusion concerning the kind of understanding they wish to yield by their incessant use of the language of science, e.g., Becker speaks of "theory" and Blumer refers to "empirical science." The fact is that any "science" that is developed in the terms of Blumer's methodological statement (1969) will not fulfill a central requirement historically associated with science, i.e., the development of general, abstract, universally applicable statements which will offer an explanation of the emergence and persistence of phenomena. A remark which can only be taken as a direct rejection of this kind of "explanatory theory" is contained in Becker's postscript to *Outsiders* (1973): "Interactionist theory grows out of a frame of mind that takes the commonplace seriously and will not settle for *mysterious invisible forces* [emphasis added] as explanatory mechanisms" (Becker, 1973:193).

Many aspects of Symbolic Interactionist Theory give rise to this preference for description over explanation. Perhaps the most important aspect is the insistence by Blumer, Becker, and Matza that the actor individually constructs his act through individual interpretive processes which are rooted in both the idiosyncratic assignment of meaning and shift of attention. Within this view, it is, of course, impossible to develop nomothetic knowledge of human conduct. Hence, such pursuits are not valued. Rather, there is an appeal for rigorous description. The research program implied by this pattern of value is the ethnographic or historical study of various social worlds. The primary difference between the ethnography of Symbolic Interaction and more traditional ethnographic programs is the emphasis upon subjectivity.

The other scholars who have been associated with the Labeling matrix adhere to values which are much closer to the Functionalists than are those of the scholars discussed above. Lemert, Scheff, and Quinney do see the possibility, and seek the establishment of, nomothetic knowledge with respect to human conduct. This quest, however, is tempered by the indeterminant element (see pages 140-141) which, as has been seen, is given some emphasis within the Labeling approach. Nevertheless, all three scholars are inclined toward the development of "theoretical systems of explanation." These attempts at explanation refer to the problem of the emergence and persistence of phenomena, as well as the question of what a particular phenomenon is. At the same time, in the work of both Quinney and Lemert, there is a good deal of emphasis upon description. In Quinney's (1970, 1973) works, the focus is upon historical description rather than upon ethnographic description. However, description for Quinney is not an end in itself. Rather, it is through description that the theory emerges and its utility is exhibited (see Quinney, 1970: Chapter 2). Lemert relies upon ethnographic descriptions of some detail. In doing so, he seeks to make cross-cultural comparisons of forms of deviant behavior. This is somewhat unique among sociologists of deviant behavior.[13] These comparisons are seen as fostering the development of a systematic theory. Lemert's goal is indicated by the following remark:

> Studies of drinking by primitive peoples have ranged from descriptive treatment in single societies to large scale uses of statistical data. . . For those who prefer to move beyond a descriptive emphasis yet seek to keep generalizations about drinking within a societal context, the modern comparative method offers a possible alternative meeting ground. (Lemert, 1972:218)

---

[13]The titles of Lemert's articles in *Human Deviance, Social Problems, and Social Control* (1972) indicate this approach: "Stuttering Among the North Pacific Coastal Indians," "Stuttering and Social Structure in Two Pacific Island Societies," "Socio-cultural Research on Drinking," and "Forms and Pathology of Drinking in Three Polynesian Societies."

In seeking to develop theoretical explanations of deviance, both Quinney and Scheff have been influenced by the "cybernetic systems theory," most closely associated with Walter Buckley's work (1967). Buckley indicates some of the objectives and strengths of the approach in the following remark:[14]

> . . . only the modern systems approach promises to get at the full complexity of the interacting phenomena . . . to see not only the *causes* acting on the phenomena under study, the possible consequences of the phenomena, and the possible *mutual interactions* of some of these factors, but also to see the *total emergent processes* as a function of possible positive and/or negative *feedbacks* mediated by the selective *decisions*, or "choices," of the individuals and groups directly or indirectly involved. (Buckley, 1967:80)

Buckley's approach also involves a highly formal and selective presentation of the theory. His method suggests that the primary components of the theory be organized as propositional statements. Further, the view of the relationships among the propositions is always interactive, including such relations as "feedback loops" and "amplification effects." Such possibilities imply that one component of the theory has an enhanced or amplified effect by its relation to the other. With respect to this approach, Quinney says:

> Any particular phenomenon, in turn, is viewed as contributing to the dynamics of the total process. As in the "modern systems approach" social phenomena are seen as generating out of an interrelated whole. (Quinney, 1970:9)

The major objective of this wing of the Labeling approach is the development of a "plausible explanation" of the relationships among relevant variables. The goal is to "make sense" out of experience with only minimal regard for the other values associated with scientific theory, e.g., prediction and control. Quinney remarks: ". . . our concern is not with any correspondence between 'objective reality' and observation, but between observation and the utility of such observations in understanding our own subjective, multiple social worlds" (Quinney, 1970:5).

c. Functionalism: Intra-Scientific Values

The examination of Functional Theory as presented thus far indicates the importance attached to the development of abstract theory within the matrix. The valued objective of science as it is done within this group is "bound up" with the importance of the role of theory. Functionalists value explanation, and what they mean by "explanation" depends upon the existence of theory as an orienting frame of reference.

It should be noted here, however, that not all science requires, as a basis for evaluation of scientific statements, that such statements "explain" anything at all. Jack Gibbs (1972), who has given some

---

[14]See also the "Methodological Note" by Buckley appended to Scheff's *Being Mentally Ill* (1966).

consideration to this issue, asks:

> On what basis are contending theories to be judged? The question is not to be dismissed lightly, for it is difficult to imagine progress in a field lacking effective consensus as to the appropriate criteria for assessing theories.

> The notion of explanation should be rejected because it does not further consensus in the assessment of sociological theories. . . (Gibbs, 1972:35)

Gibbs proposes that "theories" should be evaluated on one general ground, predictive success, rather than explanation:

> . . . in examining test results one question should be paramount: What do the results suggest about the predictive power of the theory? As the question indicates, predictive power should be the primary criterion by which sociological theories are assessed. (Gibbs, 1972:64)

Somewhat overstating the case, Gibbs suggests that Functionalists are not overly preoccupied with the power of their theories to predict:

> . . . no specific predictions flow from the typical functional explanation of a socio-cultural phenomenon. . . Consequently . . . predictive power is simply not a criterion by which functionalists assess their own theories. (Gibbs, 1972:72)

While there is some basis for Gibbs' statement, prediction is not irrelevant to the Functionalists' assessment of their theories. However, for the Functionalists, prediction is not an end in itself, as it is for Gibbs. Rather, the importance of prediction is always tied to matters of explanation, as is evident in the following remarks of Merton:

> It is well known that verified predictions derived from a theory do not prove or demonstrate that theory; they merely supply a measure of confirmation, for it is always possible that alternative hypotheses drawn from different theoretic systems can also account for the predicted phenomena. But those theories which admit of precise predictions confirmed by observation take on strategic importance since they provide an initial basis for choice between competing hypotheses. In other words, precision enhances the likelihood of approximating a "crucial" observation or experiment. (Merton, 1967:98-99)

Parsons also sees the evaluation of the adequacy of a general theoretical system as partially resting on the theory's capacity to predict. In fact, his formulation of the "ultimate goal" of science (although perhaps not his formulation of the "ultimate goal" of sociology) involves a level of theory which generates relatively precise prediction:

> We speak of an empirical-theoretical system whenever a sufficient number of relevant variables can be brought together in a single (theoretical) system of interdependence adequate for a high level of precision in predicting changes in empirical systems outside special experimental conditions. This is the long-term

goal of scientific endeavor. (Parsons, Shils, and Olds, 1951:51)

Although some value is attached to prediction by Functionalists, it is always in association with explanation. The task now is to specify more clearly what explanation entails. In so doing, it will be possible to see how the goals of the Functionalists are distinct from both description, as valued by the Symbolic Interactionists, and simple prediction, as valued by Gibbs.

First, explanation may take any number of substantive forms, e.g., causal or genetic forms, functional forms, and even predictive forms. The objection to prediction is not that it cannot be associated with explanation; it simply need not be (cf. Scheffler, 1963:43).[15] Explanation involves a particular type of comprehension of events. In presenting the essence of explanation, as the Functionalists conceive it, reference to a series of statements brought together by Gibbs (1972:26) from philosophers and sociologists will be helpful:

. . . the scientific explanation of a fact consists, from a logical point of view, in showing that it is an *instance* of a general law. (Bunge, 1959:288)

To give a *causal explanation* of an event means to deduce a statement which describes it, using as premises of the deduction one or more *universal laws*. . . (Popper, 1965:59)

. . . less general propositions, which investigators have found to hold good empirically, may be deduced from the general ones under specified given conditions. To deduce them is to explain them. (Homans, 1961:12)

The message in the above statements is clear--*explanation involves deduction.* Whether this "narrow" conceptualization of explanation is widely accepted is open to debate; however, it is the view of the Functionalists and represents the type of understanding they pursue.

The premium placed on this view of explanation is clearly represented in Cohen's "Multiple Factor Approaches" statement:

Explanation calls not for a *single factor* but for a *single theory* or system of theory applicable to all cases. It is not the attendant circumstances but the demonstration that the event and the attendant circumstances are a special case of generalized theory which constitutes an explanation. (Cohen, 1970:124)

[And, further, that] . . . explanation lies precisely in making. . . [t]heoretical assumptions explicit, showing their applicability to concretely or "pheno-typically" different "special cases" of the general theory, and demonstrating that this particular complex of circumstances fits the conditions required by the theory. (Cohen, 1970:124)

Merton views the task of science in much the same terms. Commenting

---

[15]Scheffler considers the "structural divergence" between prediction and explanation.

on the relation of empirical generalization to theory, he states that:

> Although propositions of this order are essential in empirical research, a miscellany of such propositions only provides the raw materials for sociology as a discipline. The theoretic task, and the orientation of empirical research toward theory, first begins when the bearing of such uniformities on a set of interrelated propositions is tentatively established. (Merton, 1967:95)

Even in the case where "surprising" data is observed, it is not the data which generates the proposition--the data is understood in relation to the system of propositions:

> . . . in noting that the unexpected fact must be strategic, i.e., that it must permit of implications which bear upon generalized theory, we are, of course, referring rather to what the observer brings to the datum than to the datum itself. For it obviously requires a theoretically sensitized observer to *detect the universal in the particular* [emphasis added]. (Merton, 1967:105)

There is no doubt that Parsons shares this view of explanation and that he has attached paramount importance to its development. In fact, Parsons' entire career has been spent in the attempt to develop a systematic, conceptual scheme in terms of which discreet observations can be organized.

(1) Retrodiction and Explanation

Although explanations with predictive power are valued within the Functionalist matrix, the substantive theories of deviance examined here do not meet all the requirements associated with prediction. Prediction involves a particular temporal relation between the observation of events and the positing of an explanation and involves the idea that the event can be explained and foretold. Rather than being strictly predictive, the Functionalists' theories reviewed here take a "post-factum" or, as Parsons (1965) says, a "retrospective predictive" form. This post-factum analysis is certainly viewed as acceptable within the matrix, particularly if appropriately combined with explanation. Although Merton makes a number of derisive remarks concerning post-factum analysis (and clearly favors prediction over this mode), his criticisms are qualified by the following remark which relates to the successful combination of explanation with the post-factum form:

> If the basic assumption holds--namely, that the *post factum* interpretation utilizes abundantly confirmed theories--then this type of explanation indeed "shoots arrowy light into the dark chaos of materials." (Merton, 1967:93)

Parsons is more likely to advocate "restrospective explanation" than is Merton. He sees a very thin and not too significant line separating retrospection and prediction.

> There is one sense in which explanation of past events is nothing but retrospective prediction. That consists in putting oneself in a position of an observer at the time something happened,

predicting what would have happened contingent on certain other intervening events, and then saying that the experimental check is: Did it happen or didn't it happen as predicted? In these terms the difference between retrospective explanation and prospective prediction is only that in the former case it is possible for the explainer to know what actually did happen. . . (Parsons, 1965:63)

Each of the substantive theories of deviance associated with this matrix (for example, those contained in Durkheim's *Suicide*, Merton's "Social Structure and Anomie," Cohen's *Delinquent Boys*, and Cloward and Ohlin's *Delinquency and Opportunity*) combines retrospective prediction with explanation, taking the deductive form. It should be noted that there is a sense in which retrospective prediction is more consistent with other aspects of the Functionalist gestalt than is prospective prediction. It should be recalled that there is an indeterminant element operating within the matrix. The historical process--human action--is always somewhat open. "Contingencies" operate to effect final outcomes. Expressing a position in 1964, consistent with that stated in his work *The Structure of Social Action* (1937), Parsons said:

Some people like to say that without prediction and control we have no knowledge. I take a position against that and suggest it is precisely this irreducible historical element that gives explanation an advantage over prediction. (Parsons, 1965:60)

In sum, the Functionalists' view of "doing science" emphasizes deductive explanation combined with prediction in one or another of its forms--retrospective or prospective.

(2) The Deterministic Aspect of Functionalism

In Matza's discussion of "The Positive Delinquent" (1964), he suggests that, on at least one level, there is not an important difference between earlier "positivistic-deterministic" theories of crime and modern sociological theories. Their essence is the same, for, although they focus upon different determinants, they are all deterministic. In a limited sense, Matza is correct. However, his position somewhat oversimplifies the matter. To ignore the distinct character of the determining principles of contemporary Functionalism, as contrasted with biologistic and psychologistic theories of crime, leads to fundamentally erroneous conclusions. In contrast to Matza's position, the voluntaristic (determinism-reducing) element originally set forth in Parsons' theory of action (1937) remains, although obscured, in the Functionalist theories of deviance which are being examined in this work. While the voluntaristic element is included, the substantive theories of deviance are deterministic. This apparent contradiction can be resolved by a consideration of the view of conduct and the view of scientific theory built into the matrix.

The theories of deviance that have been associated with Etiological Functionalism rest on a view of human action developed most clearly by Parsons in *The Structure of Social Action* (1937). In order to develop this argument, it is necessary to focus upon the nature of the Parsonian action scheme as voluntaristic. There is no doubt that Parsons chose this term, in part, to distinguish his approach from earlier "positivistic-deterministic" theories of behavior.[16] At the same time, he did *not* want to be fully identified with the idealist theories of conduct which, at times, have posited a level of freedom or uniqueness in action inconsistent with the application of scientific theory to the study of human behavior. Voluntarism is not to be equated with freedom—nor does it include the concept of free will. Parsons makes clear his lack of interest in such a concept in a relatively recent comment addressed to Whitney Pope in a journal exchange:

> Pope links the concept of the voluntaristic characteristics of action with a religious or metaphysical entity called free will. The belief in free will may have been a feature of theology and philosophy in the history of Western thought, but it is not the only position which is tenable. My own view has developed greatly since I wrote *The Structure of Social Action*. I regard human voluntarism as an extension of what many biologists call the self-regulating properties of living systems. (Parsons, 1975:108)

The statement indicates that Parsons has never equated voluntarism with free will, and, although his views have changed and developed over time, he indicates that there is still a place for voluntarism in his approach.

Voluntarism points to those important aspects of human action which distinguish it from the other realm of nature. First, human action is released from the control of the "conditions of action" (organism and environment). Throughout Parsons' development, he has refused to reduce human action to such terms.[17] Second, human action is goal-directed, i.e., it is guided by subjective intentions. Third, and perhaps most importantly for Parsons, persons act within and with reference to a "symbolic milieu"—the human universe of ideas, values, and norms. Voluntarism establishes this realm as not of mere epiphenomena (i.e., as not reducible to conditions), but of causal significance in human action. As Scott (1963) suggests: "In the prewar versions of the scheme, voluntarism was more than a polemic against what Parsons called 'positivism;' it was also an argument for the causal efficacy of valuation" (Scott, 1963:716). There is little doubt that Scott is correct. Parsons seeks to establish,

---

[16]It must be noted that some analyses of Parsons' work, e.g., that of John Finley Scott (1963), purport to show that Parsons deserted his earlier positions. The analysis here is based on the view that there is consistency between the earlier stages of Parsons' work and later Functional Theory—the earlier stages providing continuing foundation for the developing theory.

[17]There is a good deal of concern, particularly in Parsons' later work, for the role of conditions in *shaping* action. For example, the importance given to the functional problems represents such an interest. However, although the functional prerequisites exert influence on human conduct, they do not determine fully the character of the response to them. Action is still voluntaristic.

through the concept of voluntarism, the causal efficacy of values, norms, and ideas, and, hence, their importance in the determination of human conduct. At the same time, it is with respect to phenomena of this realm that the element of indeterminancy is introduced into the action scheme. This indeterminancy is an outcome of Parsons' unwillingness to suggest a completely determinant source of morality (norms and values) or ideas other than that which is the creation of human beings.

> Parsons also argued that a primordially creative element, independent of the natural world of "heredity and environment," was active in valuation and the choice of goals. (Scott, 1963:716)

It is with respect to this realm that human beings "make up" the human world, i.e., they are active creative agents in its construction. Hence, as Gouldner (1970) points out, there is no *science of the source of morality* in Parsons' work:

> It is precisely because moral norms serve, in effect, as *anti*-deterministic elements in Parsons' social theory, as determinism-*reducing* elements, that it is intrinsically difficult for Parsons systematically to address himself to the question of where moral norms themselves come from and on what they themselves depend. For, once this is confronted it becomes possible, in principle, to predict the *non*-normative conditions that give rise to norms; voluntarism would tend to break down in the direction of what Parsons calls a "utilitarian" social theory, in which moral forces are treated as manifestations of other real forces. Parsons wants to have his moral norms without paying the Positivist price of a deterministic universe. (Gouldner, 1970:192)

The question is, "How has this voluntaristic element carried over into Functional Theory?" First, the concept of social institution which is the focal point, the central organizing and explanatory concept of the works examined in this study, contains this voluntaristic element. Institutions emerge from two factors: (1) the conditions of action, and (2) cultural values, norms, and ideas. Neither of these factors is explicable in terms of the other. Importantly, values exist as an element independent of, and not reducible to, the conditions of action. In a general sense, the emergence of a social system is an outcome of a situation in which people face certain conditions, while oriented by a range of values and ideas.

> Action must always be thought of as involving a state of tension between two different orders of elements, the normative and the conditional. As process, action is, in fact, the process of alteration of the conditional elements in the direction of conformity with norms. Elimination of the normative aspect altogether eliminates the concept of action itself and leads to the radical positivistic position. Elimination of conditions, of the tension from that side, equally eliminates action and results in idealistic emanationism. Thus conditions may be conceived at one pole, ends and normative rules at the other, means and effort as the connecting links between them. (Parsons, 1937:732)

Both elements (ideal elements and conditions) are involved in the establishment of stabilized patterns of interaction, or a *pattern of institutions*, which comprises a social system. The character of an institutionalized system, then, is in part an outcome of an element which remains in principle indeterminant, namely, the element of cultural values. It is, of course, this concept of institutions which is central to the explanation and definition of deviance employed in Merton, Cohen, and Cloward and Ohlin, and which Parsons argues emerged in Durkheim's work.

The nature of institutions, as partially rooted in the indeterminant element, culture, does not deny order in human affairs nor preclude the application of scientific theory to the sphere of human action. Although human beings create moral values, this process and its outcome are not haphazard or senseless. In fact, culture tends toward a logically determinant order. Furthermore, the result of the institutionalization of cultural elements, i.e., bringing them to an action level, leads to problems of integration among such elements. This raises a whole set of problems concerning the relation among elements that can certainly be treated scientifically. Also, once values are given and institutionalized, they may be viewed as determinants of action. They come into play, that is, in the formation of human purpose and subjective intentions. As the preceding section indicates, the symbolic realm acts as a cause of action.

(a) Institutions and the Emergence of Culture

While Parsons does not view the emergence of norms and values as solely an outcome of determinant forces, he takes the position that it is possible to discuss their source. Furthermore, this problem can be approached without positing some supernatural explanation or reducing the explanation of the source to the conditions of action. A central part of the scheme which seems to be overlooked by many critics of Parsons, and of Functionalism in general, is that the institutionalized normative structure (itself a symbolic element derived from culture) is implicated in action in such a way as to be a factor in the emergence of cultural innovation. Notice that Gouldner's position, expressed above, suggests that, if Parsons turns systematically to the problem of the source of morality, he is forced to formulate his explanation in terms of the conditions of action. Or, as Scott (1971) puts it, in stating a position with which Gouldner is in agreement:

> While a wide variety of hypotheses about social behavior may be expressed in terms of this [Parsonian] "action scheme," one that cannot be expressed is the hypothesis that normative elements have natural causes which sociology, or any other science, can study. Such causes turn out to be part of the "means and conditions" of action, by which normative elements cannot be explained *a priori*. (Scott, 1971:9)

The point that these critics miss is that the scientific--in this instance, the sociological--explanation of normative elements need not involve a reduction to the conditions of action. Parsons' major emphasis is *not* that the ideal level is in principal indeterminant, but that there is an emergent symbolic level which has a dynamic *of its own*. The character of this level is not, as Scott suggests, such that it is simply employed as an independent variable, one which cannot itself be explained--quite the contrary. Elements of culture, once institutionalized, are the focus of the Functionalists' explanation of cultural innovation. The core of the theory of deviance involves just such a mode of explanation. This theory involves an examination of the role of the institutional structure of society, itself derived partially from the indeterminant element (culture), in the emergence of new cultural patterns. This mode of explanation is most clear in Cohen's general theory of subcultures (1955, Chapter 3). The primary element of explanation involves the social structure as an element of the situation within which the interaction (which eventuates in the *creation* of a new cultural pattern) takes place.

It should be noted that the sense in which the social structure *conditions* action most certainly does not involve a reduction of social structure *to* the "conditions of action" such as *heredity* and *environment*. The social structural arrangements to which these theorists direct are not viewed as epiphenomena, but are seen as the primary causal source of new patterns of culture from which new institutions may ultimately be fashioned. However, pointing to a factor which influences the emergence of cultural patterns does not imply that a particular innovation is a necessary outcome of those factors. The cultural innovation which emerges may still be indeterminant. That is, in reaction to the same set of conditions (including social structure--here understood as a condition), human beings may create any number of possible cultural responses; no response can be completely accounted for in terms of circumstance. In Cohen's *Delinquent Boys*, the subculture of delinquency, although a plausible response to the circumstances, need not be seen as the only possible response of youths placed in such a situation. Hence, the principle of indeterminancy is not precluded.

(b) The Logical Closure of Systematic Theory

It is suggested above that the Parsonian action scheme contains an indeterminant element and that this element carries over into the Functionalist matrix. This element, central to the approach, is the realm of values, norms, and ideas. The inclusion of this realm, as Devereux (1961:20) points out, leads to the implication "that human action systems can never become empirically closed." While this is the case, Parsons does not deny the applicability of scientific theory to the sphere of human conduct. However, scientific theoretical systems, unlike the empirical systems to which they refer, tend toward logical closure (as do other elements of culture), i.e., they are logically determinant:

> Not only do theoretical propositions stand in logical interrelations to each other so that they may be said to constitute "systems" but it is in the nature of the case that theoretical systems should attempt to become "logically closed." (Parsons, 1937:9)

Hence, Parsons' theoretical system is closed and determinant as are the substantive theories of deviance associated with Etiological Functionalism. This is the nature of theory. However, it is recognized that to assume that there is closure in the empirical system is fallacious--to do so is to commit the fallacy of misplaced concreteness. The theoretical system may not take into account the interpenetration of empirical

161

systems or, as in the case of the human action system, it may not take into account that the empirical system itself is open and indeterminant.

The development of "logically determinant theory" is not viewed by Parsons as a simple choice among heuristic principles. Rather, it is a condition of the process of developing empirically verifiable knowledge.

> . . . all empirically verifiable knowledge--even the common-sense knowledge of everyday life--involves implicitly, if not explicitly, systematic theory in this sense. The importance of this statement lies in the fact that certain persons who write on social subjects vehemently deny it. They say they state merely facts and let them "speak for themselves." But the fact that a person denies that he is theorizing is no reason for taking him at his word and failing to investigate what implicit theory is involved in his statements. This is important since "empiricism" in this sense has been a very common methodological position in the social sciences. (Parsons, 1937:10)

It is clear that the voluntaristic element remains salient in Functional Theory. However, its viability is limited and its salience is obscured by a number of factors: (1) the logically determinant nature of scientific theory, (2) the central role of the concept of institutions which assumes the existence of cultural values, and (3) the role of institutions in the emergence of cultural innovation. These factors may easily lead one to conclude that such innovations are determinant outcomes of certain institutional processes.

E. Socio-Political Value Commitments and Value Implications

1. Interactionist Theory

Labeling Theorists, for the most part, are explicitly "leftish"[18] in terms of their socio-political commitments. With the possible exception of Lemert, all express a commitment to subordinate ethnic and economic groups and suggest the necessity of changing social practices. Even Lemert's work has somewhat critical overtones in that he implicitly emphasizes the importance of power differentials, as well as focusing on the role that social-control agencies play in the stabilization of deviant behavior. This "leftish" cast within the Labeling matrix is rooted in at least three basic characteristics of the perspective. First, there is the Labelists' tendency to view the world from the vantage point of the person who (or whose action) is called deviant. Second, the theory contains an explicit critique of the agencies of social control. And third, great emphasis is placed on the role of power differentials in the construction and application of deviant labels.

---

[18]"Leftish" is employed here rather than "leftist," since the degree to which their commitment bears to the left varies among members of the matrix. The term "leftist" is reserved for those expressing explicitly Marxian commitments.

The first of these elements of orientation, taking the subordinate world-view seriously, has, at best, mildly critical implications for social practice. It involves not only "telling the story" from the point of view of subordinate members of society but, in so doing, challenging the validity of the ideology of the established powers. The established powers have a somewhat different, and better publicized, definition of the situation than those they apprehend, punish, or treat. Becker, who is only somewhat "leftish," has characterized this penchant of the Labelists as "unconventional sentimentality." The unconventional sentimentalist "assumes . . . that the underdog is always right and those in authority [are] always wrong" (Becker, 1967:5). John Lofland describes unconventional sentimentalists as those with "a disposition to assume that normals are less moral than typically portrayed and . . . that deviants are considerably more moral than is commonly thought" (Lofland, 1969:8). Unconventional sentiment is recognized by Becker and others within the matrix as a value bias, but it is a bias to which they are generally committed. Lofland further illustrates the attitudes of many Labelists, including Becker, in this remark:

> Let me say, nonetheless, that I continue to share somewhat in the unconventionally sentimental bias. What has been done in the past and is done today to those humans classified as deviant (and even to those classified as normal) is in many respects a crime against humanity. Indeed, if throughout what follows, I appear somewhat less friendly toward normals than toward some sorts of deviants, it is because I am. (Lofland, 1969:12)

Although regarded as a bias, the "unconventional" commitment is regarded as no more severe a bias than the obverse one which characterizes other sociologies; in fact, it is seen as a legitimate balance for them. Labelists regard most other sociologists of deviance as conventionally sentimental, i.e., as inclined to accept the authorities' definitions without serious question. The notion of the types of sentiment has developed as a partial challenge to the Functionalist commitment to "value neutrality" (which will be examined in the next section). Becker argues that sociologists cannot escape "telling the tale" from one point of view or the other. The issue, therefore, is not whether or not to be neutral, but, rather, whose side we are on.[19] The necessity of "declaring sides" derives from the fundamental tenets of Interactionist Theory. The focus of this theory is upon the actor's apprehension of the world which is seen as guiding his action. The basic problem is to decipher the "act," "project," or "world-view" of the actor. The result is "taking the role" and, hence, the point of view of the actor. In these terms, "Whose side are we on?" (Becker, 1967) is certainly a relevant question, particularly with regard to the confrontation between the alleged deviant and his labeler(s).

---

[19] Becker is not rejecting the fact-value dichotomy here, but, less fundamentally, suggests that the sociologist should be aware of a value bias in his work that cannot be escaped. See "Whose Side Are We On?" (1967).

This claim to unconventional sentiment can hardly be described as a radical critique of the existing order. As Gouldner (1968) points out, it can only amount to a critique of minor functionaries and subsidiary agencies:

> Becker's argument is essentially a critique of the caretaking organizations, and in particular of the *low level* officialdom that manages them. It is not a critique of the social institutions that engender suffering or of the high level officialdom that shapes the character of caretaking establishments. (Gouldner, 1968:107)

Although the critique may extend upward through the lines of bureaucracy to more important figures, it essentially reflects a reformist, rather than a revolutionary, challenge to the existing order. Again, this is rooted in the very nature of the Interactionist approach.

Interactionism focuses upon the immediate, micro-interactive situation. It does not focus upon the macro-institutional world. Indeed, it explicitly denies the existence of such a world. Gouldner (1968) notes this focus and its limitations, although he does not make much of it. Instead, he advances his "sociology of the sociological career" explanation of the value direction in Becker's work. He does state, however, that Becker:

> . . . is committed to a kind of interpersonal social psychology which, with all its humanistic merits, fails to see that men— superiors as well as subordinates--may be powerfully constrained by institutions, by history, and indeed by biology. (Gouldner, 1968:111)

The second "leftish" feature of Labeling is grounded within the *implicit* critique of agencies of social control. The focus is *not* on "the story" of the officials (i.e., not on their intentions and what they say they do), but upon the often latent and negative consequences of their actions. The reference is usually to the police and to medical personnel and allied professionals (e.g., psychiatrists and social workers) and to the personnel of judicial agencies (e.g., probation and parole officers, lawyers, judges, etc.). It is this exposition by the Labeling Theorists of the consequences of practice within the agencies of social control--i.e., the construction of deviance, the "creating" of deviants, and the resultant destruction of human beings--which is the foundation of their claim to a radical critique.

It should be noted that this focus on social-control agencies leads to a "theoretical bind" for Labeling Theorists. The existence of institutional relations is never brought to bear on the explanation of the emergence or definition of acts called "deviant." However, when the focus is on control agencies, institutional arrangements implicitly take on an independent, causal form. The way of life within the agency is depicted as patterned, as guided by a set of commitments to agency norms. But this tacit appropriation of explanation in terms of normatively governed action is never explicitly articulated within the matrix. To take such a step would, indeed, open up an institutional "Pandora's Box" and transform basic aspects of the approach. However, as a result of the refusal to take this conceptual step, the Labelists are left with a critique of the practices of minor functionaries, who are exposed as generating precisely what they do not willingly seek--the production, maintenance, entrenchment, and amplification of deviance.

Nevertheless, an incipient stage of a radical critique of society, although it does not include the element of institutions, does emerge at this level, and it is the most important basis for the claim of radicalness. In order to explain how the officials "do what they do," there is, at the heart of the perspective, a focus upon differentials in the holding of power. Becker remarks:

> . . . the interactionist approach shows sociologists that a major element in every aspect of the drama of deviance is the imposition of definitions--of situations, acts, and people--by those powerful enough or sufficiently legitimated to be able to do so. (Becker, 1973:207)

This focus on power differentials operates throughout the perspective, and its *critical* importance cannot be denied. However, just as Interactionists do not acknowledge the existence of institutional life, neither do they explicitly acknowledge the existence of a structure of power. Hence, there is an emphasis on the importance of negotiation in the immediate, interactive milieu. It is as if the crucial struggle between the accused and the official occurs in the situation itself. The distribution of social power appears to be almost random at most points in Interactionist thought (i.e., in Lemert, Becker, Scheff, in the early work of Quinney, and, to some degree, in Matza).

This view of power as randomly distributed also bears upon another phase of the approach. Aside from the role of officials in the creation of deviance, there is the important role of the sponsors of the law, i.e., the role played by Becker's moral entrepreneurs. At this level of the theory, it seems as if the lawmaker emerges and accumulates power from virtually anywhere and everywhere. The distribution of power which lies at the basis of the formulation of law appears to be haphazard. It is the result, as in the case of the "negotiation session," of individual effort and struggle. In both cases (of law and of identity), the evidence and force is mustered in the immediate, interactive context. This view of power (the Labelists'), of course, does not lend itself to a radical criticism of the character of social relations.

The Interactionist perspective's "Leftist" pretensions become much more realistic only when the view of power as structured, organized, and concentrated develops. This occurs primarily in the work of Matza (*Becoming Deviant*), whose critique begins to appear radical in his consideration of the role of the organized and systematic power of The State itself. Matza explicitly seeks to correct the view which misapprehends the relation between crime and The State; i.e., the view of The State as the pursuer and destroyer of "evil." That is, he wishes to correct the view of The State which sees it as "correctional."

> Left unassaulted, the historic misconception of the positive school--the separation of crime and the state--could remain the cornerstone of a sociological study of deviation that heeded the possibility that the correctional system's effects sometimes

boomeranged. But as long as the misconception maintained, such a possibility could be regarded as easily rectified *instead of as a profound irony lodged in the very nature of the intimate relation between crime and the state* [emphasis added]. (Matza, 1969:144)

His focus on The State certainly takes the critique to the top of the power-sphere which has been the object of Interactionist analysis. However, even Matza does not say much about the sources of power, nor about how it is structured, if at all. The reluctance remains. Interactionist Theory simply does not lend itself to the development of a radical notion of patterned, institutionalized power--power which rests in certain hands, in certain positions, and with certain classes and is exercised in a highly organized and relatively stable manner. More than this, however, in Matza, the "power of power" is limited. The victim of The State is still somehow in control. He must "collaborate" with The State in its effort to control him, if The State is to succeed in the change in his identity to that of "deviant."

However awesome the state apparatus and however active its agents may be in affecting deviation, the same general principle developed in the discussion of affiliation will maintain here: the subject mediates the process of becoming. (Matza, 1969:145)

Matza's position is reminiscent of a recurring refrain of the rebellious victims of The State. Its prisoners submit, "They can have my body, but not my mind." Really? This position is attractive, indeterminant, and leaves the individual free, i.e., "unreduced," "strong willed," even in the face of tyranny. At the same time, it diminishes the significance of the role of power. Within Interactionist thought, there is a strain between the attribution of control to the individual and the significance of power in relationships. In certain respects, the indeterminancy principle enhances the radical critique. It turns attention to those conditions under which persons may be liberated from the forces of coercive and corrupting power. On the other hand, to view man as still "free," even in the face of tyranny, ignores the devastating quality of power which makes the issue of in whose hands it rests of primary importance. Thus, the importance of the structure of power is diminished in Interactionist thought, as is the concept of institutions and their historicity, in favor of the indeterminancy principle. The Interactionist concept of power can never be truly radical, for the radical view holds that *power* determines outcomes. Being a person, unfortunately, does not in itself supply one with a viable basis of negotiation.

Matza gives his readers a critique of The State, yet he realizes the shortcomings of his analysis with respect to the development of a full-blown critique of social practice. The point of analysis that is missing in his work is the relation of The State to other important spheres of social life:[20] "'. . . I [Matza] decided that though *Delinquency and Drift* and

---

[20] Weiss interviewed Matza, and he received this response to a question. The interview is contained in *Issues in Criminology*, 6 (1) (Winter), 1971.

Becoming Deviant were defensible, each missed a key point--the relation between property and the state'" (Weiss, 1971:33). It is only in Quinney's work, and then in its later stages (1973), that a fully developed radical critique emerges in association with interactive analysis. And it emerges only when his work is tied in with a theoretical tradition which has focused upon the macro-structures which surround the micro-world of face-to-face interaction, specifically, the Marxian tradition. In *Critique of Legal Order* (1973), Quinney develops the relationship that Matza recognizes but fails to address. Quinney binds the "morality of The State" to the class structure, i.e., the institutional structure of property ownership and power in modern society. Quinney states:

> The state is . . . a political organization created out of force and coercion. The state is established by those who desire to protect their material basis and who have the power (because of material means) to maintain the state. . .

> Moreover, the legal system is an apparatus created to secure the interests of the dominant class . . . law is a tool of the ruling class. . . [Hence, T]he rates of crime in any state are an indication of the extent to which the ruling class, through its machinery of criminal law, must coerce the rest of the population, thereby preventing any threats to its ability to rule and possess. (Quinney, 1973:52)

Quinney continues by exposing the relationship of the personnel of the propertied classes to the mechanisms by which their hegemony is maintained (see Quinney, 1973: Chapters 2, 3, and 4). He focuses upon the agencies, boards, commissions, research councils, units of government, etc. by means of which the ruling class rationalizes, creates, and maintains its control over its apparatus--The State and The Law.

The solution to the "crime problem," from Quinney's view, then, is indeed radical. There is only one solution: the complete reconstitution of property relations. The task involves the destruction of Capitalist society, the Capitalist State, and property as therein conceived. The end of "property" will eliminate the basis of segmentation and diverse interest in society. Thereby, the basis from which legal order (Law) and crime emerge will be destroyed.

Although Interactionist Theory is "leftish" throughout, it does not lead to radical value implications until it is brought into a Marxian framework. It is only then that the theory as transformed can be employed to analyze macro-structural relations and face-to-face interactions as taking place within those macro-structures.

2. Values and Functional Theory

There are three major themes that will be discussed in this section: (1) the Functionalist commitment to value neutrality, (2) value implications of the Functional theory of deviance, and (3) an examination of why Functional Theory is considered conservative.

a. Value Neutrality [21]

Value neutrality is recognized by Functionalists as a political position, i.e., as a value position. It rests on two major bases, one of which is the maintenance of the Kantian distinction between judgments of value and judgments of facts. According to this view, ultimate value judgments (those which concern ends) cannot be derived in any sense from experience, i.e., from the observation of facts. Science is thus viewed as a highly limited mode of cognition--limited to nonevaluative questions concerning the existence of phenomena. The distinction between science and ideology is drawn along these lines. A scientific judgment concerns only the question of whether or not an empirical phenomenon exists and what the specification of its relation is to other phenomena. Such a judgment does not carry the weight of evaluative commitment, i.e., it does not raise the issue of whether or not the phenomenon *ought* to exist. Insofar as the actor's judgment involves commitment, in this sense of evaluation, it is ideological. Hence, science does not provide a basis of commitment to action (cf. Parsons, 1951: Chapter 8).

The second basis of the value-neutral position does not raise philosophical problems, as does the first, but, rather, political issues. It refers to the question of what the role of the scientist should be. The dominant view within Functionalism suggests that the scientist should be primarily oriented to a particular societal "sub-value" system. Parsons, commenting on Weber's position, provides the following analysis:

> It is not an advocacy that the social scientist abstain from all value-commitments. . . The point is rather that *in his role* as scientist a particular subvalue system must be paramount for the investigator, that in which conceptual clarity, consistency and generality on the one hand, empirical accuracy and verifiability on the other are the valued outputs of the process of investigation. . . Value-freedom I thus interpret as freedom to pursue the values of science within the relevant limits, without their being overridden by values either contradictory to or irrelevant to those of scientific investigation. At the same time it involved the renunciation of any claims that the scientist *qua* scientist speaks for a value-position, on a broader basis of social or cultural significance than that of his science. (Parsons, 1971:33)

In short, the value complex associated with science is seen as paramount in orienting the scientist in his scientific role. Hence, with respect to issues, other than those governing science itself, the scientist qua scientist is value neutral.

Still, the value-neutral position adopted by the Functionalists does not ignore the important role of values underpinning scientific activity. Indeed, it would be strange if Functionalists, who see values as primary determinants of human conduct, were to ignore their role in the

---

[21] This section of the book was published, with modifications, in 1980, and was coauthored with R. E. Hilbert. See Wright and Hilbert (1980).

formulation of scientific concepts and scientific problems. But this is not the case. Values, outside the peculiar value constellation directly relevant to the doing of science, form the basis of the formulation of scientific concepts. The principle of "value relevance" underpins scientific method and conceptualization. With regard to scientific interest in the actions of human beings, Parsons remarks:[22]

> . . . our interest in them [actions] is directly determined by their relevance to the values which either the scientist himself shares or which are significant to him by agreement with his own values or conflict with them. It is this "relevance to value" (*Wertbeziehung*) which constitutes the selective organizing principle for the empirical material of the social sciences. (Parsons, 1937:592)

Further specifying that conceptual schemes are rooted in values, Parsons suggests:

> . . . by relevance to such [value] systems the same concrete materials will give rise not to one historical individual but to as many as there are, in this sense, points of view from which to study it. It is, in turn, in the process of analysis of the historical individual and comparison of it with others that general concepts are built up. It follows, then, that the process will not issue in one ultimately uniform system of general concepts but in as many systems as there are value points of view or others significant to knowledge. (Parsons, 1937:593)

This position does not blur the distinction between systems of cognition (e.g., science) and systems of evaluation (e.g., ethics). Nor is science seen as reducible to the realm of the subjective evaluative judgment.

> Value judgments (*Wertungen*) cannot claim the objective validity of science, and science must as a methodological ideal, be kept free from them. Even though a value element enters into the selection of the material of science, once this material is given it is possible to come to objectively valid conclusions about the causes and consequences of a given phenomenon free of value judgments. . . (Parsons, 1937:595)

Further, insofar as scientific interest progresses from its original starting point, the role of values in the selection of scientific problems and the formulation of scientific concepts may steadily recede. This recession may take place in favor of the directions which the theoretical system itself specifies as relevant.

It is possible then, from the Functionalist's point of view, to

---

[22]This remark is a summary of Weber's position with which Parsons is in substantial agreement. His major reservation regarding Weber's position is Weber's limiting these insights to the situation of the social sciences. Parsons finds the description equally applicable to the natural sciences.

distinguish fact and value from one another. Even though this is the case, Functionalists are aware of the intimate relation between values and the formulation of scientific concepts and theories. Nevertheless, with respect to the scientific role itself, they advocate that the scientist remain primarily oriented to the sub-value system of science itself, rather than participate, as a scientist, in political disputes.

b. Value Implications of Functional Theory

(1) Introduction: The Point of View

This section begins with the assumption that deviance is taken by most as undesirable, as a problem to be diminished. Given this assumption, to find the cause of "the problem" implies that when a "cause" is located, it should at least be evaluated and perhaps eradicated. Even if the source is found to be a fundamental part of a way of life (as in the Theory of Anomie), some might conclude that it must be altered or removed. This view of deviance as something that is undesirable and which should be eliminated is certainly not clearly built into the Functionalist perspective. Functional theorists do not, by and large, advocate solutions to the "problem" of deviance. Most assuredly, the perspective is not correctional at the individual level, and Functionalists are not necessarily advocates of fundamental social change. Nevertheless, if one were to begin with the desire to reduce the level of deviance, one could discern within Functional Theory certain radical implications with respect to the structure of American society, if not all societies of the industrialized type. These potentially radical implications remain, even if specific Functional Theorists themselves are not advocates of radical change, since they see the "cure" as less acceptable than the "disease." A different value stance, in which deviance is regarded as so objectionable that its reduction is worth making significant alterations in the "American way of life," can lead to radical conclusions (e.g., the advocacy of equality in the distribution of wealth).

As pointed out in Chapter II, the core concept of Functional Theory is that of institution. Consistent with this, the source of deviance within each of the Functional theories examined in this work is a social structural element or a constellation of such elements. The substantive theories of Functionalism, drawn here from applications to the American society, each implicate institutions which are intrinsic to advanced industrialized societies. Each of these theories focuses upon the role of institutions in the generation of deviance from those institutions themselves, as well as from other institutions of the society. Viewing Merton's theory as containing the seeds of a radical critique of American society, Gouldner sees Anomie as:

> . . . the unanticipated outcome of social institutions that thwarted men in their effort to acquire the very goods and values that these same institutions had encouraged them to pursue. In its openness to the internal contradictions of capitalist *culture* few Lukacians have been more incisive. (Gouldner, 1973:xi)

This statement should not be limited only to Merton's work but should include all of the Functional Theorists examined here (even, to some extent, Durkheim and Parsons) who have pointed to the same type of "internal contradiction." At the basis of all Functional theories of deviance is the command, accepted by the actor, to conform to an institutional expectation. It is the *acceptance* of this demand to conform that provokes his deviance. Hence, at the basis of the theory is the internal contradiction--a dialectical relation, in that societal institutions provoke their antithesis in the form of departures from, and attacks upon, themselves.

In the substantive theories of deviance spawned from this perspective, it is the intrinsic aspects of the American way of life--those that are cherished, core aspects of that way of life--that are found to be the root of the problem. Thus Cohen is concerned that the "evil-causes-evil fallacy" does not obscure the explanation of the source of deviance. It is not those things which are abhorred about the American way of life-- broken homes, alcoholism, negligent parents, and other "evils"--which spawn "the problem." Rather, it is those things which are cherished.

> People are prone to assume that those things which we define as evil and those which we define as good have their origins in separate and distinct features of our society. Evil flows from poisoned wells; good flows from pure and crystal fountains. The same source cannot feed both. Our view is different. It holds that *those values which are at the core of "The American way of life*," which help to motivate the behavior *which we esteem as "typically American*," *are among the major determinants of that which we stigmatize as "pathological"* [emphasis added]. (Cohen, 1955:137)

(2) The Indicted Institutions

Turning attention to the institutional sources of the pressures toward deviance, an assessment may be made of implications for change which the problem of deviance raises for American society. In the work of Merton and Cloward and Ohlin, the origin of the pressure toward deviance is found first and foremost in the diffuse institutionalization of overarching success goals. Even if there were no class structure (i.e., even if there were equality of opportunity), persons within American society, because of the institutionalization of great stress upon the goals relative to the stress upon the means, might be motivated to deviate in the face of any obstacle, whether the obstacle were socially structured or not. Faced with a choice between adherence to the means or the goals, the "normally socialized" American actor is likely to opt to efficiently pursue goals even at expense of adherence to the legitimate means, rather than vice versa. The strength of the institutionalized goal structure of American society is sufficient to account for high rates of deviation throughout the class structure (i.e., all the way from the lower class through the higher class). Anomie is brought about by a powerful but "de-regulative" institution. The strength of this institution is the source of the "overweening ambition" which characterizes the orientation of persons in American society. Merton's critique is, of course, more extensive than this, for the second fact of American life upon which he focuses is the *structured* "inequality of opportunity." It is this second

171

source of deviance which both Merton's followers and his critics have focused upon. This is consistent with Merton's emphasis and is to be expected for two reasons. First, Merton's major objective was the explanation of the differential rates of deviance, not cross-culturally, but within the American class structure. Consistent with official statistics, he began with the assumption that deviance was concentrated in the lower classes. It was this fact which he sought to explain, and the variable in this instance is the level of legitimate opportunity. Perhaps it is Merton's liberal predilections which lead him to place his emphasis here. In fact, it can be suggested that it is Merton's liberalism, which he shares with a great many other American sociologists, which leads his critique of American society to focus upon the opportunity structure as being the primary source of deviation. Merton's mostly liberal sociological readers, as well as his radical critics have, perhaps a little short sightedly, focused here. Liberals find the indictment of inequality of opportunity consistent with their ideology. Merton's focus upon the "acquisitive impulse," itself, goes against the deeply ingrained American ideology (which Liberals share) which finds favor with acquisitiveness. To do this--to focus upon the "acquisitive impulse"--is to go to the real root of the problem and to capture the truly radical implications of Merton's thesis.

The liberal solution to the "Mertonian problem"--the problem of the "equalization of economic opportunity"--usually takes the form of the advocacy of meritocracy, i.e., the advocacy of the end of particularistic and ascriptive bases of the allocation of social rewards. It has been suggested that Merton himself proposes this type of solution. Taylor (1973) comments:

> Merton in his later more policy-oriented work would solve the problem of anomie by two strategies: first, success must be based upon merit and second (in order to implement this) there must be ample opportunities. But this assumes that there is a consensual criterion of merit and that the central dictum should be 'from those according to their merit to each according to his merit. . .' (Taylor, et al., 1973:103-104)

Whether or not Merton believed that a complete meritocracy could be structured within an industrial society, much less a capitalistic one, is unclear. What does seem clear is that a higher level of institutionalization of achievement criteria would not decrease the problem to which Cohen (1955) refers; rather, it would increase it. As was established in Chapter III, for Cohen the disabilities faced by the working-class child are the result of a pattern of socialization, the form and content of which is dictated by working-class values. If, as Cohen suggests, these values are adaptive for persons in the lower reaches of the class structure, then they are likely to remain with us as long as there is inequality in the distribution of rewards. The implication of Cohen's position seems clear: meritocracy will, if anything, aggravate the problem faced by the lower-class child. This implication will be examined later.

The liberal-reform solution here takes the form of the advocacy of a more efficient transmission of "Protestant-bourgeois" culture to the lower classes. The suggested mode of such transmission is usually such

172

ameliorative programs as "Head Start" and other welfare-state proposals designed to intervene in the transmission of the "culture of poverty." The result of these programs, as Cloward and Ohlin (1960: Chapter 8) point out, has been, at best, the destruction of the integration of slum communities, resulting in the weakening of the "illegitimate opportunity" structure. These structures of slum communities had provided not only "illegitimate opportunity" (which provided investment capital and political power), but had opened up legitimate economic opportunities as well. The effect of such "illegitimate opportunity" was not only the provision of a route of upward mobility, but also the reduction of indiscriminate violence (conflict delinquency). Ironically, the overall effect of the "ameliorative" welfare-state programs has been to destroy many of the mechanisms by which persons escaped their fate in slum communities.

In the case of the theories of Merton and Cloward and Ohlin, the origin of the pressure toward deviance is found first in "overweening" emphasis upon the overarching and widely diffused success goals instituted throughout the class structure of society. If a more endemic and characteristic feature of American social organization can be imagined, then it must be Cohen's emphasis, which finds the source of deviance in the American (and, more generally, Occidental) industrial achievement motif. In short, Merton, Cohen, and Cloward and Ohlin focus upon two *related* and essential features of the American way of life as the primary sources of deviance: (1) the widely diffused acquisitive impulse and (2) the bureaucratic ethos. Both of these, of course, have been exposed by Weber (1958) as associated with Capitalism and industry. Cohen finds in his "middle-class ethos" the locus of the problem: "These norms are, in effect, a tempered version of the Protestant ethic which has played such an important part in the shaping of American character and American society" (Cohen, 1955:87). It is, then, among the central features of modern industrial society that these theories locate the source of deviance. If the source is to be destroyed, these societies must be fundamentally reordered.

It may be suggested, then, that Functional Theory does not necessarily support the advocacy of "tinkering around" with society as a solution to the problems toward which it directs, as its liberal creators and proponents and its radical critics would have it. Its implications are, indeed, either more radical or, given a certain pessimism, more conservative than the advocacy of such "tinkering around" would indicate.

The "solutions" to the problem of deviance, given the location of its source at the core of American society, will be more thoroughly examined in the next section in which the reason for Functional Theory's so often being taken as conservative will also be considered.

c. Functional Theory's Conservative Pessimism

(1) The Consensual Starting Point

Functional Theory focuses upon institutions as the source of deviance and specifically implicates those institutions which are at the core of industrial life. Since most people take high rates of deviance to be undesirable, it would appear that the analysis of the Functionalists might have implications for radical social change. Indeed, it does. However,

Functionalism is usually taken to be a conservative doctrine: a defense, rather than a critique, of the existing institutional system. The task undertaken here is not to review all of the reasons why the general theory is viewed as a defense of the status quo. Rather, the focus is upon the implied solutions to the problem of deviance and upon the prime question, "Why, in light of the radical social changes which Functionalism implies, is this theory of deviance viewed as conservative?"

The first component of the radical's critique of Functionalism is of the theory's *analytical* starting point--the consensual group. Functionalism begins with consensus and then asks, "How does diversity, innovation, or deviance emerge?" From the start, then, it looks to those features of social life over which there is consensus and, hence, reciprocity and co-ordination--those features over which there is not *opposition*. It appears to set up a harmony of social interest and value. It is within this harmony that its theoretical problems, including the emergence of disharmony and deviance, are found. Deviance is something which takes place within an established consensus and violates it. Functional Theory does not focus at the outset on situations which involve the conflict of basic interests and values. The heuristic assumption of consensus is the analytical starting point--not segmentation, not *power differentials*, not oppression or subjugation (in Quinney's terms). But human relations are at times understood as characterized by such segmentation; groups are found in fundamental conflict with one another. For Functionalism, however, such conflicts are definitively outside "societal" life. Fundamental conflict (war) is "asocial life." It is only insofar as consensual elements exist that society exists. The absence of consensus is the absence of Functionalism's object of investigation, "social life." The "social" is the jointly held (i.e., collective) belief, value, or norm. Functionalism is concerned with how consensus is established. However, this is the limit of its concern with conflict--how, hypothetically, consensus emerges from it. It is further concerned with how this consensus breaks down, and how it might be re-established. But, by beginning with consensus as its focal point, Functionalism has systematically excluded certain politically relevant problems (e.g., the problems of war, colonization, disarticulated slave-master relationships, and, more generally, the problems of super- and sub-ordination, insofar as they involve power, rather than legitimacy, consensus, and, hence, authority). As a result, the study of crime has been brought within the framework of the Functionalist's consensual concept of deviance. The possibility that the explanation of crime has less to do with consensus than it has to do with oppression and colonization is systematically precluded within this perspective. The explanation of crime in the terms of oppression and conquest would take one completely outside the conceptual equipment and fundamental assumptions of the perspective. Such an explanation (perhaps focusing upon the clash between opposing consensual groups) would lead into the arena of fundamental disconsensus, to relations between aliens, to conflict outside the frame of institutional life, to "power" rather than to "authority," to basic disagreements of interest and value. Radical conflict, then, as opposed to institutional conflict, is outside the Functionalists' perspective. But it is with regard to radical conflict and segmentation, struggles for power, and the seeking of change that radical proposals most often

174

emerge. Radicalism, as political doctrine, comes from opposition. Functionalism's definitive focus is upon consensus. It is, therefore, not likely to "come off" as radical, except unintentionally.

(2) The Systemic Organization of Theory

A second factor, one of primary importance in the assessment of Functionalism's conservative character, is its systemic, "holistic" character. To say that Functional analysis is systemic is to say that it posits the existence of a relationship between social and cultural items such that they influence one another in fundamental ways. When relations are systemic, any change in one component will have consequences for the rest of the system, i.e., a change in one social item sets up pressures for adjustment, or even more fundamental change, in the remaining units of the system. Hence, any alterations in society may have far-reaching consequences, beyond one's desire or one's ability to foresee. Such a "realization" may, in itself, lead to some caution in the advocacy of social change.

Before continuing with various proposed solutions to the problems posed by Functional Theory--and keeping in mind the systemic nature of the theory--it would be useful to consider what Functionalists say about the positive functions of the widespread diffusion of success goals, which are at the source of the problem of deviant behavior. According to Functionalist Theory, these goals are so important that they can be eliminated only at great cost to the society. What functional role does such cross-class diffusion play in industrialized society? As Cloward and Ohlin posed the issue:

> A crucial problem in the industrial world . . . is to locate and train the most talented persons in every generation, irrespective of the vicissitudes of birth, to occupy technical work roles. Whether he is born into wealth or poverty, each individual, depending upon his ability and diligence, must be encouraged to find his "natural level" in the social order. This problem is one of tremendous proportions. Since we cannot know in advance who can best fulfill the requirements of various occupational roles, *the matter is presumably settled through the process of competition.* But how can men throughout the social order be motivated to participate in this competition. . . It is not enough for a few to make the race; *all must be motivated to strive, so that the most able and talented will be the victors in the competitive struggle for higher status* [emphasis added].
>
> One of the ways in which industrial society attempts to solve this problem is by *defining success-goals as potentially accessible to all,* regardless of race, creed, or socioeconomic position [emphasis added]. Great social rewards, it is said . . . are available to anyone, however lowly his origins. . . The industrial society, in short, emphasizes *common* or universal success-goals as a way of ensuring its survival. (Cloward and Ohlin, 1960:81-82)

A crucial function is then performed in industrialized society by the diffusion of "lofty goals" throughout the class structure. Both the

175

talented and the not so talented are motivated to perform by the promise of wealth, status, and power. Theoretically, then, persons are motivated to perform and to get into the "race" regardless of their class origins. In order to bring about the necessary motivational level, it is essential that people be made to believe that they have a realistic opportunity to succeed. That is, at least the appearance of equality of opportunity must exist. Persons in the lower reaches of society must believe that they, too, have a chance. Combined with this diffusion of goals, there is a "democratic-ethos" which states that everyone has an equal chance and, furthermore, that everyone is morally obliged to try to succeed. But, as the Functionalist Theory of deviance also emphasizes, not everyone does have an equal chance. Thus, some are frustrated in the pursuit of goals which they are induced to want and encouraged to seek. As a result, among the affected sectors of the population, the deviant way of life emerges as an attractive solution to this frustration.

Given the crucial functions of the diffusion of goals and the democratic ideology within industrial society, what can be done to alleviate the problem of deviance?

(a) The Liberal Solution

The liberal solution, consistent with American ideology, is the actual "equalization of opportunity." As has been indicated, this solution involves the establishment of meritocracy. This solution, advocated as it is by some of the liberal proponents of Functional Theory, is not viable within that framework itself. Meritocracy is impossible, given two outstanding conditions which Functionalism finds inevitable in all societies. The first is inequality in the structure of rewards (see Davis and Moore, 1945; Parsons, 1940, 1953); the second, affectivity, particularism, and diffuse role-obligation within the family. Meritocracy does not imply the establishment of "equality," only the "equality of opportunity" to perform and, hence, a promise of rewards. To establish this equality of opportunity necessitates that universalistic-achievement criteria be the sole basis of evaluation which operates in the distribution of rewards in society. But in the family and related institutions, evaluation is particularistic and ascriptive. Further, because of the character and necessity of the socialization of the young, something like the family as we know it must persist. That is, a structure characterized by diffuse and affective, hence, particularistic and ascriptive, relations must operate in society in order to accomplish the functionally relevant tasks of the historic family. Second, institutions similarly characterized and highly valued, such as friendship, must carry on (like the family) not only socialization functions within their structure, but tension-management functions as well. Such institutional relations, although perhaps hard to come by in a budding meritocracy, would fill a crucial need for the management of anxiety generated by naked competition (see *The Rise of the Meritocracy*, Young, 1961). In short, functionally inevitable inequalities of power and wealth, combined with the persistence of the functionally necessary remnants of community (family, etc.), would prevent the establishment of meritocracy and true equality of opportunity. As long as some fathers have more power than other fathers, they will see to it that their children have advantages which they do not feel obliged to provide for other children, i.e., particularistic advantage will accrue to the offspring of the powerful. Lenski suggests that this tendency also operates in the Soviet Union:

> This relative lack of job security, however, has not prevented the Soviet managerial class from becoming semihereditary. Judging from available evidence, it appears that managers who remain in the good graces of the Party elite can secure for their children special educational advantages which, as elsewhere, pave the road to membership in the managerial class or one of the other privileged segments of Soviet society. Khrushchev himself stated that only a third of the students at the university level were children of peasants or workers in the 1950s. A recently expatriated Soviet student reports that "only a handful of students attending the prestige institutions come from families outside the intelligentsia," and that "the greater the prestige of a university or institute, the more 'elite' are those who attend it." Since the managerial class is counted among the *rukovodiashchie kadry*, or leading cadres, within the intelligentsia, it is safe to assume that its sons are well represented in the best universities and institutes. (Lenski, 1966:357)

It seems, then, that even in the Soviet Union, the various sectors of the elite cooperate in locating each others' children "properly" at the expense of children perhaps more meritorious but of less powerful parentage.

It should also be pointed out that even if meritocracy could be instituted, it would be no solution to the problem to which Cohen directs. In fact, it is, itself, the problem. A strict meritocratic regime would simply enhance the bind in which the lower- and working-class child is placed. If meritocratic standards were to become more pronounced and diffused than before, the child's situation would be made more difficult, as long as he or she is not equipped by early socialization to live up to such standards. The issue at this point again refers to the Functional Theory of stratification. As long as there are inequalities of power and wealth (which this theory finds inevitable), one may expect a "culture of deprivation" to emerge as an adjustive mechanism which "cools out" and "ameliorates" the condition of those who suffer the deprivation. There is no reason to believe that those socialized within this milieu and culture should be equipped to perform in terms of the remnants of the ascetic Protestantism of the dominant class. Deferred gratification makes no sense in a lower-class world with limited opportunity for upward mobility. From a number of vantage points within Functional Theory, liberal solutions to the problem of deviance appear to be a pipedream.

(b) The Socialist Solution

The Socialist solution includes the establishment of a system of social rewards based on the proposition, "From each according to his ability, to each according to his needs." This, of course, is to be accomplished through the abolition of privately owned, productive property. From the standpoint of the Marxian framework, such property is the basis of power differentials, authority relations, and alienation. Within the terms of Functional Theory, the feasibility of such a solution meets some of the same obstacles as does the Liberal solution, although for different reasons. Again, the Functional Theory of stratification enters as a conceptual obstacle within the Functionalists' envisionment of a successful Socialist regime. Of specific importance is the role of inequality in determining a person's level of motivation to perform. If there are no differentials in reward (if human beings are rewarded "ascriptively," solely on the basis of their humanity), persons will not be motivated to undergo the sacrifice required to translate talent into skill, nor will persons be motivated to perform the functionally important tasks of society, which often require dedication and sacrifice. Only the promise of future gratification can spawn such a commitment. As a result, the technically demanding occupational positions of advanced industry will not be rationally allocated, nor will persons be motivated to perform, once they are established in these positions.

Furthermore, there is another, equally fundamental objection within Functional Theory to the Socialist solution. Operating within the legacy of Max Weber, rather than Karl Marx, Functionalists do not find the existence of private ownership of productive property to be the source of modern alienation. The definitive quality of Capitalism is not individually owned capital, but, rather, the "rational calculation of cost and gain" and, more generally, the "rational cast of mind." Socialism, rather than being viewed as a major transformation of Capitalism, is, in fact, its logical extension. Socialism is but an enhanced version of Capitalism's basic motif--bureaucratic planning, centralization, and rationality. Insofar as Socialism is so regarded, the issue is again shifted to the problem to which Cohen directs attention. That is, if Socialism cannot meet its ideal—humanistic allocation of reward--but, rather, is meritocratic (as Weber would have it), then, like Liberalism, it simply exacerbates the problem of those children who are ill-equipped to meet the performance demands of a bureaucratic social order.

(c) The Conservative Solution

The third solution to the problem, which may be referred to as conservative, is to re-establish "castelike" relations among the various strata of the population. The object in this instance would be to reduce mobility aspirations, in short, to keep the lower class and/or caste "in its place." Reducing the aspirations of those not realistically in a position to succeed would have the effect of reducing frustration. In this case, the elimination of the malintegrated social structure to which Merton and Cloward and Ohlin refer would not be resolved by the equalization of opportunity but by the "stratification of aspirations." Further, with respect to the source of deviance to which Cohen refers, this solution would involve bringing to bear different performance demands upon variously located sectors of the population. It would again be possible to speak of "successful peasantry." In the modern American case, of course, the notion of a "successful lower-class person" is a contradiction in terms, except perhaps in some relatively isolated rural Black communities

where the most successful are, even there, only "nigger rich." [23]
This solution is at least as vulnerable as the other two examined above—the Liberal and the Socialist solutions. In this case, the functionally positive, societal-wide competition for high-status position would be destroyed, because not all would be permitted to enter the race. Therefore, the talented members of the population who are cut out of the competition would not be motivated to perform, and even if they were so motivated, they would not be given the opportunity to compete. Further, the not-so-talented children of the elite would be in a privileged position to assume occupational positions for which they were not necessarily competent. In short, persons would not be allocated to appropriate, functionally important tasks on the basis of their capacity to perform. Industrial society, then, characterized as it is by highly technical work roles, would not be assured of even a minimum level of competent performance from its personnel. The sons of physicists are, as often as not, notoriously incompetent when it comes to "filling Daddy's shoes," as are the sons of kings. Somehow, monarchies get along anyway. One doubts whether modern physics would (see Cloward and Ohlin, 1960: Chapter 4).

(d) Conclusion: Functionalism's Value Implications

It appears, then, that it is not precise to suggest that Functionalism is an inherently conservative doctrine. The conservative solution is no more viable than the others which have been mentioned. All of these solutions either fail to solve the problem, exacerbate it, or fail to provide a basis for meeting the needs of industrial society. Furthermore, it is not accurate to suggest that Functionalism is a defense of the status quo. It is the existing institutional framework which generates the problem. Nevertheless, it is true that the proponents of Functional Theory tend to accept the existing structure of American society. But if it is preferred over potential structural solutions to the problems it generates, it is perhaps acceptable only by default. Gouldner, it seems, best captures the mood of Functional Analysis, if not its political orientation:

> Objectivity is the way one comes to terms and makes peace with a world one does not like but will not oppose; it arises when one is detached from the status quo but reluctant to be identified with its critics, detached from the dominant map of social reality as well as from meaningful alternative maps. (Gouldner, 1970:103)

The Functional Theory of deviance contains a critique of existing social

---

[23]The concept of "nigger rich" operated mostly among the impoverished, Southern Black population of the United States and had a complex pattern of reference. It was directed toward those Black persons who had "made it" in the aspirational terms of the Black community, but who, it was recognized, had little wealth or influence when the point of reference was shifted to the American population at large. The concept contains both points of reference and exposes the American system of stratification.

179

practice. It does not fail to be critical, but it does fail to propose modifications in existing society. Rather than being a strictly conservative doctrine, then, this mode of thought appears to be deeply pessimistic. It describes Hell, but it provides "No Exit."

The Functionalists' pessimism appears to fall at least within the framework of much of the modern Capitalist versus Socialist debate. The advocates of each of these systems take modern consciousness and modern industry for granted and seek a solution within these confines. Functionalism sees no solution within these boundaries.

Perhaps the most pointed solutions proposed from the Socialist camp are those which involve a decentralized form of Socialist organization. Some of these solutions appears to question "industry" and "rationality" and look toward the establishment of a modified version of "community." It may be assumed that, within these proposals, individualistic competition and meritocratic evaluation would at least be tempered. At the same time, the cost of these solutions would involve a reduction in the emphasis upon technique and industry, as well as upon achievement itself. This type of shift, of course, must be recognized as expensive with respect to productive and administrative efficiency.

Furthermore, although many Socialists will "hear none of it," community involves the loss of modern consciousness, of cosmopolitanism, of relativism, and of whatever degree of "de-reification" of institutions emerges in modern society. Quinney's suggestion as to what form the "new order" should take, while attractive on the one hand, is frightening on the other:

> A contemporary experience that gives support to the possibility of community custom is the case of revolutionary Cuba. . . Neighborhoods in Cuba now have their own courts, staffed by personnel elected democratically from within the community. Little emphasis is placed on sanctions of any kind. Instead, violators continue to be educated in the community. Custom plays an educative role in the community, rather than a punitive one. What is important is maintaining peace and understanding in the community rather than enforcement of a legal system. (Quinney, 1973:191)

Quinney's preference for peace and harmony over disorder is clear. His critique of "legal order" is that it is not "order" at all, but "disorder." But Quinney has a penchant for order. He does not seem to realize that one viable measure of the "freedom" of a people may be how many police and soldiers it takes to control them. "Education," as opposed to "punishment" in his description, is reminiscent of the "therapeutic mind-control state," or the not so self-conscious, but more efficient "upright and uptight" community of "conformity," "order," and dulled consciousness. The cost of community may be too great. The cost may not only be the loss of technique, industry, and achievement, which are expendable, but also individual integrity and freedom, which are not. High rates of deviance may constitute disorder, but disorder may be the price one pays for whatever degree of freedom can be attained. Quinney is right—"legal disorder" is a substitute for "moral order." What is puzzling is his preference for order.

180

Quinney's view with respect to the nature of the "new community" suffers from more problems than this. But rather than elaborating further, suffice it to say that a moral community that is "non-punitive" in response to violation is not a moral community at all (see Durkheim, 1938).

3. Excursus and Conclusion: Sociology and Values

Neither of the theoretical programs considered in this work is strictly conservative in its political implications, nor does either develop an apology for existing social practices. At the same time, neither issues a highly developed, radical critique of existing society. Even Quinney's Conflict Theory exhibits the tendency of Interactionists to inadequately take into account the role of institutions. Interactionism thus fails to focus upon the ways in which the core features of industrial life pressure human beings out of their fundamental commitments.

Functionalism, on the other hand, does not give adequate attention to the power dimension in social life, to which Labeling Theory directs. Not only do the Functionalists ignore the possibility that "crime" may be an outcome of power differentials, but they also ignore the role of power in the historical development of institutions, i.e., the role of power in the process of institutionalization (a process to which they also do not devote sufficient attention). Within Functionalist thought, it is not recognized that some parties hold more sway than do others in the "joint" creation of institutions. They do not properly acknowledge that, in the emergence of institutions, the relevant social pattern may at first be a "rule" (a pattern to which only the dominant party is committed) *imposed* upon one party by another rather than a jointly created product (a norm), only becoming jointly held through a historical process of successful imposition. At the same time, Labeling Theorists do not properly acknowledge that once an institution is established, it may have a "life of its own" and, as such, independently act upon its producers (the rule makers), as well as upon those who originally resisted its invocation. It is as difficult for the Interactionists, even when linked to Marxian Theory, to recognize the nature and influence of institutions as it is for the Functionalists to give power its due. It is in this sense that Interactionist Theory diminishes the power of power. That is, Interactionists do not acknowledge the ability of powerful groups to get their way of life diffused throughout the society. Quinney does give fleeting and narrow attention to this process in his recognition of the "diffusion of criminal conceptions" from the highest to the lowest levels of society. Matza also briefly attends this when he notes that he who commits theft can be "taught" and come to "know" that he is a thief. However, the recognition of the theoretical significance of this process in the works of both of these scholars is hazy at best. Quinney does not see that in the very process of the diffusion of conceptions, the segmentation of which he speaks is broken down, and a consensus is, therefore, established. He does not recognize that, at the point of successful diffusion, a "moral order," rather than a "legal order," is in play. But to acknowledge this is to perhaps "give the game away"--to concede the possibility that the Functionalists' conception of deviance may be an appropriate

181

conceptualization of crime. The radical implications of Quinney's thought may, nevertheless, be preserved in the recognition of the role of power in the historical process of institutionalization. Institutions to which the subordinated have become committed through coercive power and influence may not be congruent with other values and interests that they hold or with their general situation in society. It is in this context that the concept of "false consciousness" becomes meaningful. These institutions are, after all, initiated out of the interest of those in another situation in society--those with privilege and power. What is congruent with the interests of the dominant groups in society should not be viewed as easily articulated with the situation of subordinate groups. But, dominance may be asserted so as to alter subordinate groups' commitments in such a way that those commitments become congruent with the morality of the powerful. If this is accomplished, relations between these groups become institutional relations, i.e., the relations are, in an important respect, "consensual." Nevertheless, as a result of institutions' emerging in this fashion, the level of "strain" to which the Functionalists direct would be most clearly felt within the subordinate sectors of the population. Hence, there would be an expectation of higher rates of crime and other forms of deviation within this population.

Both the role of institutions and the role of power must be addressed in order to reach a full understanding of the nature of criminality and other forms of deviance. Such an understanding requires a fuller appreciation of power in the history of not only the emergence of the law and criminal conceptions, but in the emergence of other institutions as well. A theory of deviance more general, and perhaps of greater value, than either Functionalism or Interactionism would draw from both and include a focus upon institutions and the role of super- and subordination in social life.

CHAPTER IX

SUMMARY AND CONCLUSIONS

A. Introduction

The foregoing analysis of the disciplinary matrices of both Functional Theory and Labeling Theory was carried out with the primary aim of delineating the conceptual core of these two approaches to deviance. This chapter will be a review of this analysis. Further, having nearly completed the examination, a basis has been established which will now allow a discussion of the degree of commensurability between these ways of thinking. The pursuit of science is often premised upon the idea that there is a progressive development from relative ignorance about an aspect of the world to a fuller comprehension of it. It is further assumed that the object of investigation remains relatively fixed, so that knowledge concerning it is permanently valid. That is, scientific knowledge is understood as a successively greater approximation of the character of phenomena. In short, the premise is that the development of scientific knowledge is nonrelative and cumulative. [1]

What has been and remains the primary problem addressed in this study is the comprehension of the phenomenon of deviance by sociologists. The sociological attempt to comprehend this phenomenon began in the work of Emile Durkheim. The line of thought Durkheim pursued was continued, in its essentials, by Merton, Parsons, and others. The premise outlined here is that these scientists share a matrix. However, another body of thought, also oriented around the term "deviance," emerged in

---

[1] By no means do all sociologists take this position with regard to knowledge of human conduct. For example, a careful reading of the Symbolic Interactionist position suggests that social scientific knowledge is not so progressive. However, this point is in dispute within the Labeling matrix. At the same time, the development of a paradigm in which the accumulation of knowledge could take place with regard to human conduct is an explicit aim of Parsons' work. Hence, the Functionalists do recognize the possibility of nonrelative, social scientific knowledge. However, this is not, in their view, an automatic development, but must be self-consciously pursued.

the nineteen-sixties. This approach was not so clearly rooted in Durkheim's thought. An important question is, does this more recent body of thought, in any sense, represent a *cumulative* addition to the knowledge about deviance formulated within the historically prior tradition? Some of the representatives of the more modern Labeling approach, although cautious in their claims, think it does.[2] From reading Edwin Schur (1971), the impression can be received that the Labeling matrix somehow emerged from previous sociologies, and that it could not have developed unless they preceded its emergence. It is almost as if Labeling Theorists "have stood on the shoulders of giants" in order to have seen so far. But if the analysis here is correct, the Labeling approach is not, in any clear sense, an elaboration of the earlier sociologies of deviance. Rather, in Kuhn's terms, it represents a gestalt switch. The new approach poses a different universe of entities and discourse. Thus, the suggestion that the modern approach to deviance is commensurate with what has gone before raises serious difficulties. The summary of the analysis contained in the previous chapters will indicate some of these difficulties.

B. Assumptions Concerning the Nature of Human Beings

In this brief restatement of the fundamental elements underpinning the approaches to deviance, the focus will be upon the root concepts of these two matrices: for Symbolic Interactionists, "the self;" for Functionalists, "institutions" and "institutionalization."

1. Labeling Theory

The importance of the human organism as viewed by Symbolic Interactionists is that the organism is capable of supporting a "self." The human being is defined as "an organism possessing a self" (Blumer, 1969:12). The importance of the self is found in its conjunction with *mind*. Mind is viewed as, in essence, communication. Possessed of self and mind, the human being can engage in reflective thought. Reflection takes place within the confines of the processes which make up the self. Possessed of the processes of language, communication, and self, the human being is capable not only of perceiving but of *conceiving* a world in his reflective thought. Further, this reflection consists of two essential attributes--the ability to attribute meaning to objects and to selectively attend to them. Through these processes, the human being is able to "shape the environment," which he then takes into account in reflecting upon himself and in formulating his projected "Acts." Hence, the environment is not "given" in the case of human action, but is, rather, *shaped through* human action. The human being, in activity "making up

---

[2]The most extensive, although perhaps not the most cautious, work establishing this claim is Edwin Schur's, *Labeling Deviant Behavior* (1971). Schur seeks to minimize the suggestion that Labeling Theory is a fundamental departure from earlier sociologies, particularly that of Functionalism.

184

the world," is supplying the constituents of his "projects" or "Acts." The project is his *intended* action. It is formed through conceptualizing the world and selectively attending it (processes that are rooted in the mind and self). Between the "stimulus" world of the organism and human action stand the interpretive processes of mind and self. As a result, human *action* is viewed as the bringing of the project or Act into the world. In so doing, of course, the act may be "compromised" by interference from the conditions presented in the world--conditions which may militate against its fulfillment. Nevertheless, the Act must be taken into account in assessing the course of human action.

The important point to be made in assessing the distinction between Symbolic Interactionism and Functionalism is that "meaning" (interpretation) and significance (attention), which play a part in formation of the Act, are not viewed by Symbolic Interactionists as being located in an agency outside the subject. Rather, meaning and significance are *idiosyncratic creations of the individual human being.* The social (i.e., society) is not viewed as an institutional world which is the source of individual conduct. Instead, it is an accomplished "joint act." The creation of the social necessitates successfully "taking the role of the other," i.e., coming to understand the meaning of his act. In short, the social depends upon a reciprocal and successful effort to understand the intentions of the other. Once this is accomplished, as an *outcome of interaction*, it is possible for the parties to the interaction-situation to "gear" their actions into one another, i.e., in order to produce the "social act" (Mead) or "joint act" (Blumer).

From the standpoint of Symbolic Interactionism, *society is an outcome of interaction, not an antecedent influence or the cause of it.* Institutions never cause the Act or explain action; rather, society *appears* only as an outcome of interaction. Accordingly, to view society as a cause of Acts or action is to reify that which is only an *apparent reality.* Since the Act is viewed as associated with the human being's capacity to construct his world independently of causal entities (organic, environmental, or social), *it cannot be explained except in its own terms.* That is, the Act and its outcome in the world--human action--can only be *described.* Thus, the Symbolic Interactionist view of the nature of a "human science" emerges as radically distinct from that of the sciences of nature. Harold Bershady (1973) has focused upon the characteristic elements of this type of view and some of its consequences. He states of these thinkers that they say that:

> Since human life . . . is "free," it cannot be apprehended by abstractions or regularities. Human life is concrete and particular. . . In the sense of freedom from law, human life is indetermined: "meaning" is a fundamental category. . . Since there can be no development within the cultural sciences, knowledge of human life is organic rather than progressive; it does not grow by accretion but shows discontinuous, logically unrelated shifts with each of the unique constellations of meaning which is apprehended. Hence the knowledge gathered by the cultural sciences is essentially changing and dynamic. (Bershady, 1973:34-35)

It should be emphasized that Symbolic Interactionism does not locate this constellation of meaning in any source outside the subject (e.g., *Geist,* culture, etc.), but within the actor's individually constructed Act. It is, in this sense, radically relativistic with regard to human action. At the same time, Interactionists are concerned with "joint action" as the outcome of successful role taking. This focus may lead to an interest in such things as "deviant subcultures," although the use of the concept of "culture" is without real significance. Meaning, within such situations, is not received by the actor from the culture. Such "cultures" are an apparent outcome of interaction, not determinants of meanings constituting the project or Act.

It should now be clear that from the Symbolic Interactionist view of the Act, social knowledge cannot be cumulative but rather is, as Bershady suggests, organic. However, there is a strain here with regard to Labeling Theory. Whereas the Labelists are, in general, radical relativists with regard to the deviant act (or, better, the perceived act which provokes response), they do propose general theoretical categories in an attempt to develop an explanation of deviance. Specifically, whereas they do not seek to *explain* the deviant act, they do seek to explain, not just to describe, the reaction to acts as deviant. Reaction itself, of course, is an act--an act which, within the Labeling matrix, is explained by the existence of active interests and power differentials. Hence, there is a fundamental inconsistency within the Labeling matrix. There is explanation which, as has been seen, takes a conflict mode. Although it is not until Quinney that explanation finally becomes self-conscious (and explicitly associated with Marxian theory), this explanation is built into the perspective from the beginning. What is strange is that the possibility of explaining "deviant" acts is avoided, while the reactive act is found to be eminently explicable. If reaction can be explained, why cannot the act which provokes it? In short, Labeling Theory is not consistent with regard to its methodological underpinnings. There is a lack of clarity as to its methodological standing vis-à-vis the natural sciences and other sociologies.

2. Functional Theory

The aspects of the human organism given emphasis in Functional Theory are the organism's sensitivity and plasticity. The organism is not viewed as sufficient to give rise to human conduct. Its nature, however, is such that it permits commitment to a widely variable range of conduct patterns. The emphasis of Functional Theory is upon the *social sources* of the direction of conduct. For Functionalists, as well as for Symbolic Interactionists, the source of conduct is not located in the nonhuman world. But, unlike the Interactionist view, in Functionalist thought, *a source* of the act *is located* (consistently) within a strictly human milieu. The source of the Act is related to two primary concepts--institutionalization and socialization. Rather than self-forging independent projects, Functionalists direct toward the stabilization of the outcomes of human interaction. Out of interaction emerges the institution (the social), but the institution is not a mere apparition. It is an objective reality which independently acts upon its producers in such a way as to become an agency of their conduct. Institutions are the products of interactions

186

that become shared and, hence, relatively stable patterns supported by a system of sanctions. It is in this fashion that they become determinants of conduct. Given organic plasticity and sensitivity, the human being can be formed in the terms of institutions. This is accomplished via the process of socialization and its outcome, the internalization of institutional forms (e.g., norms, values, and beliefs). The institutional patterns come to be constituents of the actor's personality. As such, they take the form of internalized "need-dispositions." The actor expends effort to "live up to the patterns" which he has internalized. Operating at this level, *institutions shape the actor's projects.*

Hence, Functionalism, while recognizing human interpretive capacity and the "release" of human beings from the organic-environmental milieu, places great importance on the products of collective life. These products constitute the social milieu which is not only an outcome of interaction but is a reality *sui-generis.* The product may independently act upon its producers *as an antecedent cause* of the direction of human acts. The individual actor's interpretations and attention are viewed as influenced by this societal milieu. What meaning the individual will assign to the objects of the stimulus world (as well as to the "objects" to which he orients which are beyond nature, e.g., gods, moral principles, etc.) is institutionally given. That is, whether the actor will assign to the body of a cow the meaning "potential steak" or "sacred and inedible" is not rooted in the nature of the cow (or any other feature of the organic-environmental world), but, rather, is a determined outcome of the institutionalized cultural pattern. In this sense, the institutionalized system of meaning is implicated as the source of his Act. The same may be said with respect to the individual's "attentional modifications." Whether the actor attends this or that aspect of the environment is not given in the organic-environmental world; it is directed by the institutionalized value patterns into which he has been socialized. The institutional system is a *meaning system*, but one which is, at least analytically, external to the individual. As such, it may be viewed as the source of the actor's projects and action.

The concept of institution, then, is fundamental to the development of a human science. It refers to a human but, nevertheless, causal milieu. The development of concepts which are sufficiently general to avoid the "pitfalls" of relativism is possible within this framework. Such concepts as norms, values, institutionalized beliefs, aesthetic standards, etc. are some which have been utilized. For the Functionalists, then, a science of human conduct, one which focuses upon the social determinants of that conduct, is feasible.

Functional Theory and Labeling Theory begin their analyses with fundamentally divergent views of the relationship of persons to the social. As a result, their conceptions of the nature of the human act radically diverge. Their modes of defining and doing "science," then, also require different assumptions and methods. These differences, of course, influence the theory of deviance which emerges from their respective views.

3. Deviance

As Kuhn suggests, that which fosters the perception of the switch from one gestalt to another is, at times, a focus on a narrow component of the image. In the case of these matrices, the switch is most readily induced by a focus on the concept of deviance itself. Kuhn remarks:

> Since new paradigms are born from old ones, they ordinarily incorporate much of the vocabulary and apparatus, both conceptual and manipulative, that the traditional paradigm had previously employed. . . Within the new paradigm, old terms, concepts, and experiments fall into new relationships one with the other. The inevitable result is what we must call, though the term is not quite right, a misunderstanding between the two competing schools. (Kuhn, 1970:149)

This present analysis has shown that the incorporation of the term "deviance" into the Labeling matrix involved a fundamental transformation in its meaning from the way in which it was used in the historically prior sociological paradigm. In the Functionalist matrix, the term is always associated with a violation of normative expectations by a "member of society." (For a discussion of "membership in society," see Chapter II.) It is further associated with a conceptual scheme which focuses on consensual components as the constituents of "society." (See Chapter II.) Hence, deviance is directly associated with the concepts of institutionalized norms and values, both of which are grounded in the assumption of a consensus. As has been discussed, this consensus extends to the deviant actor himself--an actor who has *internalized*, via socialization, the normative patterns which he violates. (See Chapter II for a discussion of internalization; see also Chapters III and IV on the Functionalist concept of deviance.) It must be emphasized that the concept of deviance in Functionalism explicitly involves an actor who is fully socialized with respect to the relevant normative patterns. (See the quotation from Johnson in Chapter VIII; as well as the discussion in Chapters III and IV.) If the actor has not internalized the relevant cultural pattern, then his departure from it does not lead the Functionalist to the theoretical problem of deviance. His behavior may be "different," but it is not "deviant."

Within the Labeling matrix, on the other hand, the concept of deviance has nothing to do with a societal consensus. As previously indicated, the very nature of the social within Symbolic Interactionism is not conducive to the postulation of some stable social order which influences conduct. Further, insofar as Labeling Theory attends the relationship between the "deviant actor" and the societal group at all, it most certainly does not assume that the actor is a "genuine member of society" (in the sense intended by Levy; see Chapter II). It focuses upon persons who are geographically and "legally" *in* the group, but not morally *of* it (i.e., the focus is on "outsiders"). (For a further discussion, see Chapter V.) So, for Labelists, the concept of deviance is not associated with norms which the actor shares with others. The actor of interest here is one who may not only be *uncommitted* to the social patterns, but may not even know of the pattern which he is presumed to have violated. He is one, as Matza says, who is "innocent" in the first place. The deviant is one who is subject to rules and is related to the rule-carriers (rule-makers and enforcers) only in that he is subject to their jurisdiction. He is the "victim" of *rules*, of patterns imposed upon him by alien agents and agencies. Even if he knows of the rules, they are in no sense *of* his life, but are an alien intrusion upon it. Hence, the archetype of the social relationship which creates deviance, as conceived in this matrix, is the colonial relationship. (See Chapter VI.) In this case, the rules are imposed upon actors who must *be taught to feel guilt* in spite of their former "innocence." Rather than associating the concept of deviance with a consensual group ("society," in Functionalist terms), the Labelists generally deny the very existence of such groups. Or, if not explicitly denying such groups' existence (cf. Quinney), they deny the relevance of that consensus (the institutional milieu) to the matter of deviance. According to Quinney, consensus in modern society, when and where it does exist, is, after all, merely the consequence of "successful oppression" (see Chapter VI). The Labeling matrix, then, locates the phenomenon of deviance within the struggle between conflicting parties.

To metaphorically summarize this transformation in the conceptualization of deviance, it can be said that Functionalism is concerned with the *emergence* of the *heretic*--a member of the group gone astray. Labeling Theory recognizes no such phenomenon. It is concerned rather with the *creation* of *infidels*--those who have never known that which must be known and, therefore, must be taught. These two matrices, then, focus on radically different problems. The heretic and the infidel are distinct phenomena. The center of attention has shifted. To call both of these phenomena "deviance" easily leads to "misunderstanding." It is clear that the terms, as employed in these respective matrices, are not commensurate with one another. These two sets of scientists, as Kuhn (1970:111) suggests, are responding to different worlds. The gestalt switch here is equivalent to that which Kuhn associates with a new convert from the Ptolemaic to the Copernican system who says, "I once took the moon as (or saw the moon as) a planet, but was mistaken" (Kuhn, 1970:115). The convert from Functionalism to Labeling Theory might submit, "Whereas I once took the criminal to be a heretic, I now know him to be an infidel. And whereas I once took social patterns to be normative, I now know that these patterns are rules."

4. The Explanation of Deviance

Given that the term "deviance" is employed in radically disparate fashion within each matrix, there is no basis for suggesting that the respective explanations of deviance should address the issues posed by the other. That is, one is not necessarily faced with a choice as to which view is "right" and which one is "wrong." Since the objects of explanation are not commensurate, there is no reason to suppose that the form and substance of the understanding of them will be either. The two no only employ the term "deviance" differently, but the problems which they specify as requiring solutions are transformed as well. In Kuhn's terms, since the pieces are changed, the problems which the puzzles pose are different. In short, what is viewed as requiring examination within each matrix is different.

Within Functionalism, it is the act--the deviant act--which is the primary concern. Within the Labeling matrix, the act (which cannot be explained from the Symbolic Interactionist view) is, at most, of secondary importance. This is the case for several reasons. Important is the Labelists' insistence that the act which is called deviant *is not qualitatively distinct* from any other human act (see Chapter VI) and, hence, requires no special explanation (or even description) as a "deviant act." In fact, and more fundamentally, there is "no such thing" as a "deviant act" within the perspective (see Chapters VI and VII). The primary locus of explanation in the Labeling matrix is not deviant acts, but the reaction to acts or perceived action. Rather than asking why an act occurred, Labelists want to know why any act is reacted to as deviant. Or, to put it another way, the appropriate query does not concern itself with the emergence of the criminal act, but, rather, asks the question, "Why is ongoing action criminalized?" Consistent with the fundamental role of "the self," Labeling Theory also focuses upon the consequences of reaction for *the person* who is reacted to as deviant. Hence, some central theoretical problems of this perspective revolve around the transformation of public identity and self-concept. The question is, "How is the person made deviant?"

As has been discussed (see Chapter VII), explanation within this matrix involves two basic components: interests and power. Insiders (those who dominate) are viewed as reacting in terms of their interests and attempting, through their power, to define the *other* (an outsider) and his *activity* as *deviant*. This makes sense, of course, within a perspective which emphasizes segmentation rather than institutionalization.

The Functionalist perspective seeks to explain only indirectly the reaction to the act. The primary focus is upon the explanation of the emergence of the act itself. Great importance is attached to the explanation of the source of deviant acts, since they are viewed as distinct from conformative ones. Within Functionalist thought, deviance is characterized by a distinct motivational orientation, i.e., alienation (see the discussion of Cloward and Ohlin in Chapter III), ambivalence, or psychological guilt (see the discussion of Parsons and Cohen in Chapter III). All such elements are missing from the motivation which underlies conformative acts (see Chapter III). The Functionalists' explanation does not direct toward either segmentation or heterogeneity as the source of deviance. Rather, consistent with the importance attached to the concept of institutions and the setting in which deviance is conceived, they find deviance to be a product of institutionally-produced strain. Deviance flows from institutional sources and is a violation of institutional patterns. The actor is pressured out of his commitment to institutions by the institutions themselves. If he were not associated with an established consensus, he would not be subject to the strain which eventually leads him to withdraw support from the norms (see Chapters III and VIII).

One final comment is in order involving the distinctiveness of the array of basic concepts within these matrices. Just as the Labeling perspective denies the relevance of institutions to the problem of deviance, within Functionalism the concepts of power and interest are ignored. Rather than power, for Functionalists, the relevant concept is authority, and rather than interests, they see "vested interests." Neither of these two terms necessarily implies the existence of conflict as do the concepts of power and interest as seen from within the Labeling perspective. For Functionalists, authority is "legitimate influence" from the perspective of all parties (super- and sub-ordinate) to the interaction. "Vested interests" simply suggest the actor's level of commitment to the pattern of relevance. This includes commitments to patterns of subordination, as well as to those which involve the protection of one's privileges. Hence, a student who is well socialized into the student role has a "vested interest" in that pattern (such that he is gratified by living up to the role), even though it is a sub-ordinate role vis-à-vis the professor. There is no conflict, then, between the student and the professor over authority or the nature of what represents deviation from the student role. That is, they can "agree." Just as deviance is conceived in radically different ways in these two systems of thought, so, too, are the explanations within each system incommensurate with one another. The Labelists examine relations betwen conflicting groups (e.g., Quinney) or deny the notion of consensual groups altogether (e.g., Becker and Matza). The two systems of thought, then, can be said to: (1) direct toward different phenomena, which exist in distinguishable milieu, (2) ask radically different questions, and (3) pose explanations which involve concepts drawn from disparate universes of discourse. Since this is the case, the two matrices are incommensurate.

C. Conclusion

In closing, it is appropriate to return to a brief consideration of the objectives that have guided this study. The overarching goal has been to clarify the relationship between the two dominant theoretical approaches to deviance within the discipline of sociology. This goal has been pursued by way of an analysis of what have been referred to as the "disciplinary matrices" associated with these two contemporary schools. The isolation of the core concepts, explanatory systems, methods, and values which characterize these matrices has, hopefully, served to clarify somewhat the "misunderstanding" which characterizes the dialogue between practitioners of the respective approaches.

A secondary but, nevertheless, important objective of this study has remained largely implicit throughout this project, being systematically addressed only in this conclusion, and that is the assessment of the degree of commensurability of the two approaches--an assessment begun in this study, but by no means concluded. Since the work began with the assumption that the two approaches are distinct in important respects, it may not be surprising that they have been found to be incommensurate. It would be incorrect to conclude, baldly, that such is the case. However, the opposite suggestion--that they are, indeed, commensurable and that the Labeling matrix represents a cumulative addition built upon the knowledge established by the historically precedent Functionalist Theory--is most certainly beset by serious difficulties and is called into question by this analysis. The relationship between these approaches to deviance requires a more thoroughgoing analysis of the relationships between the general theories of human conduct which undergird them. Such an analysis of Functionalism and Symbolic Interactionism has not yet been accomplished and is long overdue.

BIBLIOGRAPHY

ALEXANDER, F. M.
1910   **Man's Supreme Inheritance.** London: E. P. Dutton.

AUERBACH, Carl
1959   "Law and Social Change in the United States." **U.C.L.A. Law Review** (July), 6: 516-532.

BECKER, Howard S.
1963   **Outsiders.** New York: The Free Press.
1967   "Whose Side Are We On?" **Social Problems,** 14 (3): 239-247.
1973   **Outsiders,** Second Edition. New York: The Free Press.

BELL, Daniel
1953   "Crime As An American Way of Life." **The Antioch Review** (June): 131-154.

BERGER, Peter
1963   **Invitation to Sociology.** Garden City, N.J.: Anchor.

BERGER, Peter and Thomas LUCKMANN
1966   **The Social Construction of Reality.** Garden City, N.J.: Anchor.

BERSHADY, Harold J.
1973   **Ideology and Social Knowledge.** New York: John Wiley and Sons.

BIERSTADT, Robert
1959   "Nominal and Real Definitions in Sociology. In **Symposium in Sociological Theory,** L. Gross (ed.). Evanston, Ill.: Row, Peterson.

BLALOCK, Hubert M. Jr.
1964   **Causal Inferences in Nonexperimental Research.** Chapel Hill, N.C.: The Univ. of North Carolina Press.

BLUMER, Herbert
1969   **Symbolic Interactionism: Perspective and Method.** Englewood Cliffs, N.J.: Prentice-Hall.

BUCKLEY, Walter
1967   **Sociology and Modern Systems Theory.** Englewood Cliffs, N.J.: Prentice-Hall.

193

BUNGE, Mario
1959   **Causality.** Cambridge, Mass.: Harvard Univ. Press.

CHAFETZ, Janet
1974   **Masculine, Feminine, Human.** Itasca, Ill.: Peacock.

CLOWARD, Richard
1960   "Social Control in Prisons." In **Theoretical Studies in Social Organization of the Prison.** Pamphlet 115. New York: Social Science Research Council.

CLOWARD, Richard and Lloyd OHLIN
1960   **Delinquency and Opportunity.** New York: The Free Press.

COHEN, Albert
1955   **Delinquent Boys.** New York: The Free Press.
1970   "Multiple Factor Approaches." In **The Sociology of Crime and Delinquency,** Wolfgang, Savitz, and Johnson (eds.). New York: John Wiley and Sons.

DAHRENDORF, Ralf
1959   **Class and Class Conflict in Industrial Society.** Stanford, Ca.: Stanford Univ. Press.

DAVIS, Kingsley
1959   "The Myth of Functional Analysis as a Special Method." **American Sociological Review** (December), 24: 757-752.
1961   "Prostitution." In **Contemporary Social Problems** (First Edition), Merton and Nisbet (eds.). New York: Harcourt, Brace and World, Inc.
1968   **Human Society.** New York: Macmillan.

DAVIS, Kingsley and Wilbert MOORE
1945   "Some Principles of Stratification." In **American Sociological Review,** 10: 242-247.

DEVEREUX, Edward
1961   "Parsons' Sociological Theory." In **The Social Theories of Talcott Parsons,** Max Black (ed.). Englewood Cliffs, N.J.: Prentice-Hall.

DURKHEIM, Emile
1933   **The Division of Labor in Society.** New York: The Free Press.
1938   **The Rules of Sociological Method.** New York: The Free Press.
1951   **Suicide.** New York: The Free Press.

ERICKSON, Kai
1966   **Wayward Puritans.** New York: John Wiley and Sons.

FRIEDRICHS, Robert
1970   **A Sociology of Sociology.** New York: The Free Press.

GIBBS, Jack
1972   **Sociological Theory Construction.** Hinsdale, Ill.: The Dryden Press, Inc.

GOULDNER, Alvin
1968   "The Sociologist as Partisan: Sociology and the Welfare State." **The American Sociologist** (May): 103-116.
1970   **The Coming Crisis of Western Sociology.** New York: Basic Books.
1973   Foreword. In **The New Criminology,** by Ian Taylor, Paul Walton, and Jock Young. New York: Harper and Row.

HALL, Jerome
1952   **Theft Law and Society.** Indianapolis, Ind.: Bobbs-Merrill.

HAMLYN, D.W.
1967   "Empiricism." In **Encyclopedia of Philosophy.** New York: Collier and Macmillan.

HANSON, Norwood Russell
1965   **Patterns of Discovery.** Cambridge: Cambridge Univ. Press.

HOMANS, George Caspar
1961   **Social Behavior: Its Elementary Forms.** New York: Harcourt.

JOHNSON, Barclay
1965   "Durkheim's One Cause of Suicide." **American Sociological Review,** Vol. 30 (6): 875-886.

JOHNSON, Harry M.
1960   **Sociology: A Systematic Introduction.** New York: Harcourt-Brace.

KANOWITZ, Lee
1969   **Women and the Law: The Unfinished Revolution.** Albuquerque, N.M.: Univ. of New Mexico Press.

KUHN, Thomas
1970   **The Structure of Scientific Revolutions** (Second Edition, Enlarged). Chicago: The Univ. of Chicago Press. (This book was first published in 1961.)

LEMERT, Edwin
1951   **Social Pathology.** New York: McGraw-Hill.
1972   **Human Deviance, Social Problems, and Social Control** (Second Edition). Englewood Cliffs, N.J.: Prentice-Hall.

LENSKI, Gerhardt
1966   **Power and Privilege.** New York: McGraw-Hill.

LEVY, Marion
1952   **The Structure of Society.** Princeton, N.J.: Princeton Univ. Press.

LINDESMITH, Alfred R. and John GAGNON
1964   "Anomie and Drug Addiction." In **Anomie and Deviant Behavior,** Clinard (ed.). New York: The Free Press.

LINDESMITH, Alfred R. and Anselm L. STRAUSS
1968   **Social Psychology** (Third Edition). New York: Holt, Rinehart and Winston.

LOFLAND, John
1969   **Deviance and Identity.** Englewood Cliffs, N.J.: Prentice-Hall.

LUCKMANN, Thomas
1965   **The Invisible Religion.** New York: The Macmillan Company.

MANIS, Jerome G. and Bernard N. MELTZER
1972   **Symbolic Interaction: A Reader in Social Psychology** (Second Edition). Boston: Allyn and Bacon.

MATZA, David
1964   **Delinquency and Drift.** New York: John Wiley and Sons.
1969   **Becoming Deviant.** Englewood Cliffs, N.J.: Prentice-Hall.

MEAD, G.H.
1928   "The Psychology of Punitive Justice." **American Journal of Sociology** (23): 577-602.
1934   **Mind, Self, and Society.** Chicago: The Univ. of Chicago Press.

MERTON, Robert K.
1949   "The Bearing of Sociological Theory on Empirical Research." In **Social Theory and Social Structure.** New York: The Free Press.
1967   **Social Theory and Social Structure.** New York: The Free Press. (The article, "Social Structure and Anomie," was originally published in 1938, in **American Sociological Review.**)

MERTON, Robert K. and Robert NISBET
1961   **Contemporary Social Problems** (First Edition). New York: Harcourt, Brace and World, Inc.
1971   **Contemporary Social Problems** (Fourth Edition). New York: Harcourt Brace Javanovich, Inc.

MILLER, Walter
  1958 "Lower Class Culture as a Generating Milieu of Gang Delinquency." **Journal of Social Issues,** 14: 5-19.

MILLIBAND, Ralph
  1969 **The State in Capitalist Society.** New York: Basic Books.

MINTZ, Morton
  1965 **The Therapeutic Nightmare: A Report on Prescription Drugs, The Men Who Make Them, and The Agency That Controls Them.** Boston: Houghton Mifflin Co.

MULLINS, Nicholas C.
  1973 **Theories and Theory Groups in Contemporary American Sociology.** New York: Harper and Row.

NAGLE, Ernst
  1965 "Types of Causal Explanation in Science." In **Cause and Effect,** Daniel Lerner (ed.). New York: The Free Press.

NISBET, Robert
  1974 **The Sociology of Emile Durkheim.** New York: Oxford Univ. Press.

PARSONS, Talcott
  1937 **The Structure of Social Action.** New York: McGraw-Hill.
  1951 **The Social System.** New York: The Free Press.
  1952 "The Superego and the Theory of Social Systems." **Psychiatry** (15): 15-25.
  1965 "The Ideas of System, Causal Explanation and Cybernetic Control in Social Science." In **Cause and Effect,** Daniel Lerner (ed.). New York: The Free Press.
  1966 **Societies: Evolutionary and Comparative Perspectives.** Englewood Cliffs, N.J.: Prentice-Hall.
  1971 "Value-Freedom and Objectivity." In **Max Weber and Sociology Today,** Otto Stammer (ed.). New York: Harper and Row.
  1975 "Comment on Pope and Cohen." **American Sociological Review** (February) (40): 106-110.

PARSONS, Talcott and Edward A. SHILS
  1951 **Toward A General Theory of Action.** New York: Harpertorch Books, Harper and Row.

PARSONS, Talcott, Edward A. SHILS, and James OLDS
  1951 "Values, Motives, and Systems of Action." In **Toward a General Theory of Action,** Talcott and Shils (eds.). New York: Harpertorch Books, Harper and Row.

POPPER, Karl R.
　　1965　　The Open Society and Its Enemies. Princeton, N.J.: Princeton Univ. Press.

POUND, Roscoe
　　1943　　"A Survey of Social Interests." Harvard Law Review (October), 57: 39.

QUINNEY, Richard
　　1970　　The Social Reality of Crime. Boston: Little, Brown and Co.
　　1973　　Critique of Legal Order. Boston: Little, Brown and Co.

RUDNER, Richard S.
　　1966　　Philosophy of Social Science. Englewood Cliffs, N.J.: Prentice-Hall.

SCHEFF, Thomas
　　1966　　Being Mentally Ill. Chicago: Aldine Publishing Co.

SCHEFFLER, I.
　　1963　　The Anatomy of Inquiry: Philosophical Studies in the Theory of Science. New York: Knopf.

SCHUR, Edwin
　　1971　　Labeling Deviant Behavior. New York: Harper and Row.

SCHUTZ, Alfred
　　1953　　"Common Sense and Scientific Interpretation of Human Action." Philosophy and Phenomenological Research (September) (14).
　　1970　　On Phenomenology and Social Relations. Chicago: Chicago Press.

SCOTT, John Finley
　　1963　　"The Changing Foundations of the Parsonian Action Scheme." American Sociological Review (October): 716-735.
　　1971　　Internalization of Norms: A Sociological Theory of Moral Commitment. Englewood Cliffs, N.J.: Prentice-Hall.

SHAW, C.R. and Henry MC KAY
　　1942　　Juvenile Delinquency in Urban Areas. Chicago: Univ of Chicago Press.

SMELSER, N.J.
　　1973　　Sociology. New York: John Wiley and Sons.

SUTHERLAND, Edwin
　　1947　　Principles of Criminology (Fourth Edition). Philadelphia: Lippincott.

SYKES, Gresham
1958   **Society of Captives.** Princeton, N.J.: Princeton Univ.
          Press.

SYKES, Gresham and Sheldon MESSINGER
1960   "The Inmate Social System." In **Theoretical Studies in the
          Social Organization of the Prison.** Pamphlet 115. New
          York: Social Science Research Council.

TAYLOR, Ian, Paul WALTON, and Jock YOUNG
1973   **The New Criminology.** New York: Harper and Row.

THOMAS, W.I.
1972   "The Definition of the Situation." In **Symbolic Interaction:
          A Reader in Social Psychology,** Manis and Meltzer (eds.).
          Boston: Allyn and Bacon.

TROYER, William L.
1972   "Mead's Social and Functional Theory of Mind" (originally
          published in 1946). In **Symbolic Interaction: A Reader in
          Social Psychology** (Second Edition), Manis and Meltzer
          (eds.). Boston: Allyn and Bacon.

VAN RIPER, Charles
1957   "Symptomatic Therapy for Stuttering." In **Handbook of
          Speech Pathology,** Lee Travis (ed.). New York: Appleton-
          Century-Crofts.

WALLACE, Walter
1969   **Sociological Theory.** Chicago: Aldine Publishing Co.

WEBER, Max
1958   **The Protestant Ethic and the Spirit of Capitalism.** New
          York: Scribners.

WEISS, J.G.
1971   "Dialogue with David Matza." **Issues in Criminology**
          (Winter), 6 (1): 33-53

WHYTE, William Foote
1943   **Street Corner Society.** Chicago: Univ. of Chicago Press.

WRIGHT, Charles and R.E. HILBERT
1980   "Value Implications of the Functional Theory of Devi-
          ance." **Social Problems** (December), Vol. 28, No. 2:
          205-219.

YOUNG, Michael
1961   **The Rise of the Meritocracy.** Baltimore: Penguin Books.

INDEX

general Methodological Position, 134-137
weakness in Methodological Underpinnings, 186
focus on Power Differentials, 165
"Self" as a root concept, 184-185
irrelevance of Societal Consensus, 188-189
intra-scientific Values, 150-153
socio-political Values, 162-167
(see also Becker; Lemert; Matza; Quinney; Scheff)
Language, 55, 125
Law
within Labeling Theory, 74-77
discussed by Lemert, 93
discussed by Quinney, 113-117, 120
within Colonial Systems, 76-77
of Theft, 115-116
Repressive and Restitutive, 21, 22, 75
Legitimacy, 26
Lemert, Edwin, 2, 3, 4, 80, 98
critical overtones, 162
emphasis on Description, 152
non-reliance upon Determinism, 143
and Deviance, 61, 66, 67-70, 71
explanation of Secondary Deviance, 89-95, 141
Law, 93
Self-Concept, 93-95
Social Control, 92-93
Lenski, Gerhardt, 177
Levy, Marion
and Institutions, 14
Membership in Society, 17-18
Lindesmith, Alfred F., 93, 124
Lofland, John, 2, 163
and emergence of the concept of Deviance, 9-10
Luckmann, Thomas, 125

Malinowski, Bronislaw, 63, 87, 144-145
Manis, Jerome G., 54

Marijuana, 65, 73, 81-85, 85-86n, 88, 93, 101, 103, 106
Marijuana Tax Act, 88
(see also Marijuana)
Market, 41-42, 43, 45
Marriage, 41
Marx, Karl, 4
Marxian Sociology, 3, 5, 53, 74, 111, 112, 120, 167, 177
Matza, David, 2, 3, 4, 11, 91, 189, 191
discussion of Affiliation, 104-105
preclusion of the concept of Cause, 141-142
emphasis upon Description, 150-152
and Determinism, 143, 157
and Deviance, 61, 72-74, 79-80
and Consciousness, 99-111
and Meaning, 129, 130
general Methodological Position, 134
discussion of The State, 107-111, 165-167
McKay, Henry, 46
Mead, G.H., 3, 4, 53, 54-59, 64, 91, 124-125, 126-127, 141, 185
Meaning
in relation to Causation, 139-140, 141-142, 146-148
within Symbolic Interactionist Theory, 56, 57, 129-130, 185
Means, 43-44, 46, 52
Mechanical Solidarity, 21, 22, 23, 37
Meltzer, Bernard N., 54, 57-58
Mental Illness, 61, 70-72, 95-99, 114
Merton, Robert, 2, 4, 9, 18, 32, 35, 131n, 178
in contrast to Becker, 62-63
limitation of concept of Causation, 146
on Components of Systems, 144-145
and Deviance, 10, 24-26, 27, 28, 52

204